The
Emergence of
Standard English

Besechinth mekely semu to thir reyntors of ...
late ago be boght of ... thrampton of ... he
... to the ... noght ... lyndy of the
of the Roller above ... porty thereof being the
to his ... grthoire pouce gracious ...
the ... Willm comuntoying hym by the ...
... by tyme ... to the other Willm ...
... hym in place prinebard ...
in this ... the ... like it you ...
... to smrve a ... of proclamaron ...
... Ship that ye ... Willm ...
... to the ... Suppliant of the in
... here ... setimyne the ... untu
... the ... beforehor in ... parrie ... be ...
... by the ... proclamaron the ...
... to ... in the forme ...
... for the ... time vnto the ...

THE
EMERGENCE OF
STANDARD ENGLISH

John H. Fisher

THE UNIVERSITY PRESS OF KENTUCKY

Library of Congress Cataloging-in-Publication Data

Fisher, John H.
    The emergence of standard English / John H. Fisher.
        p.   cm.
    Includes bibliographical references and index.
    ISBN 0-8131-1935-9 (cloth : alk. paper). — ISBN 0-8131-0852-7
(paper : alk. paper)
        1. English language—Middle English, 1100-1500—Standardization.
    2. Great Britain—History—House of Lancaster, 1399-1461.
    3. English language—Middle English, 1100-1500—History. 4. Great
    Britain—Officials and employees—Language. 5. English
    language—19th century—Standardization. 6. Language policy—Great
    Britain—History. 7. Chaucer, Geoffrey, d. 1400—Language.
    8. England. Court of Chancery—History. 9. English language—
    Standardization. I. Title.
    PE524.7.F7 1996
    427'.02—dc20   95-16425

For
Jan, Jack, and Judy

CONTENTS

ACKNOWLEDGMENTS

"A Language Policy for Lancastrian England." *PMLA* 107 (1992): 1168-80.

"Chancery English and the Emergence of Standard Written English." *Speculum* 52 (1977): 870-89.

"Animadversions on the Text of Chaucer." *Speculum* 63 (1988): 779-93.

"European Chancelleries and the Rise of Standard Languages." *Proceedings of the Illinois Medieval Association* 3 (1986): 1-33.

"Chaucer's French: A Metalinguistic Inquiry." *Chaucer Yearbook* 1 (1992): 33-46.

"Piers Plowman and Chancery Tradition." *Medieval Studies for George Kane.* Ed. E.D. Kennedy. Cambridge, Eng.: Boydell and Brewer, 1988. 267-78.

"Caxton and Chancery English." *Fifteenth-Century Studies.* Ed. R.F. Yeager. New Haven, Conn.: Archon, 1984. 161-85.

"The History of Received Pronunciation." *The Ring of Words: Essays Presented to Henry Kratz.* Ed. Ulrich Goebel and David Lee. Lampiter, Wales: Mellen, 1994. 41-62.

I

INTRODUCTION

For more than a quarter of a century I have become increasingly convinced that Standard Modern English did not just "happen" but that it was, and is, the result of formal institutionalization, that is, of deliberate planning and management. This idea is anathema to the Anglo-Saxon temperament, which resists the notion of social engineering, but the institutionalization of language is supported by the experience of other cultures, particularly those of France and Spain. In 1253 Alphonso X of Spain decreed that the usage of the Chancellery of Toledo should be the standard for all official documents. In 1257 St. Louis of France indicated that official correspondence was to be written in the French of the Chancellerie Royale in Paris, and the 1539 ordinance of Villers-Cotterets legally established chancellery French as the language of law and administration.

Linguistic historians, preferring to believe that languages live and die by social evolution, have a hard time allowing for influences such as these. Besides, we have no record of any such formal promulgations in England. Professors Baugh and Cable in their *History of the English Language* have an interesting discussion (259ff) of the seventeenth-century movement in England for the establishment of an academy, like the academies in Italy and France, to control the development of the language. Years of foot-dragging, however, eventually left management of the language in the hands of entrepreneurial lexicographers and grammarians, where it still rests today in Great Britain and America. This congenital resistance to official control of the language is reflected in contemporary resistance to making English the legal language of the United States. A recent article by Jack Citrin and others, "The 'Official English' Movement and the Symbolic Politics of Language in the United States," is particularly interesting. It summarizes the "U.S. English" lobby, sponsored by S.I. Hayakawa, for amending the Constitution to make English the official language of the United States. By 1988, forty-eight states had considered this proposition and eighteen had passed laws making English the official language. Thirty states rejected the proposition, mostly on the ground that it was unnecessary. Tables in Citrin's article show that the proposition was in direct response to the influx of non-English-speaking immigrants after World War II, that the states enacting laws were those with the smaller numbers of immigrants, and that the movements both for and against English as an official language were largely symbolic, supported by abstract notions of "national identity."

In spite of this tradition of resistance, I have grown increasingly convinced that the standardization of English began and continues as more than a casual drift. At the end of chapter four I refer to congressional action toward simplified spelling. *A Manual of Style Prepared by the U.S. Government Printing Office* states: "By act of Congress the Public Printer is authorized to determine the form and style of Government printing. . . . Essentially it is a standardization designed to achieve uniform word and type treatment. . . . It should be remembered that the *Manual* is primarily a Government Printing Office printer's stylebook. Easy rules of grammar cannot be prescribed, for it is assumed that editors are versed in correct expression" (xi). Thus, even in the United States today, there are laws that support a standard language.

Conventions of grammar and expression are controlled by an establishment of government bureaucrats, men of letters, teachers, and publishers who have inherited from Henry V and the English Chancery of the fifteenth century. It is the regularity of their writing that creates a standard language. My interest has been in the process by which this regularity emerged, a process which I think is more authoritarian than historians of the English language have traditionally allowed.

For many years, I have been a voice crying in the wilderness. Language historians assumed that regularity developed simply as a convenience with the accumulation of literacy, was eventually imposed by the decisions of printers, and was codified by lexicographers and grammarians. But it has always been a matter of looking at the partially full glass: is it half empty or half full? On the one hand, standardization of the written language (I won't even consider the problem of standardization of the spoken) has not yet been achieved or there would be no need for English composition classes, dictionaries, rhetorics, and the individual manuals of the Government Printing Office, the Modern Language Association, the University of Chicago Press, and indeed the individual style sheets of every publisher and printer. On the other hand, as one whose professional life has been devoted to the study and teaching of Old and Middle English, I am impressed by the degree of standardization that has been achieved since 1400. Until that time there was no standard English; there were only the Old and Middle English dialects. The reason for this is obvious. During the Middle Ages the official language throughout Europe was Latin. The history of the emergence of the modern era is coterminous with the history of the emergence of written standards of the European vernaculars.

In 1920, in his important pioneer study *A History of Modern Colloquial English*, H.C. Wyld discussed the emergence of an English standard. He assumed the existence of a "London official or literary English" (76, 82, etc.) but, like most linguists of the period, he believed that the only genuine language was the oral, and that writing was merely an effort to represent pronunciation. He had nothing at all to say about writing as an independent medium or the process by which the "official" written language emerged. He was interested only in the first evidences of a spoken standard in the sixteenth century (chap. 4). Like Wyld, E.J. Dobson began his authoritative essay "Early Modern Standard English" (1955): "That there was a standard form of literary English in the sixteenth century is obvious and commonplace," but he, too, had nothing more to say about the emergence of the written standard, and devoted the rest of the essay to preliminary indications of the emergence of an oral standard in London and the Court. (I discuss the emergence of the oral standard in the final essay in this volume.) Baugh's observation of 1935, preserved in the 1993 edition, concerns a written standard:

> By far the most influential factor in the rise of Standard English was the importance of London as the capital of England. Indeed, it is altogether likely that the language of the city would have become the prevailing dialect without the help of any of the factors previously discussed [i.e., the importance of the Midland area of England in contrast to the North and South, and the influence of an important writer like Chaucer]. In doing so it would have been following the course of other national tongues—French as the dialect of Paris, Spanish as that of Castile, and others. [This ignores the influence of the French and Spanish chancelleries—see the fourth chapter]. London was, and still is, the political and commercial center of England. It was the seat of the court, of the highest judicial tribunals, the focus of social and intellectual activities of the country . . . The history of Standard English is almost the history of London English. (189)

This is a confused account: the "language of the city" and the contrast with the North and South imply spoken dialects, but the reference to Chaucer implies writing. The appeal to parallels with the French and Spanish chancelleries carries the same confusion as the appeal to London English; these chancellery dialects were written, not spoken.

Wyld's, Baugh's, and Dobson's observations, and others like them, evince obfuscations that impair nearly all discussions of the emergence of standard languages. First, they are chiefly concerned with the emergence of spoken standards, whereas evidence indicates that written languages were regularized long before the spoken and are, indeed, much more regular than the spoken today. If I may paraphrase Baugh's last sentence: the only standard language is a written language. Differences in spoken dialects involve prestige rather than standardization.

Wyld, Baugh, and others make an unwarranted leap from the importance of centers like London and Paris to the establishment of written/spoken standards. London (to narrow the generalization to my topic) is a large and various city, with many spoken dialects, ranging from Cockney to Received Pronunciation, and many written modes, ranging from the language of journalism and popular poetry to sermons and parliamentary prose. "London English" to Wyld and everyone else means the oral and written language of the court and central bureaucracy, but this is seldom made clear. Nor is the *process* by which court usage was promulgated ever spelled out.

In making such generalizations, Wyld and Baugh assume that the London model would influence the broader populace by a kind of osmosis—standardization would just happen. Dobson discusses the importance of "education" in communicating the standard in the sixteenth century, as I do for the nineteenth, but this has little relevance to establishing a written standard in the fifteenth century. Everybody from the king to the milkmaid spoke in regional English dialect in the fifteenth century. Schools did not teach English; there were no dictionaries or textbooks that recorded standard English forms. There were elaborate tools like the texts of Donatus and Priscian for teaching standard Latin. Especially relevant were the tools of the "writing masters," independent tutors not unlike modern music teachers, who taught Latin, French, and, presumably, English, in the age of Latin grammar schools (H.G. Richardson). The tools of these masters were their "formularies," collections of appropriate models that they set before the students to be copied and emulated. We have Latin and French formulary collections, but none of English, even though they must have existed. On page 64 of *The Importance of Chaucer* I quote from the statues of Rivington grammar school (ca. 1450) showing how the formularies were used. These collections were devised for teaching clerks the skills of *ars dictaminis*, that is, the writing of business letters. Their models displayed the practices of the great chancelleries, beginning with the Roman curia. In the second essay I explore the way in which this sort of official writing provided the model for the normalization of written English.

Until recently, generalizations like those of Wyld and Baugh have dominated the field. The first discussion of how English writing might actually have been institutionalized began with M.L. Samuels's essay "Some Applications of Middle English Dialectology" (1963) in which he distinguished "four types of language that are less obviously dialectal . . . [that] cast light on the probable sources of the written standard English that appears in the fifteenth century" (407). The first type is the language of the Wycliffite manuscripts, a literary standard based on the dialects of the central Midland counties. This language was evidently taught in Lollard centers like Lutterworth and Leicester. Until after 1430 it was used throughout Midland and Southern England for Lollard and other writings.

The second proto-standard is the language of non-official writings in and around London, such as the Auchinleck manuscript, the early English prose psalter in BM Addit 17376, and other mid-fourteenth-century manuscripts identified by Samuels (417n7). He finds variation in the language of these manuscripts, but enough consistency to constitute a "type." The third proto-standard is the language of selected manuscripts of Chaucer, Gower, Langland, Lydgate, and Hoccleve, and a number of documents from the turn of the fourteenth century in Chambers and Daunt's *Book of London English*. There is variety in these manuscripts, particularly in the orthography, but consistency in the inflections and syntax.

The fourth proto-standard, "which I shall call 'Chancery Standard,'" writes Samuels, "consists of that flood of government documents that starts in the years following 1430. Its differences from the language of Chaucer are well known [he says, but gives only four differences], and it is this type, not its predecessors in London English, that is the basis of modern written English" (411).

Inspired by Samuels's statement, I applied for an National Endowment for the Humanities fellowship and, with my wife Jane Law Fisher, spent the winter of 1975-76 in the Public Record Office poring over the Chancery files. Nearly all of the Chancery records have been calendared, but the summaries are in English and do not indicate the original language of the velum. We found a typewritten list of the English records, no doubt compiled as Chambers and Daunt were making their search of the files, but it turned out to be not nearly complete. The Public Record Office keepers became interested in our activity and asked us to note in pencil in the catalog the language of the English entries. We returned to Knoxville in the spring of 1976 with a mass of photostats that became the basis for the final two thirds of *An Anthology of Chancery English* (1984) and for the second essay in this volume, "Chancery and the Emergence of Standard Written English."

As indicated in that essay, I still had very little notion as to what motivated the Chancery scribes to begin writing in English in the 1420s. Malcolm Richardson was looking for a dissertation at the time, and he elected to explore the relations of the Chancery clerks to Henry IV and Henry V. He quickly turned up the English Signet missives of Henry V that comprise the first third of the Chancery anthology and went on to discuss the similarities between the language of Henry V and Chancery English in his dissertation and in his 1980 *Speculum* article, "Henry V, the English Chancery, and Chancery English."

The final stage in this intellectual odyssey was my realization that the Chancery documents, the royal missives, and the early literary manuscripts might form a continuum that suggested a deliberate policy on the part of the Lancastrian administration. If this is a plausible idea, there is a great deal more work to be done on it. It will be interesting to identify more fully the scribes and patrons of the literary manuscripts and the relationships between the political and literary establishments, as A.I. Doyle, Malcolm Parkes, Paul Strohm, Thomas Cable, Paul Christianson, A.S.G. Edwards, Derek Pearsall, John Bowers, Seth Lerer, and others are beginning to do. (Malcolm Richardson's catalogue of the Chancery clerks has just been accepted for publication by the Public Records Office).

One very interesting development since the publication of the article on an official language policy is Sylvia Wright's identification of portraits in the Bedford Psalter, B.L. Add. MS. 42131. This handsome manuscript, commissioned about 1410 by John, Duke of Bedford, the younger brother of Prince Henry (as he then was), contains portraits of Henry IV, Henry V, Gower, Chaucer, Hoccleve, and probably Henry Beaufort and Lydgate. And there are some 120 other extremely realistic portraits of kings and magnates still to be identified! Those individuals identified by Wright so nearly match the affinity of Prince Henry discussed in the first essay that I am eager to study the manuscript further. The text of the psalter is Latin liturgy and seems to have nothing to do with Lancastrian politics or the English language policy, but why then does the manuscript contain the portraits of the English poets?

Meanwhile, it is gratifying to see the idea of a fifteenth-century institutionalization of English becoming more widely accepted. In the third edition of *A History of the English Language*, Thomas Cable added to Baugh's text that "a factor more difficult to assess is the influence which the Chancery clerks may have had [upon the establishment of a London standard]. By the middle of the century they had developed a fairly consistent variety of London English in both spelling and accidence, and as the language of official use it was likely to have had some influence in similar situations elsewhere" (194). Cable cites the second essay in this collection and goes on to discuss the influence of printing. In the fourth edition, he adds further material about Chancery influence on the development of language: "This influence emanating from London can be seen in the variety of English used in documents of the national bureaucracy as written by the clerks of Chancery. By the middle of the century a fairly consistent variety of written English in both spelling and grammar had developed, and as the language of official use it was likely to have influence in similar situations elsewhere" (190).

Norman Blake in the *Cambridge History of the English Language* likewise observes that "the growth of the civil service in London and the rise in patronage from the court made London a centre for English" (II: 7). He cites the influence of Chancery language on writing throughout the country but says that "it was not felt immediately in the writing of literary texts, where other traditions continued to prevail for some time" (19). In *An Outline History of English*, Jacek Fisiak is more specific. He observes (83ff) that the generalizations about London English by Wyld and Baugh "require some qualification" and cites articles and *An Anthology of Chancery English* by the Fishers and Richardson as evidence that what emerged in the fifteenth century was a written standard that "had no spoken correlate" (83)—a conclusion more absolute than Dobson or other British scholars would allow. He summarizes Samuels's article and suggests that Chancery Standard became the basis for the language of Caxton and the sixteenth-century writers and printers, and the authors of the first dictionaries and rhetorics. In his fine book *Chaucer and His Readers*, Seth Lerer connects the fifteenth-century "laureation" of Chaucer with "the years between the victory at Agincourt and Henry V's death [that] marked a new interest in the possibilities of English as the medium of official communication" (48). Similarly, Derek Pearsall in his "Hoccleve's *Regement of Princes*: The Poetics of Royal Self-Representation," observes that "the story of Henry V's encouragement of the use of English in government documents and correspondence is well known and has been well told" (398) and cites the essays in this collection and Malcolm Richardson's *Speculum* article.

In the essays in this collection I treat the origins of Chancery Standard (and something of its relations to Henry V), Chaucer, the *Piers Plowman* manuscripts, and Caxton. In the final essay, I discuss the development of Received Pronunciation from the court and bureaucratic London dialect at the end of the eighteenth century. Finally, by bringing these essays together in a single volume, I hope to demonstrate the influence of Chancery English upon the continuing movement towards a written standard between 1500 and 1700.

My contention throughout these essays is that language is standardized by government and business rather than by literary usage. I do not mean to imply that clerks innovated and expanded the capacities of language but that it was their habitual usages that created a "standard." This was particularly true before the introduction of paper and the steel pen. The mechanical process of writing was very difficult in the era of quills that had to be sharpened every few lines and of rough surfaces that blotted ink.

Virtually all writing was dictated. The puissant connotations of the terms *dictator* and *auditor* derive from this era; *ars dictaminis* was the art of taking dictation (Julius Caesar is said to have dictated to five secretaries at the same time). Language and matter were spoken by the dictator, but the graphemic representation was produced by the clerk. The master may have sometimes provided written drafts and corrected the documents, so that as the clerk grew accustomed to the dictator's verbal habits, his style became essentially that of the dictator. However, it was the clerks' copies that were widely distributed and preserved. This is the story of the Signet missives of Henry V. They reveal at least thirteen different hands, but all of them employ the same style, syntax, and orthography. The style and syntax, although not the orthography, are the same as those of the two holographs by Henry himself (see Malcolm Richardson's *Speculum* article and *An Anthology of Chancery English* 13, 122). Henry must have sometimes given the clerks rough drafts and/or approved the finished versions.

My second generalization is that the distinction between government, business, and literary languages is artificial. These languages were produced by the same people. This was especially true in classical times: Julius Caesar and Cicero, who together are said to have "created" classical Latin, were both rulers and writers. Tacitus was a consul, Seneca was tutor to Nero and virtually ruler of Rome in Nero's minority; Ovid studied law but was a drop-out; and Horace was a notary. The same ties between government, law, and literature existed at the time English began to be standardized: Chaucer was a bureaucrat; Gower studied, and probably practiced, law; and Hoccleve was a clerk in the Privy Seal office. Lydgate studied at Oxford, but, like Vergil, held no bureaucratic position. My point is that Chancery English was created by government officials as the language of government, business, and literature in the fifteenth century. The same process continued as written English was "improved" and further standardized in the sixteenth century. Of the "creators" of Elizabethan English (the language Dr. Johnson regarded as the beginning of cultivated English—I am confining myself to writers born before 1600), we lack records of formal education for only Shakespeare and Izaak Walton. Henry Howard, Earl of Surrey, was privately educated as befitted a duke's son; Ben Jonson got only as far as Westminster School; and John Webster may have studied in the Inns of Court.

For the rest of the writers of this period, the record is clear. Thomas More, John Donne, and Francis Bacon studied both at the university and the Inns of Court. John Lyly, Philip Sidney, Walter Raleigh, John Foxe, Richard Hooker, and Thomas Hobbes all went to Oxford. John Skelton, Thomas Wyatt, Christopher Marlowe, Edmund Spenser, George Herbert, John Milton, and Robert Herrick were all at Cambridge. (Lyly and Skelton studied at both Oxford and Cambridge.) Surrey, More, Bacon, Sidney, Raleigh, Skelton, Wyatt, Spenser, Milton, and probably Marlowe held important positions at court or in the government bureaucracy.

This was even more true of the scholars and educators who compiled the first textbooks and dictionaries. Roger Ascham, author of *Scholemaster* and *Toxophilus*, was educated at Cambridge, tutor to Princess Elizabeth, and Latin secretary to Queen Mary. Richard Mulcaster, author of the early textbook on English composition, *Elementarie*, was educated at Oxford and headmaster of St. Paul's School. Thomas Wilson, author of *The Art of Rhetorique*, was educated at Cambridge and served as Privy Councillor and Secretary of State. George or Richard Puttenham, whichever was the author of the *Arte of English Poesie*, was educated at Oxford and in constant trouble with the government, if not a part of it. Richard Carew, author of *The Excellency of the English Tongue*, was educated at Oxford and the Middle Temple and served as High Sheriff of Cornwall and Member of Parliament. Thomas Smith, author of *De recta et emendata linguae Anglicanae scriptione*, educated at Cambridge and in Padua for law, was Regius Professor of Law at Cambridge and Secretary of State and served in many public offices. Unfortunately, we know less about the first lexicographers: Robert Cawdrey, author of the first dictionary, *A Table Alphebetical*, was a schoolmaster; John Bullokar, author of *English Expositor*, was a physician; and Thomas Blount, author of *Glossographia*, was an attorney. So, as these listings attest, many of the writers and scholars who presided over the shaping of the language in the sixteenth century were university-educated men of affairs.

The language that had originated with the authority of King Henry V and the Chancery clerks continued to develop under the aegis of writers and scholars who were important government officials. Language was standardized by wide and habitual usage—i.e., by clerks and then printers—but these people worked under the supervision of the dictators, or rulers, who were at the same time the premier authors and educators. Autodidact Vergils and Shakespeares are the exceptions that prove the rule. Since the time of John Dryden and Samuel Johnson, it has been men of letters like Vergil, Shakespeare, and Ben Jonson who have come to represent linguistic authority through their belletristic, non-utilitarian writing rather than through their political power. But beneath the idea of correctness, of standardization, still runs an awareness of power. Rulers and writers receive the same sort of linguistic education, which rulers employ (and have employed for them) for bureaucratic communication, and which men of letters employ for imaginative creation. We are intrigued by the experimentation of James Joyce and e. e. cummings, but until the IRS forms begin to spell *through* as *thru* and employ the useful negative *ain't*, we will continue to use the forms that began to be established in Chancery English and continued to evolve in bureaucratic composition.

What sort of changes did Tudor English make in Chancery English? I do not pretend here to provide a full analysis, but let me explain the major differences. The most important development was in punctuation. Punctuation in the era of manuscript publication was largely an oral phenomenon. Until the nineteenth century, reading was an oral activity (see the remarks and references in the last essay in this collection and in M.B. Parkes's *Pause and Effect*). When one reads aloud, the text does not make sense unless the voice punctuates. Latin rhetoric had analyzed the intonations of pauses and conclusions under the heading *cursus*. Essentially, however, it was assumed that a passage would be read aloud repeatedly until it made sense. Parkes shows (35) that in the Middle Ages, Latin was more carefully punctuated than the vernacular, particularly liturgical texts where misreading might produce heretical meanings. The humanists began to convert punctuation from rhetorical to logical and developed the full range of symbols. With the advent of printing, readers grew more proficient at reading silently. Logical punctuation had to be introduced for silent readers to serve as intonation did for oral readers.

English vernacular manuscripts were very sparsely punctuated. The handsome Hengwrt and Ellesmere manuscripts of *The Canterbury Tales* have only medial virgules marking the caesuras. The Chancery velums interchange (carelessly) virgule, period, and *punctus elevatus* (the upside-down semicolon) to set off phrasal elements. There is very little sense of the end of a sentence. Caxton's and Wynkyn de Worde's punctuation is essentially that of the English manuscripts, setting off (more carefully) phrasal units with virgules and occasional periods. But by the 1520s commas, introduced into Latin manuscripts by the humanists, began to replace virgules in printed texts, and commas and periods began to distinguish between phrases and clauses. By the 1560s the modern semicolon began to be used in printing, and soon thereafter question marks and exclamation marks begin to appear. By 1600 printed pages began to look very much like they do today, only with heavier punctuation and more capitals. Plates of a holograph page by Richard Hooker and the same page set in type (Parkes, *Pause and Effect* 258-60) show that educated authors were using the same punctuation as the printers, or perhaps vice versa. But displacement of the virgule, more regular use of capitals, and more logical employment of periods, commas, and semicolons made pages created in 1600 look very different from those produced in 1500.

A second difference between Chancery Standard and Tudor English is some regularization of spelling. Chancery spelling was extremely diverse, but the important development was that the variations no longer represented dialectal differences in pronunciation. In the glossary to *An Anthology of Chancery English* I have recorded all of the spellings of all of the words in the documents, indicating the number of times each spelling is used. Usually the form that has come down into Modern English is already the favorite form in

Chancery, *e.g.*, *abide* (8), *habyde* (1); *abouesaid(e)* (29), *abouseid* (10), *abousayde* (1); *any* (130), *eny* (104), *ony* (16). Sometimes, however, this is not the case, *e.g.*, *ayenst* (18), *ayens* (18), *aʒeyns* (8), *ageyns* (1), *ageynst* (1); *bitwene* (8), *betwene* (6), *between* (1). The chief difference is variation in the spelling of the unaccented vowels (schwa) *e/i/o/u/* (see *Anthology* 31-34). For example, *fader/fadres* (154), *fadir/fadris* (14), *fadur* (1); *people* (45), *pepil* (7), *pepul* (4); *costes* (6), *costis* (4); *goodes* (41), *goodis* (6), *goodus* (2). The maddening thing is that an individual scribe can use any of these variants within a word or a line. They were clearly regarded as graphemic rather than phonetic, just as we still use different shapes of *s* or *f* within a word or line. Variations between *i/y* and *u/w* were likewise graphemic; *y* and *u* were somewhat preferred with minims, *e.g.* *knyght* (26), *knight* (9), *nygh* (4), *nigh* (1); *in* (1683), *yn* (199); *doun(e)* (11), *down* (10), *toun(e)* (53), *town* (33). Another graphemic variation is in the joining of words, principally prepositions and headwords such as *by cause, vn to, wel beloued*. All of these variations continued in Tudor English but appeared less frequently as printing became more established. Erasmus spent his career copyediting and proofreading Latin. Caxton clearly did the same for his English, and his successors were even more concerned with establishing regularity.

A convenient way to follow the gradual regularization of the English is to look at *The Triumph of the English Language*, in which Richard Foster Jones excerpts quotations, carefully preserving the original spellings and punctuation, from most of the books of the sixteenth and seventeenth centuries. We can see the appearance of the passages growing more "modern" as time progresses. There is, however, still no marked regularity until preferred forms were codified in the eighteenth-century dictionaries and grammars. Even now, though, we still have variations embalmed in modern dictionaries: *plow/plough, controller/comptroller, caesarean/cesarean, per cent/percent, et cetera/etcetera*, and the British/American variants, *re/er, mme/m, s/z*, and so on.

Elision of the article or preposition with the following word is very frequent in Chancery English (*thende, teschewe*), in Caxton, and in some early examples in Jones (*cf.* Sir Thomas Elyot's 1534 sample, 13n25). By the time of Jones's discussion of these practices in his chapter "The Useful Language" (ca. 1600-1650), spelling and word separation had become much more modern and regular. The chief difference by this time was the presence of absence or final *e*: *he/hee, be/bee, defens/defense, becaus/because.*

The disappearance of thorn (þ) and geoc (ȝ) are another very visible difference between Chancery and Tudor English. The Chancery velums freely exchange þ and *th*, and ȝ and *gh/z*. Caxton and Wynkyn de Worde likewise exchanged these forms, but less frequently. The ȝ form disappeared shortly after 1500 but þ continued occasionally in print until the end of the century because it helped to justify the line. It was represented by *y* in script, and occasionally in print as late as a 1632 title page, "Argalvs and Parthenia: The Argument of Ye History" (Fisher, "Ancestry" 241 Fig. 9), and we still see "Ye Olde Tea Shoppe."

Finally there is the regularization of inflections and syntax. Again, a convenient way to follow the gradual standardization is to follow the selections in Jones. In Chancery the plural is usually *s*, but sometimes *n*, and we find *shoys* (shoes)/ *shone* in a 1525 example in Jones (6). The plural/possessive *eȝ* is very common in Chancery (indicating that the final *s* was beginning to be voiced) *kinges/kingeȝ*, but I have not found this usage in either Caxton's or Jones's examples. The objective *me*, *I recommende me/Ye declared me/me thoughte*, is frequent in Chancery and Caxton (*me semeth/now take me this panyr* [basket]—I am taking my Caxton readings from Lenaghan, which preserves the original text), but I have not found it in Jones's examples after 1600. The second person singular pronoun *thou/thy/the(e)* (usually þu/þi/þe) is regular in Chancery and Caxton but very infrequent even in the early Jones examples. Baugh's *History* lists it as a form that disappeared during the sixteenth century. This might be partly because the context so seldom calls for the singular. It was, of course, used regularly in the King James Bible (perhaps under the influence of Continental languages). I find an example in Francis Bacon (Jones 61) but in none of the other Jones examples. An important difference between Chancery and the early printers is the disappearance of the *h* forms for the plural pronoun. *They* was already regular in Chancery, but *her* (variously spelled) was as frequent as *their*, and *hem* more frequent than *them*. In Caxton *their/them* forms are already regular. *Hit* is regular in Chancery and Caxton, but it is gradually replaced by *it* in the Jones selections.

In Chancery verbs, the third person singular inflection *-eth/-eþ* is more formal than *-es/-s* (Fisher, *Anthology* 45). I find no example of

-*s* in Caxton. Throughout the succeeding century -*s* grows more frequent. In the King James Bible the third singular inflection is regularly -*th*. Shakespeare is famous for his mixed forms: stage direction in *Henry VIII* I.ii reads, "kisses and placeth her by him"; *The Merry Wives of Windsor* III.ii reads, "Has Page braines? hath he any eies?"; *Pericles* I.iv reads, "Who wanteth food and will not say he wants it?"

This brief summary suggests the sorts of developments that distinguish Chancery Standard from Early Modern English. Further changes have been made and continue to be made in style and lexicon as well as in orthography and punctuation. But they have continued, and still continue, under the aegis of "influential" writers and publications, and therefore carry with them the imprimatur of authority. English has never been governed by laws or academies, but its "standard" usages have been, and still are, dictated by the "authority" in the culture.

The essays in this volume were written on different occasions over a period of some twenty years. They should be considered in the context of the introduction to *An Anthology of Chancery English* and the final chapter of *The Importance of Chaucer*. Because of the nature of their creation, there was a good deal of repetition, which I have tried to remove in my revisions for collected publication.

II

A LANGUAGE POLICY FOR LANCASTRIAN ENGLAND

How did English become the national language of England? From the Norman Conquest until after 1400, French was the official language of England—not because any law had been passed to make it so but because it was the native language of all those who held office. As Sir John Fortescue explained in 1460, in *De Laudibus Legum Anglie* (I give the English translation by Stanley Chrimes of Fortescue's Latin):

> [A]fter the French had, by duke William the Conqueror, obtained the land, they would not permit advocates to plead their causes unless in the language they themselves knew, which all advocates do in France, even in the court and parliament there. Similarly, after their arrival in England, the French did not accept accounts of their revenues, unless in their own idiom, lest they should be deceived thereby. They took no pleasure in hunting, nor in other recreations, such as games of dice or ball, unless carried on in their own language. So the English contracted the same habit from frequenting such company, so that they to this day speak the French language in such games and accounting. (115)

From 1066 until 1217, England was the property of the dukes of Normandy, who were in turn subjects of the kings of France. The French connection was so strong that when Pope Innocent III divested Duke Jean, whom we call King John, of his lordship, he ordered the French king to carry out the sentence. When the barons fell out with John over the implementation of the Magna Carta, they offered the English crown to King Louis of France, who came over to England to take possession. England ceased to be a province of France when William Marshall defeated Louis in the Battle of Lincoln in 1217.

We think of the period from 1066 to 1350 as culturally barren in England, but some of the most important literature of that period was produced for the Anglo-Norman aristocracy that flourished on both sides of the Channel. The *Chanson de Roland*, Arthurian romances, troubadour lyrics, the first French play, French sermons, saints' lives, and chronicles are found in insular manuscripts and were probably composed in England. Moreover, some of the finest French writers—Chrétien de Troyes, Marie de France, Robert Grosseteste, and in Chaucer's time, Jean Froissart, John Mandeville, and John Gower—wrote French in England for Anglo-Norman audiences (Merilees; Legge).

The fourteenth century saw the beginning of the rebirth of English cultural independence, but the reigns of Edward III and Richard II, 1327-99, were the high point of the influence of French culture in England (Johnson; Vale; Matthew). As Ruskin observes in *The Stones of Venice*, it is when a culture is decaying that it articulates itself most clearly. After King John lost Normandy, he and his successors still claimed lordship over France south of the Loire, for which they were obliged to do homage to the French king. Beginning with Edward III, however, for a hundred years the English kings asserted, and tried to implement, their sovereignty over France.

This was the great era of French influence throughout Europe. The geographical centrality of France, the wealth and population its fertile lands generated in an agricultural economy, and its supremacy in chivalry (when a knight in armor was equivalent to a modern tank) made France the superpower of the Continent. But superpower in the medieval tribal sense. Until long after Chaucer's death there was no unified "France," only a kaleidoscope of competing dukedoms, of which the English were merely the most disruptive. French nationalism is not considered to have begun to emerge until the rise of Joan of Arc, ca. 1430, whereas English nationalism began to emerge in the 1340s with Edward III. Even though most of the energy of France during this period of cultural ascendancy was spent on internal conflict, enough was left to spill over onto its neighbors. When the pope and his curia moved to Avignon in 1309, France became the seat of religious as well as secular supremacy. Its modes of combat, architecture, religion, literature, dress, food, and manners set the standard everywhere, especially in England, which had for so long been an integral part of France.

Men of the English aristocracy regularly married Continental wives and married their own daughters to Continental husbands. King Edward's wife, Philippa, came from Hainault in modern Belgium. Froissart served as her secretary from 1361 until her death in 1369, and while in England he began collecting material for his chronicle of the Hundred Years' War. Chaucer's wife, Philippa, and her sister Katherine were the daughters of a French knight, Sir Paon de Roet, who came to England in the retinue of Queen Philippa. One wonders what the domestic language was in Sir Paon's household, in which Philippa grew up, and what Chaucer's own domestic language may have been when he married the daughter of a French knight. Katherine married Sir Thomas Swynford and later became the mistress and eventually the wife of John of Gaunt and mother of Henry Beaufort and his brothers who, I believe, played an important part in the re-establishment of English.

Below this aristocratic stratum, the English commoners were beginning to assert their own culture. It was English-speaking longbowmen who had cut down the French chivalry at Crécy and Poitiers. An argument used in the English parliaments of 1295, 1344, 1346, and 1376 to raise support for the wars against France was that French victory would annihilate the English language ("Chancery and the Emergence"). The Rolls of Parliament were regularly in Latin and French, but occasional entries indicate that the oral discussion was in English. In an entry of 1426, the exposition is in Latin but the lines spoken by the witnesses are in English. In another of 1432, the clerks of the Royal Chapel present a petition in Latin but the introduction is in English. In 1362, the clerks admitted for the first time that parliament was addressed in English, and in the same year parliament decreed that all legal proceedings had to be carried on in English because the litigants could not understand French. As a matter of fact, this statute was not enforced, and the common-law courts continued to plead in French until 1731, but that is another story.[1]

Evidently by the 1360s most oral exchange in commerce and government must have been carried on in English, but the records were still kept in Latin and French. Formal education was in Latin, and the writing masters who taught English clerks the secretarial skills of *ars dictaminis* taught them in Latin and French. Virtually all religious and cultural writings intended for any kind of circulation were in Latin or French. Such records as we have of the libraries of Edward Ill and Richard II and other books mentioned in wills and inventories before 1400 indicate that the books are exclusively in Latin and French. A.S.G. Edwards and Derek Pearsall estimate that there are extant only some thirty manuscripts of secular poetry in English written before 1400 and that nearly all are personal productions, like Cotton Nero A.X of the *Gawain* poems, King's College 13 of *William of Palerne*, and Bodley 264 of the *Alexander*. A.I. Doyle has pointed out that these few extant manuscripts are by household scribes writing in provincial dialects, not by professional scribes in London. The courtesy literature that distinguished the gentle from the churl was virtually all in French (Nicholls).

It is the politics of the movement of the written language from Latin and French to English that concerns me here. We are not now talking about when secular poetry began to be *composed* in English. From 1300 on, and particularly after 1350, more and more literature was composed in English, but clearly there was no audience that caused these English writings to be copied and disseminated. All the manuscripts of Geoffrey Chaucer, John Mandeville, John Trevisa, John Barbour, Laurence Minot, and other fourteenth century secular English authors date from after 1400. Gower might be regarded as an exception because one of the two earliest manuscripts of *Confessio Amantis* (the Stafford manuscript, now Huntington El 26.A.17) seems to have been dedicated to Henry Bolingbroke before he became king in 1399, but that is grist to my mill.

A great deal has been written about the emergence of writing in English after 1350, perhaps best in *A History of the English Language* by Albert Baugh and Thomas Cable, but like all others, Baugh and

Cable write as if English just happened. They trace a gradual accretion of statements about and documents in English that reveal an undirected, populist movement. Chaucer used to be given much credit for the transition in the language, and Derek Pearsall gives Lydgate almost as much importance in conferring prestige on literary English. But neither Baugh and Cable nor Pearsall, nor any others who have discussed the matter, point to the significance of the relation between the specific date at which manuscripts of English writings began to multiply and the date of the Lancastrian usurpation of the throne, September 1399. Until 1400 we have virtually no manuscripts of poetry in English that were commercially prepared and intended for circulation. Immediately after 1400 we have the manuscripts of Gower, Chaucer, and other fourteenth-century writers and the compositions and the manuscripts of Lydgate, Hoccleve, Clanvowe, Scogan, John Walton, Edward, Duke of York, and other fifteenth-century writers. After 1420 the libraries of Sir Richard Beauchamp, Sir Thomas Chaworth, Sir Edmund Rede, and Sir John Paston contained manuscripts by Chaucer and Lydgate as well as other courtly and didactic writings in English (Doyle).

I do not believe that this sudden burst of production of manuscripts written in English after 1400 was simply a natural evolution. I believe that it was encouraged by Henry IV, and even more by Henry V, as a deliberate policy intended to engage the support of government, business, and the English citizenry for the questionable Lancastrian usurpation of the throne. The publication of Chaucer's poems and his enshrinement as the perfecter of rhetoric in English were central to this effort. The evidence for this policy is circumstantial. King Henry, Prince Henry, Henry Beaufort, John Lydgate, Thomas Chaucer, and Thomas Hoccleve did not keep diaries about their plans and motives, but the associations and dates warrant examination.

The fragility of the reign of Henry IV is well known (Wylie, vol. I; Harriss, *Cardinal* ch. 2). During the first four years he had to contend with three rebellions of barons who rejected his title to the throne. He countered these by appealing to the commons for support, thus ultimately strengthening parliamentary government. One aspect of his appeal was the increased use of the English vernacular. The earliest English entry in the Rolls of Parliament is the 1388 petition of the Mercers Guild printed by Chambers and Daunt, but the next English entries are the 1397 address of Judge Rickhill concerning the impeachment of the duke of Gloucester, which precipitated the downfall of Richard II; two 1399 addresses by Chief Justice Thirnyng regarding the deposition of Richard; and—most important of all—Henry's own challenge to the throne on 30 September 1399 ("Chancery and the Emergence"). The only conceivable reason for these entries to be recorded in English at a time when the official entries in the Rolls were still uniformly in Latin and French was that they were meant to appeal to the commons.

John Gower says that Richard II encouraged him to write the *Confessio Amantis* in English (Fisher, *Gower* 9-11), but the earliest manuscript (Huntington El.26) appears to have been presented to Henry Bolingbroke upon his return from France in 1399. It is illuminated with the lion recognizance of John of Gaunt and the swan of Thomas of Gloucester, a symbol that Bolingbroke assumed immediately after Gloucester's murder. The absence of royal emblems indicates that the manuscript was completed before Henry's coronation. Immediately after the coronation, Gower composed *In Praise of Peace*, a poem in English warning Henry not to presume on the right of conquest but to seek peace and to rule with pity (Fisher, *Gower* 132-33). Between the time of Henry's accession and Gower's death in 1408, Gower commissioned perhaps ten manuscripts of his *Confessio* and other English poems. Richard Firth Green in *Poets and Princepleasers* has a good deal to say about Gower's support of Henry's usurpation.

In 1393 Henry had given Gower a collar with a swan pendant, apparently as a reward for Gower's support of Thomas of Gloucester, and soon after his coronation Henry granted Gower two pipes of wine yearly (21 Nov. 1399). At nearly the same time (13 Oct. 1399[2]), the King doubled Chaucer's annuity from Richard to £20 and granted to Hoccleve, then a young clerk in the Privy Seal office, an annuity of £10 (12 Nov. 1399). Henry IV may have made these grants for the writers' civil service rather than for their poetry, but his benefactions to Gower, Chaucer, and Hoccleve all three certainly qualify him as a supporter of poets writing in English.

Our attention now shifts to Henry V, who came to the throne in 1413. The entries in the Rolls of Parliament under Henry IV continued to be mostly in French, and Henry V continued to use French for his correspondence as Prince of Wales and during the first three years of his reign. His effort to secure the support of the Commons in parliament was even more strenuous than that of his father: in 1414 he granted that their statutes should be recorded without altering the language of the petitions on which they were based. There is no evidence that this elevated the use of English, but petitions and the actions upon them are the primary constituents of the Rolls of Parliament. Henry V's success at Agincourt in 1415, after so many years of failure in the wars with France, reinforced English nationalism. In 1416, as the king began to assemble his forces to make good his claim to the French throne, he addressed five proclamations in English to the citizens of London, requesting supplies and commanding soldiers and sailors to assemble for the invasion.[3] These are the first royal proclamations in English since the proclamation of Henry III in 1258, and that had been the only royal document in English since the a proclamation of William the Conqueror in 1087. Most significantly, upon reaching France on 12 August 1417, Henry addressed his first missive in English to his chancellor. From that time until his death in 1422, he used English in nearly all his correspondence with the government and the citizens of London and other English cities. Henry V's use of English marks the turning point in establishing English as the national language of England. Its effect is reflected in the familiar entry of 1422 in the abstract book of the Brewers Guild explaining their change of record keeping from Latin to English:

> Whereas our mother-tongue, to wit the English tongue, hath in modern days begun to be honorably enlarged and adorned, for that our most excellent lord, King Henry V, hath in his letters missive and divers affairs touching his own person, more willingly chosen to declare the secrets of his will, for the better understanding of his people, hath with a diligent mind procured the common idiom (setting aside others) to be commended by the excercise of writing; and there are many of our craft of Brewers who have the knowledge of writing and reading in the said English idiom, but in others, to wit, the Latin and French, before these times used, they do not in any wise understand. For which causes with many others, it being considered how that the greater part of the Lords and trusty Commons have begun to make their matters to be noted down in our mother tongue, so we also in our craft, following in some manner their steps, have

decreed to commit to memory the needful things which concern
us [in English]. (Chambers and Daunt 139)

This momentous decision is recorded in Latin, but in the 1420s
the Brewers and other guilds did switch their record keeping to
English, and the Chancery dialect, modeled in many ways on Henry's
own grammar and idiom (Richardson; Fisher, Richardson, and
Fisher), became the prestige written language (Samuels). Chambers
and Daunt edited many of these documents in their *Book of London
English*, and Malcolm Richardson, Jane Fisher, and I edited Henry's
Signet letters and other English Chancery documents in *An Anthology
of Chancery English*.

This is the documented historical record, but I believe that the
transformation of the language of government and business would
not have been possible without more than a decade of preparation
and propaganda. Let us go back to 1398 when Prince Henry was
eleven years old. According to a tradition commencing with the
Chronicle of John Rous, completed in 1477, Henry Beaufort (son of
John of Gaunt and Katherine Swynford and therefore half brother to
Henry IV, son of John of Gaunt and Blanche of Lancaster) was tutor
to Prince Henry at Queen's College, Oxford. The relationships with
Beaufort and the university are not mentioned in any other chronicle,
and Rous's account—coming, as it does, some eighty years after the
event—is regarded as questionable evidence. But it may be pointed
out that since Rous was born in 1411 and at Oxford by 1425, his
testimony is more current than the 1477 date of the completion of
his chronicle might indicate. Nineteenth-century biographers accepted both relationships (e.g., Armitage-Smith 414; Towle 170-71),
and recent biographers accept the tutorship but not the prince's
residence at Oxford (e.g., Harriss, *Cardinal* 9; Hutchinson 18; Seward
4). The careful conclusion of the entry on Henry Beaufort in the
Dictionary of National Biography suggests why Harriss and others have
accepted the tutorship: [Beaufort] "is said to have been the tutor of
the Prince of Wales. He certainly exercised considerable influence
over him. While the king was in a great measure guided by Arundel,
the prince attached himself to the younger and more popular party
of which [Beaufort] was the head." In the entry on Henry V,
the *DNB* narrows the inference: "The tradition that he was educated at Queen's College, Oxford, under the care of his uncle Henry

Beaufort . . . first appears in the 'Chronicle of John Rous' (ed. Hearne 207). Beaufort was chancellor [of Oxford] in 1398, and, if the statement is correct, the prince's residence at Oxford must have fallen in this year. There is, however, no record relating to Henry at Queen's College."

Again the evidence is circumstantial. The political association between the Prince and Beaufort from 1403 onward, abundantly detailed and documented in Harriss's *Cardinal Beaufort*, was so constant and familiar that biographers feel they must accept a personal relationship, hence the tutorship; the lack of any record at Oxford, however, makes them hesitant about the Queen's College association. One might ask, Why accept one half of Rous's statement but not the other? Furthermore, would it have been so unusual for the college records not to mention a boy of eleven—even a prince—staying with his uncle and having no official connection with Oxford? Hutchinson (17) and Seward (3) never consider where and when the tutorship that they accept might have occurred. As the *DNB* observes, the best possibility for the tutorship is 1398, when Beaufort was chancellor of Oxford.

In the fall of 1398, at the age of twenty-three, Henry Beaufort was made Bishop of Lincoln and began his service with the king. But G.L. Harriss surmises that Beaufort still spent a good deal of time in Oxford until 1403, when he was appointed chancellor of England for the first time (*Cardinal* 8, 12, 19). He served as chancellor four times—under Henry IV, V, and VI—becoming the richest man in England and supplying enormous sums to support the war in France. According to the historian William Stubbs, until his death in 1447, Beaufort "held the strings of English policy" (3: 143). K.B. McFarlane's essay "At the Deathbed of Cardinal Beaufort" is a fascinating overview of Beaufort's wealth and influence (*Collected Essays* 115-38).

Prince Henry was not at Oxford continuously after 1398. In October of that year King Richard, after banishing Henry Bolingbroke and confiscating the Lancastrian holdings, called the prince to court, and in January 1399 he took young Henry with him on his expedition to Ireland. There Henry remained until his victorious father sent a ship for him the next October. After Henry had been made Prince of Wales on 15 October 1399, he was reported to be at Chester and in Wales with the troops from time to time, but until 1403 his connection with the Welsh wars was nominal. The actual operations were in the imperious hands of Sir Henry Percy (Hotspur). It was the rebellion of the Percys that led to Prince Henry's appointment in March 1403 as King's Lieutenant of the Marches of Wales, making him commander-in-chief in fact as well as in name at the age of sixteen (Harriss, *Cardinal* 15; Seward 18). We have no continuous account of Prince Henry's whereabouts between October 1399 and March 1403. In the same month that the prince assumed military command, Henry Beaufort was named Chancellor of England for the first time. So whatever period there could have been for Henry Beaufort and Prince Henry to contemplate the place of English in Lancastrian policy would have been in whatever intervals they may have passed together at Queen's College and elsewhere between 1398 and 1403.

During this five years, Thomas Chaucer was settling into his manor at Ewelme, about ten miles from Oxford.[4] Thomas was the son of Philippa Chaucer, the sister of Katherine Swynford. I will not here go into the question of whether his father was Geoffrey Chaucer or John of Gaunt, but Thomas was at least first cousin to the Beauforts and may have been an unacknowledged half brother of both the Beauforts and the king (Fisher, *Importance* 19-23). His amazing career points in this direction. In 1395 he was married to a wealthy heiress, Maud Bergersh, through whom he acquired Ewelme and many other valuable properties, and he was showered with honors from the moment Henry IV assumed the throne: in 1399 he was appointed Constable of Wallingford Castle; in 1400 Sheriff of Oxfordshire; and in 1402 King's Butler, a position carrying the responsibility not only for procuring and dispensing the wine for the royal household but also for collecting petty customs, the tax on wine imports throughout the kingdom. He sat as member of parliament for Oxfordshire in 1401 and in thirteen other parliaments. He was speaker for the Commons in the parliament of 1407 and in three other parliaments. And he remained until his death in 1434 an important intermediary between the Commons and the king.

A third member of Prince Henry's putative Oxford circle between 1398 and 1403 may have been John Lydgate. We know that he was at Gloucester College, Oxford, in 1406 from a letter by the prince to the abbot and chapter of Bury Saint Edmunds asking them to allow Lydgate to continue his studies at Oxford (Pearsall 29). John

Norton-Smith believes that Lydgate was in residence there from 1397 to 1408 (195).

Thomas Chaucer was one of Lydgate's longtime patrons, and by all accounts the two sustained a pleasant relationship at Ewelme (see Schirmer; Pearsall; Ebin). Thomas's manor was the salon for a literate Lancastrian circle much interested in English poetry, and from these patrons Lydgate received several commissions. In the complimentary *Balade at the Departyng of Thomas Chaucer into France*, he extolled Thomas as his "maister dere," the same term he had applied several times to Geoffrey. The ballad to Thomas Chaucer, like the friendship between Prince Henry and Henry Beaufort, is circumstantial evidence for an association dating back to college. An Oxford association of the prince, his tutor, his cousin, and the budding poet-apologist for the house of Lancaster could have been the time and place when the seeds for the self-conscious cultivation of English as the national language were planted. The first sprout of that momentous plan may have been the decision to organize and publish the poetry of Geoffrey Chaucer.

There are no extant manuscripts of Chaucer's poems dating from before his death in 1400, and it is the general (though by no means universal) opinion that he died without commissioning a presentation copy of a single one of his works ("Animadversions"). Why this was apparently the case we do not know, since presentation of an elaborate manuscript to a patron was the accepted method of publication in the Middle Ages (Root). Chaucer's failure to publish, or the loss of all his presentation manuscripts, is one of the great mysteries of early English literary culture. Furthermore, the textual evidence seems to indicate that Chaucer fully finished very few of his works, either poetry or prose ("Animadversions"; Blake; Windeatt). He was living in Westminster during the first two years of the fateful 1398-1403 period, presumably surrounded by copies of works that were well known to the courtly and commercial circles of London from oral presentations dating back over thirty years, which had never been published because of Chaucer's own diffidence and because of the lack of prestige of English as a cultivated language. Everyone spoke English, but writing in English was simply not couth.

This is not an unusual sociolinguistic situation. It was exhibited in Montreal, Canada, and in India and Norway at the beginning of this century.[5] In Montreal, most of the population spoke French, but business and commercial writing was largely in English. In Norway most of the population spoke Norwegian dialects but wrote Danish. In India, most of the population spoke Prakrit dialects, of which Hindi was the most widespread, but official writing was in English. In these cultures in the nineteenth century and for some time afterward, the populace generally spoke native dialects, but official and polite writing was in non-native prestige languages. So it was with England until after 1400.

French, Norwegian, and Hindi are now official languages in these cultures and are exemplified by increasingly sophisticated literatures. But the elevation of these languages is not merely the result of demographic and economic evolution. It reflects deliberate political decisions. Today we have ample evidence about how such linguistic decisions are made, but the absence of recorded evidence for linguistic change in England in 1400 does not mean that the process was different at that time. England had persisted in its bilingual situation, with French as the official language and English as a patois, for four hundred years—two hundred years after the Battle of Lincoln made the country politically independent and sixty years after the beginning of the Hundred Years' War made France its enemy. It seems likely that bilingualism might have persisted for much longer if it had not been for a deliberate decision by some influential authority.

Henry V was such an authority. Much has been made of his charisma as a national hero, of his cultivation of nationalism, and of his communication with Parliament and the citizenry (Harriss *Henry V*). It took him three years after his accession to implement the use of English in his Signet letters. This action could hardly have been casual and unpremeditated. There was a persistent medieval tradition that official languages were implemented by kings—by King Alfred in Anglo-Saxon England (Richards), by Philip the Fair in France (Brunot 1: 370), Alphonse X in Spain ("European Chancelleries"; Wolff 178). Modern linguists tend to discount this tradition and to attribute sociolinguistic developments to impersonal demographic and economic forces. I do not deny the importance of such forces, but I think that, whatever the process in Montreal, the development of Norwegian would not have proceeded as it did without the leadership of Knud Knudsen and Ivar Asen, nor of Hindi without the leadership of B.J. Tilak and Mahatma Gandhi (see note 5). Einar Haugen specifically discusses the role of the language planner and cites the names of language planners in northern European countries and in Greece and Turkey (168-70). The history of the developments of all official languages for which there is documentation shows that such developments do not occur without influential leadership and deliberate political process.

The outburst of copying and composing in English that began soon after 1400 can best be explained as an intentional activity that laid the groundwork for the political actions of 1416-22. That Chaucer should be chosen as the cynosure for this movement would not be at all surprising. He was of both the royal and the commercial circles, son of a vintner and a close relative by marriage to King Henry IV, Prince Henry, and the Beauforts. His vernacular poetry had already attracted the attention of Thomas Usk, Henry Scogan, John Clanvowe, and other contemporaries in England, and of Eustach Deschamps in France. Norman Blake, developing the arguments of J.S.P. Tatlock, Germaine Dempster, A.I. Doyle, Malcolm Parkes, and others, has given a persuasive account of the evolution of the text of *The Canterbury Tales* from the initial effort to make sense of the foul papers in the Hengwrt manuscript to the fully edited text in the Ellesmere manuscript. Blake envisages the development of five or six versions under the direction of a group of editors working to give a veneer of completeness to papers that Chaucer had left in disarray at the time of his death.

The most sumptuous of all Chaucer manuscripts and written by the same scribe as Hengwrt, Ellesmere is associated by its illuminations and scrimshaw with Thomas Chaucer, whom Manly and Rickert propose as "logically the person to have made what was clearly intended as an authoritative text" (1: 159). Thomas would presumably have had opportunities to visit his father during the poet's last years in Westminster and to arrange for the Hengwrt scribe to begin making an initial compilation from the foul papers. He and his friends (Henry Beaufort, Prince Henry?) could have gone over the result with the scribe and engaged another scribe to produce the Corpus version. Thomas and his friends would have then gone through a similar editing process with this new version and then with the Harlean, Lansdowne, and two Cambridge versions—I am following Blake's scenario. With the last two manuscripts the editors approached completion: Cambridge Dd achieved the Ellesmere order for the tales, and Cambridge Gg introduced the first illustrations of the pilgrims. Having gotten to this stage, Thomas Chaucer could have arranged for the original scribe to produce the Ellesmere manuscript, incorporating all the editorial "improvements" arrived at throughout the several versions.

This process would have been expensive, but Thomas Chaucer had the money to pay for it. Doyle and Parkes give a fascinating account of a group of five scribes working in London and Westminster in the first quarter of the fourteenth century who produced eight of the earliest manuscripts of *The Canterbury Tales*, including four of those that Blake treats in his scenario of the evolution of the text (Hg, El, Cp, and Ha). One or more of the same group of scribes also produced a copy of *Troylus and Criseyde*, seven copies of *Confessio Amantis*, a copy of *Piers Plowman*, a copy of John Trevisa's translation of *Bartholomaeus Anglicus*, and three manuscripts of the writings of Thomas Hoccleve. Indeed, as one of the group himself, Hoccleve cooperated in producing the Trinity College manuscript of *Confessio Amantis* that Doyle and Parkes use as the touchstone for their analysis.

Doyle and Parkes's evidence indicates that the London book trade at the beginning of the fifteenth century was still very informal. The shifting associations among the scribes militates against the notion of bookshops employing regular staffs of copyists. It appears that books were produced under individual contract. The contractors were called "stationers" because they were stationary; that is, they had shops where they could be reached. Paul Christianson is assembling evidence that these shops were clustered around Saint Paul's Church in London. There the stationers accepted commissions from patrons for books or other documents, which they copied themselves or hired other scribes to help with. These assistants operated on a piecework basis, fascicle by fascicle, in their own rooms. When the copying was complete, the stationer would assemble the fascicles and send them out to the limners to be decorated and eventually to the binders to be bound. Most of the piecework clerks would be, like Hoccleve, regularly employed in government or commercial offices. Some, like Doyle and Parkes's scribe D, might be freelance scriveners.

This commercial method of book production had begun long before 1400, but until then its products in England had all been in

Latin or French. We have no evidence that the switch to English was stimulated by any policy of Henry IV, Prince Henry, or Henry Beaufort. None of the manuscripts by the five scribes identified by Doyle and Parkes reveals any connection with royalty, but royalty and aristocracy were patrons of English manuscripts. The Morgan manuscript of *Troylus and Criseyde* has on its first page the arms of Prince Henry while he was still Prince of Wales. Additionally, English poetry composed at the beginning of the century shows that Prince Henry was considered a patron and Geoffrey Chaucer the initiator. G.L. Harriss observes that Hoccleve's *Regement of Princes* was completed in 1411 and Lydgate's *Troy Book* was commissioned in 1412, precisely the years "in which the prince, at the head of a council of his own choosing and virtually without reference to his father, was carrying through a sustained programme of 'bone governance' to which he had pledged himself in the parliament of January 1410" (*Henry V* 9). Part of the "bone governance" may have been the enhancement of the position of English.

This takes us back to the third member of the putative Oxford circle, John Lydgate. Lydgate's dedication of the *Troy Book* comes as close as anything we have to attributing to Prince Henry a "nationalistic" policy for enhancing the use of English. The prince, Lydgate says,

> Whyche me comaunded the drery pitus fate
> Of hem of Troye in englysche to translate
> . . . .
> By-cause he wolde that to hyge and lowe
> The noble story openly wer knowe
> In oure tonge, aboute in every age,
> And y-writen as wel in oure langage
> As in latyn or in frensche it is;
> That of the story the trouthe we nat mys
> No more than doth eche other nacioun:
> This was the fyn of his entencioun.
> 　　　　　(*Troy Book*, Prologue 105-6, 111-18)

Schirmer identifies the Tanner D.2 manuscript of this poem as the possible presentation copy to Henry himself (50). Lydgate's *Life of Our Lady* is likewise in one manuscript ascribed to the "excitation and stirryng of our worshipful prince, kyng Harry the fifthe." Even though Pearsall doubts the validity of this ascription because the work was never finished and contains no internal reference to the patron such as Lydgate usually makes (Pearsall 286), the ascription manifests recognition of Henry's patronage of English letters.

What most supports my argument, however, is Lydgate's acknowledgment that his version of the Troy story is based on Chaucer's model:

> The hoole story Chaucer kan yow telle
> Yif that ye liste, no man bet alyve,
> Nor the processe halfe so wel discryve,
> For he owre englishe gilte with his sawes,
> Rude and boistous firste be olde dawes,
> That was ful fer from al perfeccioun,
> And but of litel reputaticoun,
> Til that he cam & thorug his poetrie,
> Gan oure tonge firste to magnifie,
> And adourne it with his elloquence—
> To whom honour, laude, & reverence
> Thorug oute this londe yove be & songe,
> So that the laurer of oure englishe tonge
> Be to hym yove for his excellence,
> Rigt as whilom by ful hige sentence
> Perpetuelly for a memorial.
> (*Troy Book* 3.4234-49)

Two of Lydgate's earliest poems, *The Complaint of the Black Knight* and *The Flour of Curtesye*, which are dated by Schirmer between 1400 and 1402 (during the fateful 1398-1403 period) are acts of homage to Chaucer (Schirmer 34, 37). The acknowledgment in *The Flour of Curtesye* suggests that they may have been composed very soon after Chaucer's death:

> Ever as I can supprise in myn herte
> Alway with feare betwyxt drede and shame
> Leste oute of lose, any worde asterte
> In this metre to make it seme lame,
> Chaucer is deed that had suche a name
> Of fayre makyng that [was] without wene
> Fayrest in our tonge, as the Laurer grene.

We may assay forto countrefete
His gay style but it wyl not be;
The welle is drie, with the lycoure swete . . .
                    (Spurgeon 1.15)

In *The Churl and the Bird* (ca. 1408), a beast fable somewhat like the
Nun's Priest's Tale, Lydgate again does obeisance to Chaucer's prece-
dence in creating an English that could stand beside French:

Go gentill quayer, and Recommaunde me
Unto my maistir with humble affectioun
Beseke hym lowly of mercy and pite
Of thy rude makyng to have compassioun
And as touching thy translacioun
Oute of frensh / houghever the englisshe be
Al thing is saide undir correctioun
With supportacioun of your benignite.
                    (Spurgeon 1.15)

Schirmer observes that these poems, like most others by Lydgate,
must have been written in response to commissions, but he does not
venture who the patrons might have been (31, 37). I would like to
think that the poems were commissioned by Henry Beaufort and
Prince Henry at the same time that they were encouraging Thomas
Chaucer to bring out his father's works.

The *Temple of Glas*, another early work acknowledging
Chaucer's inspiration, could likewise have been composed in response to the Oxford inspiration. In addition, Lydgate pays tribute
to his master Chaucer in the *Serpent of Division* (ca. 1420) and the
Siege of Thebes (ca. 1422), works whose patrons are not identified;
in the *Pilgrimage of the Life of Man* (ca. 1427), written for Thomas
Montacute, the husband of Chaucer's granddaughter Alice; and in
the *Fall of Princes* (ca. 1431), written for Humphry, Duke of
Gloucester, the youngest brother of Henry V. The list of Lydgate's
patrons reads like a *Who's Who* of both the courtly and commercial
circles in England, suggesting influential support stemming from
the Lancastrian affinity for the cultivation of English. If this
support was the result of policy inaugurated at Oxford about 1400
by Henry Beaufort and Prince Henry—a resolve to elevate the
prestige of English and to display Chaucer's poetry as the cynosure

of this elevation—then John Lydgate could be considered the public relations agent for this policy.

Lydgate was not alone in his promotional efforts. I have already mentioned Thomas Hoccleve as one of the scribes in the cohort that was turning out commercial manuscripts in English. Hoccleve's relation to the emergence of English is peculiar. As a clerk in the Westminster office of the Privy Seal, he should have been party to the introduction of English into Chancery. But after he retired from the office, about 1425, he compiled a formulary with examples of different kinds of instruments issued by the Privy Seal office. These examples are all in French or Latin, but between folios 36 and 37 there is a scrap of vellum in Hoccleve's hand with one of the earliest statements about Chancery procedure, showing that Chancery was a cultivated style: "In a precedende write word by word and leter by leter titel by titel as the copie is & than look ther be aplid ther on in the chauncerie & that the write be retourned unto the chauncerie and begin thus . . . " (Fisher, "Chancery Standard" 141). The instructions go on, in increasingly illegible script, to address themselves to Latin formulas. Hoccleve's professional languages, like Chaucer's, were always Latin and French while, as did Chaucer, he wrote his poetry in English. Like Lydgate, Hoccleve acknowledged Prince Henry as the patron of English and Chaucer as its initiator. *The Regement of Princes* begins with a warm dedication to "[h]ye and noble prince excellent" (l. 2017) and speaks of the prince's grandfather, John of Gaunt, and father, Henry IV (ll. 3347-53), indicating that the poem was completed before Prince Henry ascended to the throne in 1413. Halfway through the dedication comes the first reference to Chaucer: "Mi dere maistir—god his soule quyte!—/ And fadir, Chaucer, fayn wolde han me taght; / But I was dul and lerned lite or naght" (ll. 2077-79). The dedication ends with more compliments to the prince and good wishes for his reign and leads into what Jerome Mitchell has called "virtually the first full-fledged English manual of instruction for a prince" (31), which was a subject of great interest to the public (more than forty manuscripts are extant) since the behavior of the king was the only context in which people of that period could conceive of social amelioration. The discussion continues to be punctuated with exhortations to Prince Henry both to be virtuous and to pay Hoccleve his annuity. Near the end, under the heading "take counsel," comes the most explicit tribute to Chaucer, accompanied by the famous picture that is thought to be the exemplar for the Ellesmere and other contemporary portraits:

> The firste fyndere of our faire langage,
> Hath seyde in caas semblable, & othir moo,
> So hyly wel, that it is my dotage
> For to expresse or touche any of thoo.
> Alasse! my fadir fro the worlde is goo—
> Be thou my advoket for hym, hevenes quene!
> (*Regement* 4978-83)

Hoccleve wrote five other poems addressed to Henry V after the king ascended to the throne.

Much more could be written—and indeed, has been written (*e.g.*, Bennett)—about the efflorescence of compositions and multiplication of manuscripts in English in the first quarter of the fifteenth century. I have said nothing about Henry Scogan's *Moral Ballad*, addressed to Prince Henry and his brothers, which also acknowledges "my maister Chaucer," but my line of argument is by this time evident. Hoccleve, no more than Lydgate, ever articulated for the Lancastrian rulers a policy of encouraging the development of English as a national language or of citing Chaucer as the exemplar for such a policy. But we have the documentary and literary evidence of what happened. The linkage of praise for Prince Henry as a model ruler concerned about the use of English and for master Chaucer as the "firste fyndere of our faire langage"; the sudden appearance of manuscripts of *The Canterbury Tales*, *Troylus and Criseyde*, and other English writings composed earlier but never before published; the conversion to English of the Signet clerks of Henry V, the Chancery clerks, and eventually the guild clerks; and the burgeoning of composition in English and the patronage of literature in English by the Lancastrian court circle are all concurrent historical events. The only question is whether their concurrence was coincidental or deliberate.

All linguistic changes of this sort for which we have documentation—in Norway, India, Canada, Finland, Israel, or elsewhere—have been the result of planning and official policy. There is no reason to suppose that the situation was different in England. Policy in the Middle Ages originated with the king, who worked with the advice of influential counselors (Scanlon). As we look at England between 1399 and 1422, we see Henry IV and Henry V attempting to establish their shaky administrations by appealing to parliament; the Beaufort brothers and Thomas Chaucer providing counsel and support; the poetry of Thomas's father being cited as the cynosure for cultivated English; and Henry V beginning to use English for his official missives. An association of Prince Henry, Henry Beaufort, Thomas Chaucer, and John Lydgate at Oxford and Ewelme between 1398 and 1403 would have offered an appropriate opportunity for the initiation of a plan to cultivate English as the official and prestige language of the nation. Oh to have been a cricket on the hearth at Queen's College and Ewelme Manor to have heard the talk that went on around the fire in those years!

III

Chancery
and the Emergence of
Standard Written English

Descriptive linguists and sociolinguists have debated the nature of "standard" English, the first group tending to deny the existence of a standard because of variations in the spoken language, and the second arguing that standard language is an elitist shibboleth erected to perpetuate the authority of the dominant culture.[1] Neither of these positions recognizes the historical fact that in every society there is a formal, official language in which business is conducted, which is different from the patois of familiar exchange. The more stable and enduring a society becomes, the more regular its administrative procedures become. Part of the process of regularizing the procedures is the standardization of the official language in which they are transacted and recorded. The official language thus very early achieves a regular written form.[2]

Official languages have always been the prerogatives of ruling hierarchies, from Mandarin Chinese to Sanskrit to classical Latin. The "standard" West Saxon used throughout England in the tenth and eleventh centuries was evidently the product of King Alfred's royal secretariat.[3] That this language was different from the spoken Old English dialects may be deduced from the rapidity with which it disappeared as soon as the central administration turned to Latin and French.[4] My interest is in the re-emergence of English in the fifteenth century as an administrative language, independent of the spoken dialect of any region or class. In the long run, this language imposed its own structure and idiom upon those who conducted the affairs of the nation. Curiously, the rise of standard written English has never been studied in terms of the emergence of an official language. Evidence has been collected by H.C. Wyld, A.C. Baugh, and others about the re-emergence of spoken English among the middle classes and aristocracy in the fourteenth century.[5] Parliament was opened for the first time in English in 1362, and this evidence, in addition to the fact that Chaucer and Gower began to write their pieces in English to be recited before the royal court and the Inns of Court, clearly indicates that English had become the first language for a majority of the population. However, historians of the language have discussed only in the most general terms the transition from speaking colloquial English to writing clear, business-like English prose. Take, for example, Wyld's explanation in *A History of Modern Colloquial English*:

> If we examine the records of our language in the past, it appears that from the thirteenth century onwards a large number of writings exist which were produced in London, and apparently in the dialect of the capital. These documents are of various kinds, and include proclamations, charters, wills, parliamentary records, poems, and treatises. Among the latter we may reckon the works of Chaucer. The language of these London writings agrees more closely with the form of English which was later recognized as the exclusive form for literary purposes than does the language of any other mediaeval English documents.... London speech, then, or one type of it, as it existed in the fourteenth century, is the ancestor of our present-day Received Standard.[6]

This sort of generalization is found in many histories of the language. It contains two inaccuracies. First of all, it identifies the language of official proclamations, charters, and parliamentary records with spoken language. I noted earlier the universal dichotomy between formal, official language and the colloquial. It is hard at this distance to know how much difference or just what differences there were between royal proclamations and the speech of London citizens in 1400, but all history points to the fact that they were not the same.

Second, Wyld identifies official proclamations, charters, and parliamentary records with London. This is too loose an interpretation of English administrative history. Official documents of this sort were not associated with the City of London; they were instead compositions by the national government. By the fifteenth century, when written English began to be standardized, this national government was located mainly in Westminster, just outside of London. But its activity and bureaucracy were quite independent of that of the city. Its members were not predominantly Londoners. They looked to the country at large—indeed to all of Europe—for the recruitment of staff and transaction of their business. Their primary concern in language, whether Latin, French, or English, must have been to maintain a comprehensible official idiom for communication throughout the kingdom. This distinction between civic English and government English was first attempted by Lorenz Morsbach in 1888.[7] His discussion, however, had no appreciable influence upon subsequent historians of the language, partly because the documents to support his case were not then accessible either in print or in the Public Record Office, but even more for what A.A. Prins refers to as his "humanistic shortcoming."[8] Morsbach could never get beyond "Lautlehre" and "Formenlehre" to discuss the intellectual significance of the question he posed. In 1931 R.W. Chambers and Marjorie Daunt followed up on Morsbach's work, providing the examples of London English that his work had lacked. Unlike Wyld, they recognized that their guild and corporation records were local. This collection, as Chambers and Daunt state in their introduction, is only part "of a much bigger question—the question of what was recognized as Standard English in the later Middle Ages." They proposed to go about tackling this larger question by collecting "all the official documents in the English tongue from the time of the Conqueror to that of Henry VI."[9] However, as it turned out, they never went ahead to make such a collection.

Historical Background of Chancery

Chancery was the agency that produced most of the official proclamations and parliamentary records cited by Wyld as among the ancestors of Modern Standard English. When the term Chancery is used today, it carries with it restricted implications of a certain kind of law court, since after the fifteenth century Chancery came to be limited to its juridical functions, and the activities of the national bureaucracy were departmentalized into the various "offices" of the government. But until the end of the fifteenth century, Chancery comprised virtually all of the national bureaucracy in England except for the closely allied Exchequer. Thomas Frederick Tout, who made a lifetime study of the workings of Chancery and its affiliated offices, began his six-volume *Chapters in Mediaeval Administrative History* by quoting Palgrave's observation that "Chancery was the Secretariat of State in all departments of late medieval government."[10]

As Tout and others have pointed out, all medieval administration grew out of the household of the king.[11] The ruler trusted the administration of his dominions to his household servants. Chancery grew out of the little office connected with the chancel, or chapel, where the chaplains of the court occupied themselves between divine services by writing the king's letters. In an age when writing was a rare art with laymen—even with kings—executives authenticated their letters not by signing them but by affixing their seals. The most responsible of the chaplains was entrusted with the king's seal and inevitably came to be trusted with the responsibility for composing and authenticating the royal correspondence. As the royal administration grew more complex, the "chancellor" who handled the king's correspondence became the most trusted of his ministers, in effect prime minister. To discharge his work he had to gather about him a staff of skilled assistants. These assistants, in turn, would look to the chancellor rather than to the king as their master, and so the household of the chancellor began to separate itself from the royal household. As the tasks of the chancellor's clerks became more technical, the clerks became more indispensable. Orderly functioning of government services could be maintained only by a permanent staff that carried on its activities regardless of changes in kings and ministers. Hence, by the middle of the thirteenth century the household of the chancellor would become the household of Chancery, where the continuity of the office was emphasized rather than the importance of the person ruling over it at any given time.

Until the fourteenth century, there was little association between Chancery and Westminster. Like the rest of his household, Chancery followed the king in his peregrinations about the country, and correspondence up to this time may be dated from York, Winchester, Hereford, or wherever the court happened to pause (as the king's personal correspondence continued to be dated throughout the fifteenth century). It is important to observe that in its movement about the country, the court as a whole must have reinforced the impression of an official class dialect, in contrast to the regional dialects with which it came in contact.

For two centuries this court dialect would have been spoken French and written Latin; after 1300 it would have been increasingly spoken English and written French. Presumably the English spoken in court then and for a long time afterwards was quite varied in its pronunciation and structure. E.J. Dobson has presented evidence that the pronunciation of English among the educated classes was not standardized until the eighteenth century.[12] Written Latin, however, had been standardized in classical times, and by the thirteenth century written French also began to be standardized in form and to achieve the lucid idiom that English prose was not to achieve until the fifteenth century. Increasingly throughout the fourteenth century, Latin and French were written by clerks whose first language was English. Latin was the essential subject in school, but the acquisition of French was more informal, and by the end of the century we have Chaucer's satire on the French of the Prioress, Gower's apologies for his own (quite acceptable) French, and the errors in legal briefs which betoken Englishmen trying to compose in a foreign language.[13] By 1400 the use of English in speaking and Latin and French in administrative writing had established a clear dichotomy between the colloquial language and the official written language. For the Chancery clerks using English in their official writing after 1420, this separation of language must have made it easier to create an artificial written standard independent of the spoken dialects.

The Hundred Years War between England and France brought into play forces that influenced the evolution of Chancery as an office and allowed for the beginning of the standardization of Chancery English. When Edward III was absent from the realm, Chancery came to be localized at Westminster. By 1345 the recognized location of Chancery was "the southwest angle of Westminster Hall where said chancellor commonly sits at the marble table among the clerks of Chancery discharging the duties of his office."[14] The last full-scale removal from Westminster was at the time of Richard II's quarrel with London in 1392-93, which led John Gower to change the dedication of his *Confessio Amantis* to Henry of Lancaster. When Chancery returned from York to Westminster in 1393, it was spared the inconvenience of working in one corner of Westminster Hall while the two benches were sitting in the other corners of the same hall. Chancery was now assigned "a place newly appointed in the white hall of Westminster for the office and session of the chancellor and the clerks of Chancery."

This move represented the beginning of the division between the administrative and judicial functions of Chancery, and a second recognition of this division was made in the same period. In 1232, Henry III had assigned 700 marks a year for the support of a *domus conversorum*, a house for converted Jews, to be created in what is now known as Chancery Lane. Never in great demand, this house fell into almost complete disuse after the Jews were banished from England in 1290. After this date, the chancellor began to use the house as a residence for the Chancery clerks when the court was in Westminster. As crown property, the rolls were supposedly stored in the Tower of London, but during the fourteenth century the *domus conversorum* became the place in and near which the clerks lived and copied the new rolls. Several Keepers of the Rolls during the fourteenth century were named keepers of the *domus conversorum*, and finally in 1377 the *domus* was officially deeded to the Keeper of the Rolls. From this time forward the *domus* was the recognized center for Chancery business and was called the Rolls Chapel and (with its adjacent buildings) the Rolls House until the Public Record Office was built on the same site between 1845 and 1895.[15]

In addition to having offices separate from the royal household, Chancery developed into an independent and self-perpetuating bureaucracy during the fourteenth and fifteenth centuries. From the time of the Magna Carta onward, the rivalry between the king and the barons for control of the government had modified the character of the chancellorship so that by the fourteenth century, the chancellor had become nearly as much an instrument of the magnates as the chief ministerial agent of the crown. During this time, kings attempted to create new personal offices for administration, and these offices were absorbed one after another into the bureaucracy of the civil service. The chancellor and the Great Seal were the king's personal instruments until they were formalized during the bad reigns of King John and Henry III. The Wardrobe and Privy Seal were then developed as personal offices until the Privy Seal began to be used as the secretariat for the king's Council in the bad rule of Edward II. After this, the Signet was devised as the king's personal secretariat until it declined in importance at the end of the reign of Henry VI. The king's secretary was a personal officer until he, too, was formalized into secretary of state in the time of Henry VIII.[16]

Chancery was the oldest, largest, and most independent of these national administrative offices. As custodian of the Great Seal, it was the central agency for the administration both of justice and of national affairs. No action could be begun in the king's courts and no action concerning inheritance or the transfer of property could be begun anywhere without a writ originating in Chancery, which served as the justice's warrant for entertaining the action.[17] A mass of written petitions to the king and Council for letters of remedy and grants of land and money passed through Chancery annually and the ensealed writs and charters issued in response to these petitions.[18] Both the original petitions and the responses were written by the Chancery clerks.[19] The clerks had in their charge the complicated system of indentures by which Henry V freed his military organization from the instability of the ancient feudal levy.[20] They issued the summonses that brought parliaments together and the writs of expenses that sent knights and burgesses home with proof of their claims for wages. Chancery clerks both wrote and received the petitions to parliament and classified and presented them to the magnates who were the "triers" of petitions.[21] They kept the rolls which recorded the proceedings of parliament and drafted and enrolled the statutes that emerged from these proceedings.[22] Chancery was likewise responsible for the administration of customs, taxes, and subsidies (since these derived from parliament). All of the most important administrative officials looked to the chancellor for their commissions of appointment and for authorizations for their most important actions.[23]

By 1400 this was all routine. The same clerks acted year after year for parliament; the same names appeared year after year signed to writs and warrants, no matter what political changes might occur at the top. In 1388 the Lords Appellant ordered a reform of the abuses of Chancery. This led to a codification of its personnel and organization, still extant, although in a form dating from 1410-26. This document, entitled "Ordinaciones cancellarie domini regis facte anno duodecimo regni regis Ricardi secundi,"[24] makes no reference to the role of the king in appointing the clerks of Chancery or in the authorizing or verifying of writs. The chancellor was to appoint his subordinates only with the advice of the senior clerks. No clerk was to be received into the first or second form save by "due election and judgment of the clerks of the first form there present." There were twelve major clerks of the first form, who were called "Masters of Chancery." Each of these had under him three clerks except for the most dignified who was designated "Keeper of the Rolls" and had six clerks. There were twelve clerks of the second form who had one subordinate each, except for special officers such as the Keepers of the Petty Bag and Hanaper, and the two Clerks of the Crown, who had two clerks apiece. Finally, there were twenty-four cursitors, writers of ordinary writs, who were allowed no assistance, except that when incapacitated by sickness or old age, they were allowed "a sufficient, unmarried clerk" to write and seal under their names. All told, Tout estimates, on the basis of the *Ordinaciones cancellarie*, Chancery in 1400 was composed of about 120 clerks.

Transition from Latin and French to English

This compact, disciplined, hierarchical body of civil servants is not merely an antiquarian curiosity but a fact of capital importance in the evolution of standard written English since this is the group who introduced English as an official language of central administration between 1420 and 1460. Latin had been the original official language of Norman government. In 1066 writing in the colloquial Romance languages had only just begun to emerge, and Latin was still regarded as the most formal and correct way of writing French.[25] Furthermore, in Norman as in Anglo-Saxon society, official writing was almost wholly in the hands of the clergy. Whereas the Anglo-Saxon clergy had been quite independent and inclined to translate scripture and learning into English, the Norman clergy were strong adherents of Rome and were inclined to conduct all of their affairs in Latin.[26] Throughout the Middle Ages, the first language of the royal secretariat continued to be Latin. Instruments under the Great Seal executed in Chancery were almost universally in Latin, and nearly all of the business of the Exchequer was carried on in Latin. These traditional functions continued in Latin into the sixteenth century, and sometimes well beyond. Entries in the Pells accounts of the Exchequer of Receipts were made in Latin until this file came to an end on October 10, 1834, at which point someone wrote in pencil "Diem mortis Scaccari."[27] It was the introduction of English by the royal secretariat for the new functions of Chancery in the fifteenth century that created the new official language.

While Latin was the language of bureaucracy from 1066 onwards, French was the language of parliament and the law. The Anglo-Norman nobility wrote (or had scribes write for them) in Latin, but they spoke in French. Latin was used for laws and ordinances from the time of Norman Conquest until the middle of the thirteenth century, but the king and his Council, parliament, and the Anglo-Norman nobles in their manorial courts carried on all oral discussion in their native language.[28] For a while English maintained some status in the common law courts. In 1258 Henry III declared in both French and English his acceptance of the provisions that were forced upon him by the Parliament at Oxford. But the legal reforms of Henry II and Edward I made everyone eager to seek the king's justice, and by the fourteenth century French had superseded both English and Latin as the language of parliament and the law courts.[29]

Latin continued to be used in the ecclesiastical courts and by the municipal government, but since trade involved communication with the Anglo-Norman gentry and with the Continent, French became the language of commerce. In the fifteenth century when domestic business and government began turning to English, French remained the language of diplomacy. One mark of this development was Henry IV's appointment of secretaries for the French language. Such officers had not existed before this time, but by 1425 there were at least eight of them who acted as liaison between the English government and its French possessions. It became the custom for the royal secretariat to answer diplomatic correspondence in the "language of the recipient," i.e., French for French-speaking rulers and Latin for the pope and non-French-speaking rulers.[30]

French continued as the spoken language of some members of the nobility and merchant class into the fifteenth century. My concern is not with the revival of spoken English, although we may be sure that by the time Chaucer wrote his poems and Richard II commanded Gower to write the *Confessio Amantis* in English, English had become the domestic language for all classes.[31] But there is also sporadic evidence in the *Rotuli Parliamentorum* of the beginnings of the use of English for official debate. An argument repeatedly used to whip up parliamentary support for the continuing war with France was that a French victory would annihilate the English language. This argument appears in the Latin account of the opening address to parliament in 1295, and in the French accounts of the opening addresses of 1340, 1344, 1346, and 1376.[32] It is hard to believe that such an argument could have been made to the assembly in either Latin or French. More likely the discussions of parliament were already being carried on at least partly in English, although recorded by the clerks in the traditional languages.

The clerks for the first time admit in 1362 that parliament was addressed in English.[33] This information may have been recorded because this was the parliament that enacted the famous statute requiring that all court proceedings be conducted in English since the litigants could not understand French.[34] Although this statute was not enforced and the common law courts continued to plead in French until 1731, from its inception around 1394, the court of Chancery conducted most of its proceedings in English. The *Rotuli Parliamentorum* reports that the parliaments of 1363, 1364, and 1381 were opened in English.[35] We are unsure how many parliaments in between or after these years were addressed in English because the clerks did not bother to include the phrase "dit en Engleis."

The first English entry in the *Roluli Parliamentorum* is the 1388 petition of the Mercer's guild (RP III.225), which Chambers and Daunt print as an example of London English.[36] In 1397 the address of Judge Rikhill concerning the impeachment of Gloucester is recorded in English (RP III.378). Chief Justice Thirnyng's two speeches regarding the deposition of Richard II and accession of Henry IV and Henry's own challenge to the throne in 1399 are in English (RP III.424, 451, 453). There are English entries in 1403,

1404, 1405, 1411, and 1414 (two), and two from the last parliament of Henry V in 1421. But beginning with 1422, the first year of the reign of the infant King Henry VI, English entries begin to be more frequent, and by 1450 they are the rule.[37]

Characteristics of Chancery English

(Since this article was written in 1976 Jane Fisher, Malcolm Richardson, and I have edited from the original velums all of the texts here cited from the *Rotuli Parliamentorum*, and much else, in *An Anthology of Chancery English* [1984]. At the time of this article, I was not aware of the personal influence of Henry V on the development of the language. Malcolm Richardson discovered the Signet letters of Henry V and discussed their similarity to Chancery Standard in his dissertation and *Speculum* article, and we included them in the *Anthology*. The discussion of the language here does not differ substantially from that in the *Anthology*, but here it shows no awareness that Chancery Standard was based upon the personal language and style of Henry V.)

The English of the *Rotuli Parliamentorum* may be taken as a yardstick against which to measure the evolution of Chancery Standard. The Rolls of Parliament were entirely in the hands of the Chancery clerks, and nothing they wrote could be more official or prestigious.[38] The petition of the Mercers in 1388 is even more regional in morphology than the contemporary English of Chaucer and Gower. Its adverbs regularly end in the southern *lich* (*frelich, openlich*), and its past participles often take the completive prefix *y* (*ybe, yhidde*). As with Chaucer, its third person pronouns are regularly *they, hem, her*; the plural verbs often, but not always, end in *n* (*they compleynen, they wolden*, but *we biseche, we knowe*). Many past participles are likewise marked by *n* (*holden, founden*).[39]

As late as the petition of the Physicians in 1421 (RP IV.158) some of these characteristics appear, particularly the pairing of participle with *y* (*y suffred, y lerned*). In this entry, *high* is spelled phonetically *hey*. Phonetic spelling of the native English palatals (*high-hey, though-thow, right-rit[e]*, etc.) was a characteristic of non-Chancery writing during the first half of the fifteenth century.[40] The refusal of the Chancery scribes to accede to this phonetic re-spelling is one of the distinctive contributions of Chancery Standard to Modern English orthography. After the initial word, this petition goes on "Hey and most myghty Prince," and subsequently we find three conservative *gh*'s (*ought, slaughtre, nought*), with only repetitions of *hey* representing the simplified form. In addition, the 1421 petition shows several other characteristics of Chancery Standard. The *they, them, their* forms (variously spelled) are used throughout; *shuld(e)* is more frequent than *shold(e)*, and the distinctive Chancery spelling of *eny* has replaced *any*.

By 1430 Chancery English had assumed its mature form. It may be worthwhile to look closely at the beginning and end of a typical example. (See Table 3.1.)

This is the text of the original petition brought before parliament. It is in Chancery script, presumably prepared from dictation or based upon a preliminary draft brought in by the petitioner, but it had to be copied over and presented by a sworn clerk as attorney, since the Chancery clerks had a monopoly on presentations to parliament and to the chancellor.[41] After a petition had been voted on by parliament and accepted by the king (or by members of the Council acting in his name), it would eventually be carefully inscribed on the roll pertaining to that particular parliament. The differences between the original form and the inscribed form give us a glimpse of the drift towards standardization, for along with a neater hand in the enrollment goes a tendency towards regularization, or modernization, in our terms. The enrolling clerk for the preceding entry (C65/90/21) modernizes in six categories (21 individual instances) by: (a) dropping *e* where it is not found in Modern English (4, 37, 74, 133, 162); (b) changing *seid* to *saide* in every instance (11 times); (c) changing *hadd* to *had* (142); (d) changing a plural inflection from *ez* to *es* (199 *damagez* to *damages*); (e) changing þ to *th* (41, 116 *that*); (f) changing *monoie* to *monay* (75, but see 153 where both scribes spell it *money*).

On the other hand, in five categories (11 instances) the enrolling clerk regresses (in our terms) by: (a) adding *e* where it is not found in Modern English (36, 117, 161); (b) changing *i* to *y* (12, 63); (c) doubling *t* (42, 93 *butt*; 117, 161 *atte*); (d) dropping *l* (166 *shal*); (e) using short *o* for *u* (201 *theropon*). The greater number of modernizations and the relatively greater importance of modern forms like (b), (d), and (f) in the first group support what is evident in the handwriting; apparently the enrolling clerk, working more leisurely

TABLE 3.1.
(Ancient Petition SC8/25/1238)

```
            1   2    3    4      5        6            7       8      9  10  11
[Heading] To the kyng oure soueraigne lord [Text] Besechith mekely leuin le Clerc

     12   13   14  15    16    17     18    19 20  21      22       23  24  25
Burgeis of Gand to consider by encheson of the trewe acquitaille that the seid

   26   27   28  29   30   31 32    33      34   35   36 37     38        39
towne hath doon and doth dayly in diuerse maners vnto yow oure soueraigne lord

   40    41  42   43 44  45   46   47   48        49      50  51      52     53 54
howe þat but late ago he boght of Robert Brampton of Caleys attorney to his

     55     56      57     58     59     60   61    62    63     64 65 66 67
brother William Brampton of Chestreville in Derby shire certein wolles to the value

68 69  70 71   72    73     74       75    76   77    78      79 80  81  82 83  84
of xijc and xv nobles the whiche monoie the same leuin paied in hand to the seid

   85     86     87      88   89 90  91     92     93 94 95    96      97     98 99
Robert noght having liuery of the seid wolles But the seid Robert bonde his seid

    100   101  102   103  104 105  106     107    108   109 110  111    112 113 114  115    116
Brother and hym self  in  the aboue seid somme to the same leuin to the entent þat

117 118 119    120 121  122    123  124    125 126 127  128     29    130        131
at   a certain day he shuld have had lyuery of the wolles aboue seid Notwythston-

       132    133     134    135 136 137  138 139 140 141 142    143       144 145 146
dyng the whiche bonde the seid leuin hath not as yet hadd noþer lyuerey of the

147   148    149 150 151 152   153        154    155    156 157    158     159    160 161
seid wolles ne of the seid money . . . and thowe the seid William appere not at

  162   163 164 165 166   167 168 169 170       171     172 173    174     175    176
suche day as he shall have by the seid proclamation the seid Chanceler have power

177   178 179    180      181 182 183     184      185   186 187    188     189 190
to procede to Iuggement for the seid suppliant ayenst the seid William by his

  191   192 193 194 195   196    197 198  199    200     201 202 203      204
defaute as well of the Principall as of Damagez and thervpon to awarde execucion

205 206   207   208    209
in  the  fourme afore rehersed. . . .
```

and less under the influence of the client's oral statement or the bill drawn up by his notary, was more careful in his language. At this stage in the history of the written language, more careful means more modern. The clerks' same general practice becomes evident when nearly any enrollment is compared with its original petition.

The printed version of this text in the *Rotuli Parliamentorum* (IV.372) is a reasonably faithful transcription of the enrolled version. The changes do not affect the validity of the printed text as a basis for linguistic study. All capitalization and punctuation are modern (according to the principles of the eighteenth century); abbreviations in English tend to be expanded more often than in French and Latin; consonantal *u* is often transcribed *v*; and þ is transcribed *y* or *th*. Other than these general changes, there are four differences in the *Rotuli Parliamentorum* version: *Clerc* (11) is *Clerk*; *diuers* (33) is *diverse* (*diurse* in the original); *butt* (42) is *but* (*but* in the original); and *such* (162) is *sich*. The first three changes are probably lapses in transcription. The last is probably an accident, and in no sense an example of northern dialect. It is *suche* in the original, but on the roll the *u* is in ligature with the *s* and was misread.

Taken together, the Ancient Petitions and the Rolls of Parliament reveal the degree of standardization achieved by Chancery English before the advent of printing. It was not the standardization of a "taught" language like Latin or, to a lesser degree, French,[42] but more nearly like the standardization of the Chancery script in which the documents were copied. This hand had not been deliberately contrived but had developed by an unselfconscious "drift" as the conduct of national business grew more centralized and professionalized during the first half of the fifteenth century.[43] While there were differences in the ways clerks shaped individual letters, the overall appearance of Chancery hand, or court hand, as it is sometimes called, is unmistakable. The same apprentice system that produced this tendency to graphic uniformity produced a corresponding tendency to linguistic uniformity.

This uniformity was greater in morphology than in orthography. In pronouns, the second person singular is always *ye/you*,[44] and the third person plural is quite regularly *they, them, their*, though *hem* and *her* occur sporadically in official documents until the advent of printing. The reflexive with *self/selves* is frequent. *Tho* as a plural for *that* is infrequent, and *those* even less frequent. Adverbs never end in *lich*.

Verbs rarely have the plural *n* except in stereotyped phrases (in many bills the petitioners "bisechen" or "compleynen" in the first line but never use a plural *n* afterwards). The participial *n* is found on many words that no longer have it in Modern English (*founden, stonden*), but the participial prefix *y* (*ydo, ybe*) has been completely lost. The preterit is always with *d* (*asked, washed*) and never with the northern, phonetic *t* (*asket, washet*). The negative particle has come to be placed after the verb ("they that be noght able" instead of "they that ne be able").

Spelling was less regular than was accidence. We have already mentioned the preference of the Chancery scribes for *gh* spellings of the native palatals (*high, through*) and for the preterit *d*. The variations between non-distinctive pairs like *i/y, u/v, u/w, ou/ow* and the presence or absence of final *e* were not only matters of individual preference but matters on which an individual scribe could vary from word to word, just as we may today find ourselves using different strokes for *f*, *s*, or capital *t*. Yet in orthography there were preferred forms, most of them the forms we use today: *I* was seldom spelled *Y*, as it continued to be in the west and south of England; *which* was seldom spelled *wich/wech* as in the north; initial *wh* was never spelled with *q*; and common words like *shuld, such, much, but*, and *ask* usually appear in nearly their modern spellings. (See the glossary in *An Anthology of Chancery English*.)

Not all of the forms found in Chancery English have been adopted by Modern English, however. Most noticeably, the third person singular continued to end in *th* until after the advent of printing, although we find *s* in northern documents in the fourteenth century and in the non-Chancery documents in London and the southern region by the 1450s. *Be/ben* continues to be used where the northern dialect and Modern Standard use *are*. *O* continues to appear before *n* in words like *lond* and *stond*. The spelling *eny* for *any* appears to be a Chancery shibboleth, along with *shew*. The semivowel appears in forms of *ayen* and *yive*, often spelled with ʒ. *From* is *fro*; *one* is *on/oon*; and *between* is usually *betwix*.

That Chancery written English had ceased to be a representation of any spoken dialect may be seen from the spelling of palatals (*high*), preterit *d* (*asked*), *ig* in French words (*reign, foreign*), and the cavalier treatment of the final *e*. In addition, the preferred Chancery forms are representative of various dialects. *They, them, their* and the adverbial *ly* are northern, while third person *th* and preterit *d*, the *be/ben* forms, and *yive/ayen* forms are southern. The explanation usually given is that this amalgam represents a spoken language in London based upon the original southern dialect of the city as modified by northern immigrants. Bertie Wilkinson has pointed out that from the time of Edward III, a majority of the Chancery clerks came from the northern counties, and these particular Chancery forms were maintained throughout the long Lancastrian hegemony.[45] An even stronger influence, however, must have been the fact that the new official language was a combination of the two earlier written standards that M.L. Samuels distinguished in his study of Middle English dialects.[46] The first of these dialects is the language developed in the centers of Wycliffite activity such as Lutterworth and Leicester in the central Midland counties. This is the language of the majority of Wycliffite manuscripts, and the Lollards spread it throughout England. Eventually this language was used for secular prose works in such various parts of the country as Somerset, Dorset, and Wales, and it survived virtually unchanged into the latter part of the fifteenth century.

The second written basis for Chancery Standard was the writing in London at the end of the fourteenth century. As used by Chaucer, Gower, and Hoccleve (themselves civil servants or closely involved with Chancery), one form of this language may indeed have been a proto-Chancery, already distinguished from the civic language of the Mercer's guild by the use of *ly* for *lich* and the reduction in the *y* participles.[47]

Whatever the relative influence of the oral usage of northern clerks mingling with the local population versus the influence of written Wycliffite and London models, the more modern tone and appearance of Chancery English is due not only to its accidence and orthography but also to its style and idiom. Chancery English's style and idiom are based on the those of the written documents that the trilingual clerks continued to copy in Latin and French at the same time that they were creating an official language of correspondence in English.

Until the end of the fifteenth century, non-Chancery prose continues to be characterized by the paratactic constructions that distinguish Chaucer's own prose from his poetry.[48] These tendencies may be illustrated by a sentence from the 1388 petition of the

Mercers: "And lordes, by yowre leue, owre lyge lordes commaund-
ment to symple & unkonnyng men is a gret thyng to ben vsed so
famulerlich withouten nede, for they, unwyse to saue it, mowe
lyghtly ther ayeins forfait" (Chambers and Daunt 36). The chief
difficulties here, aside from the meaning of "vsed" and "saue it," are
the reference of "they" and "it," and the shift in structure (ana-
coluthon) of "withouten nede" and "ther ayeins."

Long before 1300, Latin had provided official French prose
with a model for compact, logical expression. In turn, by 1300 French
had achieved a businesslike clarity of expression that English was
not to achieve for another century.[49] The simple directness of the
Anglo-French official style that Chancery clerks copied daily may be
illustrated by a short plea to Henry IV (ca. 1406): "Plese a nostre
tresexcellent seigneur le Roy grantier a vostre humble servant Jehan
Hethe, un des poevres clercs escrivantz en l'office de vostre prive
seel, l'empension annuel quelle celui que serra primierement crees
en Evesque de Norwich serra tenuz de faire avoir a un de voz clercs
luiquel vous lui ferrez nommer. Pur Dieu et en oevre de charite."[50]
The non-restrictive modifier and the references of "quelle celui" and
"luiquel" are here quite specific. This style sets the model for
hundreds of equally simple and direct paragraphs in English. For
example, a petition to Henry VI (1438): "Please it to the king oure
souerain Lord of youre benigne grace to graunte to youre humble
seruunt and ouratoure Sir William Wakysby, Tresorer with the Quene
youre moder, the denery of Hastynges in the dyose of Chichester,
the whiche Prestewyk, Clerke of youre parlement, late had, on who
sowle god assoile; and youre saide oratour shal pray God for you"
(PRO E28/58/B, punctuation added). As in the French, the antecedents of "the whiche" and "youre saide oratour" are quite specific
and the references of the non-restrictive modifiers clear.

This style can grow into more complicated narrative, as illustrated by the plea of John Frebarn (ca. 1435):

> Mekely besecheth your povere oratour John Frebarn of London,
> lighterman, pitously complaynyng how that the vij day of Sep-
> tembre now last past . . . as his servantz, called John Scotte,
> William Spencer, [etc.], were comyng from Seint Katerine's by
> the Tour wharf homeward toward the house of your seid be-
> secher in Pety Wales, ther cam upon them on the seid Tour

wharf oon John Davy Squyer, marchall of the Admiralte, and at
sute of partie arrested the seid servantz of your seid besecher . . .
and therupon had them in to the Tour of London, and there
were in prison by iij dayes in grete duresse, and your seid
besecher coude not have them out of prison there, but as he was
fayn to take them to baile, under surete for to brynge them to
their answer there atte court day. (PRO C1/2/36, punctuation
added)

With the exception of one ellipsis—"and there [they] were in
prison"—this reads almost as clearly as Daniel Defoe three hundred
years later.

The Earliest English Documents

This variety of fairly modern, fairly standard prose, nearly
always in the script of the Chancery clerks, was in wide use in the
Westminster offices by the 1430s. Again, as with linguistic drift, in
discussing the contents of the Public Record Office collections we
are dealing with tendencies rather than with absolutes. Not only has
there been a disordering of documents over the years, but it also
appears that the original distribution by the receivers of petitions
must have been fairly arbitrary. Exactly the same sorts of documents
are found in different collections.

First and most uniform in both hand and language are the
petitions and actions connected with the judicial side of Chancery:
the Ancient Petitions addressed to parliament (SC8), Chancery and
Parliamentary Proceedings (C49), the Early Proceedings of the Court
of Chancery (Cl), and related files.[51] The second category is the
administrative paperwork classified under Council and Privy Seal
(E28), Ancient Correspondence (SC1), and related files.[52] Both hand
and language are more mixed in these than in the documents controlled directly by the Chancery clerks. Finally, there are the indentures and agreements grouped under the heading of Ancient Deeds
(E40, E210, E326, E327, etc.), which seldom originated in Chancery
and continue to show frequent traces of regional dialect through
1461.

To elaborate upon the earliest English documents in the first
two categories, the Ancient Petitions are the originals of petitions

presented to parliament. As Francis Palgrave observed, parliament was originally called not for the purpose of legislation and taxation, but to hear the complaints of the commonwealth and of individuals. It was the king's great and extraordinary court of justice.[53] During the reigns of Henry IV, V, and VI, most petitions came to be addressed to parliament instead of to the king and council.[54] As is evident from the uniformity of the hands and styles, the petitions presented to parliament are the handiwork of the same clerks who received them and dealt with them as clerks of parliament.[55] The typewritten list of Ancient Petitions in English in the Round Room of the Public Record Office gives an indication of the movement of this activity from French and Latin into English. Before 1400, there are only two petitions in English; 1401-10 none; 1411-20 eight; 1421-30 sixty-three; 1431-40 one hundred and thirty-two; 1441-50 one hundred and thirty-five; and in 1451-60 one hundred and forty-two. But after 1455 the collection begins to peter out as the judicial functions of Chancery become more independent of parliament[56] (between 1451-55 there are one hundred and twenty-six English petitions; between 1456-60 only sixteen).

The Early Proceedings are petitions and depositions concerned more directly with Chancery as a court of law. According to the preface of the printed Calendars (1827), these proceedings commenced in 1394 (17 Richard II) when the chancellor and his clerks, at the behest of the council, began to hear petitions directly during the interims between parliaments. The questioning of witnesses appears at first to have been oral, but very soon (by Henry VI, 1422) all Chancery judicial procedure had been reduced to writing. All of the materials preserved from the reign of Richard II are French. None have been preserved from the reign of Henry IV. The few from Henry V are mostly French and Latin. But from the beginning of the reign of Henry VI, the proceedings of the Court of Chancery appear to have been preserved more systematically, and nearly all of them are in English. The Chancery hand appears less regularly in these than in the Ancient Petitions even though it was necessary for every suitor to employ a Chancery clerk to act as his attorney before the court.[57] A study of the files reveals the reason for the appearance of the non-Chancery documents. They appear to be the originals of complaints submitted to Chancery, which had then to be re-written by the clerks before being officially presented. For example,

C1/6/318 and 321 are depositions concerning the divorce of Lady Margery of Langford in a non-Chancery legal hand whose most noticeable characteristic is its northern spelling of the preterit as *t* (*asket, assemblet, anoydet*). Items C1/6/319 and 320 are Latin redactions of these English depositions in neat Chancery hand. C1/19/491 is an interesting complaint by Thomas Bodyn, apprentice, that his master had not, as agreed in the indenture, sent him to school to learn to read and write. C1/19/492 is the same complaint copied over in Chancery hand with Chancery spellings.

The next categories of material, Council and Privy Seal papers and Ancient Correspondence, appear to be petitions addressed to the king and Council, responses to these petitions, and memoranda and instructions dealing with the king's personal business and the administration of the realm. Much of this is Privy Seal and Signet material, so it is not directly from the hands of Chancery scribes. Many of the clerks in the king's personal secretariat were university graduates, and some had been educated abroad. They were men of learning and intelligence who tended to end up as deans and bishops.[58] But such rising magnates had not been subjected to the rigorous training in the Households of Chancery, and they did not write in Chancery hand.[59] Hence, we begin to find in this material the scrawled secretary hand of which we see so much after the advent of printing. What we find in these collections are largely what would today be called "file copies"—rough drafts, models, and copies of originals which were sent out. The language of many of the documents from the periods of Henry IV and V, like the *Rotuli Parliamentorum* material before 1425, shows similarities to the language of the civic materials printed in Chambers and Daunt's *Book of London English*. Through the 1420s, however, documents in Chancery Standard become more frequent, and by the 1430s they are the rule. After this time, missives to the king and council dated from Cornwall, Wales, Chester, or Calais are likely to be in nearly the same hand and language as missives dated from Westminster.

There continue, of course, to be differences. Civic authorities remain more regional than Westminster clerks, even when their scribes write a good imitation of Chancery hand. In 1431 the citizens of "Cardagyn," Wales, still use the forms *yhold, hynesse* (for highness), *tho*, and *wheche* (for which) (E28/51/AA); in 1434 the people of "Huntyntonshire" use *liggyng* and *mykkill* (E28/54/40). Though non-standard forms continue to appear in documents in Chancery hand, there is a perceptible correlation between the standard hand and the standard language.

Although we have little information about the training and working conditions of the scribes, there is from time to time evidence of a sense of error. On one parchment we find *wile* with a caret and *h* inserted above the line (E28/60); in another *warf* with a caret and inserted *h* (E40/A1779); in another *iooardie* crossed out followed by *iupardie* (E28/57); and in another "Itm þ it nys vnknowyn" is corrected "ys not vnknowyn" (Cott. Vesp. F. VII, fol. 56). Presumably changes such as these betoken a sense of "correctness." Then there are the exemplars in the files with lists of names attached that show how a master copy would be reproduced to go to the barons or mayors throughout the country.[60] Such letters then turn up in the letter books of York or London, showing how the Chancery style could penetrate and influence the writing of provincial officials.[61]

The memoranda in the Ancient Correspondence and Proceedings of the Council indicate that the business of the king's council was by the 1430s conducted very largely in English, even though the secretary might take the minutes in Latin or French. There is more than one French summary which begins "Il dit en Englais."[62] The free hands of some of these memoranda indicate what we know from other sources—that the king's secretaries were university men and not Chancery clerks. We find accordingly that they are somewhat more inclined to use non-Chancery forms. Their hands reveal how much skill in handwriting in the fifteenth century resembled skill in typewriting today. We must recognize that the magnates and university trained secretaries never made the final drafts of writs and letters that were sent abroad. These were produced by the "typing pool," the Chancery, Privy Seal, or Signet clerks who made fair copies in due form and submitted them for sealing.

It was the language of these professional clerks that circulated about the country and established the model for official English between 1420 and 1460. Because of the tight hierarchy in Chancery, the idiom and form of the official documents was controlled by a very few people. In theory, only the twelve masters in Chancery were empowered to originate new language or to sign important letters.[63] There is ample evidence for the supervision exercised over the writing of the under clerks.[64] So the favorite forms of Chancery

English—and ultimately many of the forms of modern written English—originated as the conscious or unconscious choices of a handful of men in a strategic position at the moment of the creation of the official language.[65] The biographical and social factors that led to the selection of the forms of language is less important than the political and administrative situation that led to their establishment as "official."

The Influence of Chancery English

This variety of written English grew up outside the orbit either of the church or the schools, nearly all of whose reading and writing continued to be in Latin until well into the sixteenth century. In the absence of any other national model for writing in the vernacular (and in view of the enormous prestige and ubiquitous presence of Chancery writing), it is not surprising that Chancery set the fashion for business and private correspondence.

Chancery provided a system of education for both its own clerks and for the common lawyers. Each of the twelve major clerks had his own house in which minor clerks and candidates for clerkships lived. These "hospiciae cancellarie" were the origin of the Inns of Chancery, which were the preparatory schools for the Inns of Court through the eighteenth century.[66] The mysteries of writs and pleas, and the other formal procedures of administration into which the Masters of Chancery were inducting the aspirants to Chancery were also essential knowledge for the legal clerks who would have to deal with the same matters at the other end. Hence, we find that from the beginning, aspirants to the legal clerkships sought places in the Households of Chancery, and the *Ordinaciones* forbad Chancery clerks to mingle with "omnes allei clerici qui dicte cancellarie propter doctrinam et scripturam adherere voluerint."[67] "Scripturam" no doubt here means the technical forms of writs and perhaps the formal Chancery hand as well, but it must inevitably have meant, also, the correct use of the official language, be it Latin, French, or—after 1420—English.

The influence of Chancery reached into Oxford itself. Although formal education continued to be in Latin, a statute of 1432 indicates that private tutors were provided at the university for students who wished to pass on to the Inns of Court.[68] These tutors taught the art of composition and writing in French, the art of composing charters and other scripts, the art of holding law courts, and the art of pleading in the English manner. Since these were exactly the subjects taught in the Inns of Chancery, we may infer the influence of Chancery upon these extra-curricular offerings at the university. As in the *Ordinaciones cancellarie*, there is no evidence in the Oxford statute that the tutors taught composition in English. However, John Fortescue suggests in *De Laudibus Legum Anglie* (1466) that some of the instruction in the Inns of Chancery and Inns of Court was in English: "In the universities of England sciences are not taught unless in the Latin language. But the laws of [England] are learned in three languages, namely, English, French, and Latin."[69] Fortescue is not clear as to just what form this learning takes, and he spends much of his time justifying the use of French and Latin. But clearly some study in English is implied when he reiterates:

> Thus, since the laws of England are learned in these three languages, they could not be conveniently learned or studied in the universities, where the Latin language alone is used. But these laws are taught and learned in a certain public academy, more convenient and suitable for their apprehension than any university. . . . For there are in this academy ten lesser inns, and sometimes more, which are called Inns of Chancery. To each of them at least a hundred students belong, and to some of them a much greater number, though they do not always gather in them all at the same time. These students are, indeed, for the most part, young men learning the originals and something of the elements of law, who, becoming proficient therein as they mature, are absorbed into the greater inns, which are called the Inns of Court.[70]

Fortescue does not elaborate on the curriculum of the "originalia" in the Inns of Chancery. No doubt it was mostly French and Latin, but if the English law was really studied in three languages, there must also have been instruction in English. Students would have to have some elementary education, probably including reading and writing in English, before they entered the Inns of Chancery.[71] This education was likewise influenced by Chancery. Tout notes grants to John Tamworth (ca. 1374-75) and after him Geoffrey Martin (ca. 1376-84) for the conduct of what Tout thinks were schools for would-be Chancery clerks.[72] A.F. Leach records that the Owestry Grammar School in Shropshire, one of the earliest instances of a school staffed by a mixed faculty of laymen and clerics and not part of an ecclesiastical foundation, is said to have been founded by a Welsh lawyer David Holbeach, who Leland credited with the foundation of Davy's (or Davies) Inn of Chancery.[73]

No doubt the formal curriculum at Owestry, as at Oxford, was Latin grammar and rhetoric. Every reference I have found to school books or subjects taught in the formal curriculum of the fourteenth and fifteenth centuries is to Latin. When Edmund Stoner sent his son to Ewelme Grammar School in 1380, the only text mentioned is a Donatus.[74] When books were purchased in 1395 for the education of young Henry of Monmouth (the future Henry V), they are all Latin.[75] When new schools were demanded in London by petition to Commons in 1447, they were for the amending of the study of Latin grammar (RP V.137).[76] The innovation credited to John Cornwall and Richard Pencrich (ca. 1350), who "chaunged þe lore in gramer scole and construccioun of Frensche into Englische,"[77] was merely that *recitation*, which up until that time had been in French, was changed to English. The grammar being construed was still Latin.

Writing in English grew up outside of this educational framework. Like other business skills—accounting, the clerical hand, business law—it was a subject learned throughout this period either by apprenticeship in the houses of the Masters of Chancery, in the houses of guild masters, or by extra-curricular tutorials designed to impart these practical skills to academic students hoping to enter the business community.[78] We have already observed in the *Ordinaciones cancellarie* that the Inns of Chancery served two social groups, those who aspired to become professional clerks and those who were acquiring a preparatory education to enter the Inns of Court. From the way Fortescue described them, students headed for the Inns of Court represented inherited wealth,[79] whereas the apprentice clerks would have been from less wealthy classes and had their livings to earn. Those who did not find places in Chancery or in the Westminster offices found service as clerks with municipal corporations or wealthy households or established themselves as public scriveners. Chancery clerks themselves were loaned out from time to time,[80] and the clerks of the Exchequer regularly travelled throughout England preparing the handsome Ministers' Account Rolls preserved in the Public Record Office (SC6).

Historians of the English language are agreed that the genesis of the standard language is not literary, even though our predilections as literary scholars lead us to study most closely and to take examples largely from belletristic materials. The truth of the matter is that written literature (poems, plays, tales, sermons, treatises) bulked as small in the lives of most people in the fifteenth century as they do now. Furthermore, in an age of patronage, such *belles lettres* were likely to be addressed to a localized audience.[81] The writing that an ordinary person would most often read and the sort of writing most likely to carry a sense of authority would be bureaucratic (licenses, records, etc.), legal (inheritance, transfer of property), or commercial (bills, agreements, instructions).

In the Middle Ages, most bureaucratic and legal writing related either to the church or the king. That relating to the church continued to be in Latin until after the sixteenth century, but that relating to the king began to appear in English in the fifteenth century. Perhaps the notion of "the King's English," suggested for the first time by Chaucer in *The Treatise on the Astrolabe* (1392),[82] had a personal dimension in that Richard evidently preferred to read in English.[83] More importantly, after the Norman Conquest the whole legal and administrative machinery of England centered about the king and was carried on in his name. As Pollock and Maitland have stated, "In its final form almost every message, order or mandate that came, or was supposed to come, from the king, whether it concerned the greatest matter or smallest, whether addressed to an emperor or an escheator, whether addressed to all lieges or one man, was a document settled in Chancery and sealed with the great seal. Miles of parchment, close rolls and patent rolls, fine rolls and charter rolls, are covered with copies of these documents, and yet reveal but part of Chancery's work, for no roll sets forth all those 'original' writs that were issued 'of course.' "[84] Most of this writing was in Latin and French, but there is no question that Chancery established the standard for bureaucratic and legal language and that this linguistic authority was recognized by the courts.[85]

It is easy to see how this official language would influence private business writing. Except for the small quantity of writing related to literature and learning, virtually all writing before the seventeenth century is related to business. Nearly all of the many Paston, Stoner, Cely, and Plumpton papers are what we would now call "business letters," many of them to or about officers of the central administration. Indeed, the Stoner and Cely papers found their way into Chancery as the result of extended lawsuits.[86] The indentures and agreements classified in the Public Record Office under the heading Ancient Deeds (E40, etc.) continued to show regional dialect through the 1450s and 1460s, long after Chancery and the other government offices had begun to settle into regular forms. One of the most interesting things that Norman Davis observed about the language of the Pastons is the way that John II and John III began to use Chancery forms in the 1360s after they went to London and took service in the court. After this point their usage shifted. They began to use *them, their* forms more frequently; they used the *n* plural for verbs less frequently; and they began to use the *ght* spelling more commonly, *right, thoght* for *rith, thowte* (sometimes mistakenly, *wright* for *write, dowght* for *doubt*). The members of the family who went to the university instead of taking service in the court do not show these changes, but continued to write the English of their Norfolk relatives, indicating that the influence was London/court, not Eton/Cambridge.[87]

Skill in writing and accounting in the fifteenth century was confined to a small, highly professional group. C.L. Kingsford's optimistic observation that "the wives and sisters of country gentlemen could often write as well as their husbands and brothers, and both they and their servants could and commonly did keep regular household accounts"[88] is simply not borne out by the evidence. For example, Norman Davis has pointed out that about one half of the Paston papers are not in the handwriting of their authors, and that none of the women's letters are autograph, although references in the letters indicate that some of the women could read.[89] It is all too easy in the Public Record Office files to detect the missives from uneducated stewards and bailiffs to their masters at court about affairs at home on the farm. We are still in the era when a good hand and proper language were the monopoly of a small body of professionals likely to have been educated in and to continue to operate under the influence of the Chancery tradition.

Speaking institutionally, we may see the modern written standard emerging from conventions established by the clerks in Chancery between 1420 and about 1440, and spread by professional scribes throughout England by 1460. Undoubtedly, though, this process was under way some time before 1420. Tout has pointed out that Chaucer, Gower, Hoccleve, Usk, Richard of Bury, and other fourteenth-century authors who wrote in English most like the Chancery Standard were themselves members of the civil service or closely involved with the civil service.[90] To secure their positions, most of them would have had to be trained scribes, although in their day, their professional writing would have all been in Latin or French.

Chancery English and London English

Finally, is Chancery English simply a development of London English, as implied by Wyld and other historians of the language, or can the impulse be identified more precisely? This is a subject for continuing investigation. Yet it does appear that we can distinguish differences between examples of London English printed by Chambers and Daunt and Chancery English of the same period. The basis of comparison is the summary of the characteristics of Chancery English rehearsed above. I omit from consideration here the features that continue to show fluctuation in Chancery English before about 1430 (such as verb plurals in *n* and past participles with *y*) and compare only features that in Chancery were already well standardized.

In the Ordinances of the Grocers' Company, 1418-25 (CD 195-205), the customary form of the relative is non-Chancery *wich(e)* (*which* does occur; once *wich* is corrected to *wiche*); except in one entry (1418) the third-person plural is always *her*, *hem*; and we find the non-Chancery verb forms *ar* and *sholde*. The orthography shows several phonetic features: shifted *e* is *ie* (ei), *bien* (been), *quien* (queen), *theis* (these); silent or unstressed sounds are dropped or modified, *ys* (his), *hye* (high), *weytez* (weights), *apon* (upon), *clotyng* (clothing); and pleonistic letters are added, *hawns* (owns).

William Porland, the clerk who wrote the entries in the Brewer's First Book, 1422-25 (Chambers and Daunt 140-91), always used *her*, *hem*; sometimes *hese* for *his*; *arn* and *shold* alongside Chancery *ben* and *shuld*; *betwene* for Chancery *betwix*. Most characteristic of Porland's language is the substitution of non-Chancery *e* for *i*, *wete* (wit), *reden* (ridden, but *to riden*,) *bregge* (bridge), *deden* (did), *wendowes*, *prevy*, etc.

Ony appears as frequently as Chancery *eny*; *nouth* (nought), *thow* (though), *owre* (hour), *ageyns* (Chancery *ayens*). Some of these differences suggest a northern tinge to Porland's dialect.

The language of the Guildhall Pleas and Memoranda, 1412-23 (Chambers and Daunt 119-36), written by clerks in the different wards of the city, show several differences from Chancery Standard: *her*, *hem* is regular (*þame* appears once in 1422); *wich* appears alongside *which*. But the most characteristic feature of the memoranda concerning "nuisances" in the wards is the appearance of the voiceless dental preterit, *stoppit* (stopped), *paiet* (payed), *sellit* (sold), etc. This never occurs in Chancery. One scribe uses *s* as a third-person plural ending, *þai bringes*, etc. Again, there are phonetic spellings not found in Chancery: *erbys* (herbs), *hie* (high), *ost/ostrye* (host), *þorowe* (through), *neybours*, *feest a* (of) *cristemasse*, *ȝer a Regne*, and pleonistic spellings *whif* (wife), *dunghe* (dung). *Betwene* is regular (*betwix* only once).

When we turn to the Guildhall Letter Books, we find the usage closer to Chancery Standard. The letters to the king and proclamations having to do with the French wars, 1415-24 (Chambers and Daunt 64-89) have very few variations. *Them*, *their* alternate with *hem*, *her* as they do in the *Rotuli Parliamentorum* of the same period; *tho* and *wich* appear rarely, again as in the *Rotuli*. Forms do occur like *those* (once only) and *ar(e,n)* that are seldom found in the *Rotuli*. The regular use of *betwen* (betuene) is non-Chancery. There are a few more phonetic and pleonistic spellings than in the *Rotuli*: *hie* (high), *euynesse* (heaviness), *ierarchies* (hierarchies), *hall* (all), *habondance* (this does occur in Chancery), *hough* (how). The Guildhall proclamations not relating to the war, 1418-23 (Chambers and Daunt 93-115), show nearly the same variations.

These comparisons point to two conclusions. First, there was no London "standard" before the advent of Chancery Standard. Writing continued to be in the dialect of the individual scribe and differed from guild to guild and ward to ward. Second, the closer City writing got to the central administration, as in the Guildhall Letter Books, the more it resembled Chancery.

Finally, we have an explicit acknowledgment of the Chancery influence in the familiar statement by the Brewers, quoted in the first essay, as to why they changed their record keeping from Latin and French to English in 1422. This passage deserves careful study.

Although it follows English tradition by crediting the king with personally inspiring the use of English,[92] it actually looks to the model of "the Lords and trusty Commons" (in other words, to parliament), as recorded by the clerks of Chancery, for the real justification for the change.[91]

More remains to be done so that we may more fully understand the development of official English in the fifteenth century and its relation to various authors and segments of the writing public. The dominance of the scribal tradition lasted only until the advent of printing. By the end of the fifteenth century, printers and educators began to assume dominant roles in codifying the approved forms and idioms of written English, just as educators had for centuries controlled the approved forms and idioms of Latin. During the crucial period between 1420 and 1460, before the advent of printing and before English became part of the educational establishment, English first began to be used regularly for government, business, and private transactions. The essential characteristics of Modern written English were determined by the practice of the clerks in Chancery and communicated throughout England by professional scribes writing in Chancery script and under the influence of Chancery idiom. When Caxton returned to England in 1476, he established his press not in London but in Westminster, under the shadow of the government offices where, by that time, Chancery Standard was the normal language for all official communications. Caxton printed in a language strongly influenced by Chancery Standard, but within a few years printers were introducing *are* for Chancery *be/ben* (found in London documents before 1420) and *s* for Chancery third-person *th* (found in London documents by the 1450s).

And so it goes. Modern English is not Chancery English. In its style, its forms, and particularly in its capitalization and punctuation, it has continued to evolve. But Chancery English of the early fifteenth century is the starting point for this evolution, and it has left an indelible impression upon the grammar, spelling, and idiom of Modern English.

IV

EUROPEAN CHANCELLERIES AND THE RISE OF WRITTEN LANGUAGES

The decline of dialects and the emergence of standard languages in Europe at the close of the Middle Ages is a familiar chapter in the histories of the individual languages. However, I do not know of a discussion that points out how similar this process was in various countries and discusses the implications of this similarity for our general understanding of the nature of standard languages.[1] A comparative study reveals that standard languages all emerged as written and not oral forms; that these written standards were created by government secretariats, not by literary figures; and that when spoken standards began to emerge in the seventeenth and eighteenth centuries, their grammar and pronunciation were based on the written standard and not vice versa.

One of the reasons that these historical patterns have not been recognized more clearly is the continuing ambiguity about the relation between speech and writing. During the last century, linguists have made a fetish of speech as the primary form of language and have treated writing as a merely subsidiary representation of speech.[2] Psychologically and philosophically, there is much to be said for this point of view, although even here it has its limitations. Some forms of language, such as mathematics, are impossible without written notation. Such a simple concept as 777 is impossible to grasp without the figure 7.[3] The logical processes of thought advanced by Plato and Aristotle, such as definition of terms, classification, and formal logic, are very heavily dependent upon writing. Aside from the psychological relation between writing and thinking, it is historical nonsense to equate standard languages with speech. In A.D. 950 there were in Europe six "languages": Latin, Greek, Hebrew, Arabic, Anglo-Saxon, and Old Church Slavonic.[4] In 1937, the *Atlas Linguisticus* identified fifty-three languages in Europe, twenty-three of which had emerged since 1900. This would appear to indicate that the languages in Europe are multiplying and growing more diverse. But of course that is not true. All studies show that dialects, especially during this century, have become less widely used and that standard languages are becoming more popular throughout Europe, when the *Atlas Linguisticus* would appear to indicate that the greatest number of new languages have come into existence.

The historical fact is that both in 950 and today, spoken dialects in Europe represent a continuum in which, from north to south and east to west, each village can understand the speech of its neighbor, although at the extremes the speech is mutually unintelligible. W.J. Entwistle has observed that clear linguistic frontiers are always the results of war and politics.[5] In contrast, areas with uninterrupted cultural development have blurred linguistic frontiers. The fixing of sharp linguistic boundaries in Europe began with the centralization of government, the growth of nationalism, and the self-conscious creation of official written languages. As these written standards emerged, dialects continued to be spoken and, indeed, in many cases are still spoken. When literacy and education grew more widespread after the seventeenth century, governments took steps to establish and teach uniform pronunciation, but in large measure, the "languages" of Europe are still the written standards established by government edicts at the end of the Middle Ages. Therefore, understanding the historical process through which these standards came into being is important to understanding languages today.

The historical situation is further obfuscated by the fact that some of the earliest writing in each of the European vernaculars is in local dialects and is devoted to poems, stories, sermons, and other non-official, non-utilitarian literature. This tends to reinforce the impression that, like speech, writing is a private medium and its primary aspect is subjective and expressive. This notion, however, overlooks the fact that in the Middle Ages the official language was Latin, and unofficial speech and writing was in local dialects. Standard Latin was essentially a written language. Philippe Wolff observes that the characteristic linguistic feature of the Roman world was bilingualism: bilingualism between Latin in the West and Greek in the East; bilingualism between Latin and the native dialects; and bilingualism between Imperial Latin and the vulgar Latin dialects that became the romance languages.[6] These bilingualisms have different histories in different areas, but in all of them written Imperial Latin (which we today call Classical Latin) lived on as the language of administration, liturgy, jurisprudence, historiography, learning, commerce. The extent to which government and business slipped back into oral tradition following the overthrow of the Empire is a moot point. Germanic tribesmen were apparently slow in learning to write. Not until the reign of Charlemagne in the eighth century do we have evidence of writing used for secular government. Erich Auerbach in *Literary Language and its Public* argues that from the sixth to the twelfth century writing was purely ceremonial.[7] M.T. Clanchey in *From Memory to Written Record* argues that the Anglo-Saxon charters and Alfred's interest in writing were magical and ceremonial. Even the compilation of the Domesday Book Clanchey views as largely symbolic since there are no references to it in legal proceedings until after 1250.[8]

The principal bilingualism of the European Middle Ages was between speech and writing. Latin writing was inextricably linked with the spiritual and secular ambitions of the Roman Church, which had inherited the mantle of the Empire. For the Church, Latin was an instrument of vital political importance. As Elliott Goodman observed, a national language is the nerve center of national memory, the most important medium through which national traditions are nurtured and transmitted.[9] As long as administration, worship, jurisprudence, education, learning, and literature were carried on in the language of Rome, the Empire lived. As the vernacular languages of the European countries displaced Latin, Rome's authority declined.

In the tenth century King Alfred was the first European ruler to try deliberately to replace Latin with writing in the vernacular, and his secretariat went some distance towards creating a national standard. Helmut Gneuss, in the fullest study yet made, discounts Alfred's personal involvement and attributes the standardization to Aethelwold's school in the Old Minster in Winchester.[10] However, Gneuss discusses only literary and ecclesiastical manuscripts. He mentions in passing that Aethelwold may have introduced a new kind of charter in Anglo-Saxon, but he offers no comment on the language of the Anglo-Saxon laws and charters, which Mary Richards has begun to study. The evidence of later developments in the language indicates that it is in connection with such civic documents as these that standardization begins. Winchester would have been the location of an Anglo-Saxon chancellery. Until the official documents have been further studied, we will not know to what extent the activities of the Anglo-Saxon chancellery foreshadowed those of Toledo, Paris, and Westminster.

Gneuss attributes the creation of standard Anglo-Saxon to the Benedictine reform, and it is true that some of the earliest writings in the other European vernaculars are associated with religious movements that reflected implicit resistance to the domination of Rome. In his *Admonitio Generalis* in 789, Charlemagne urged the clergy to make more use of the vernaculars for meeting the needs of the laity. At the Council of Frankfort in 794 he stated that "no one believes that God should only be worshipped in the three languages [i.e., Latin, Greek, and Hebrew]. God is worshipped and man's prayers are heard, when his demands are just, in any language." Despite the fact that they are recorded in Latin from the lips of an emperor who aspired to the imperial diadem, these words serve as the birth certificate of nationalism and of national languages.[11] Nineteen years later the Council of Tours confirmed this movement by ordering priests to translate their sermons into vulgar Latin or German ("rusticam romanum aut þeotiscan," þeod = tribe) for the benefit of the lay people. These sentiments lie behind Alfred's preface to the Anglo-Saxon translation of Pope Gregory's *Pastoral Care* and his program for translating other Latin works into English. This sort of religio/linguistic resistance to Rome is also found in the vernacular poetry of the Franciscans in thirteenth-century Umbria,[12] in the development of the Wycliffite written tradition in England[13] in Luther's translation of the Bible into German,[14] and in Calvin's insistence on composing his theological treatises in French.[15] No doubt ecclesiastical writing was more utilitarian and official in the Middle Ages than we regard it today. Nevertheless, in no case does this early ecclesiastical writing represent the tradition from which modern vernacular standards emerged. The monastic scriptoria, devoted to producing masterpieces of calligraphy and painting, reveal the magical and ceremonial aspects of writing, not the official.[16] This aspect is not unimportant since magic and ceremony are attributes of power. But standard languages emerge from government and business, not from magic and ceremony.

In contrast to the statements recorded in Latin at Frankfurt and Tours advocating the use of the vernacular, the two earliest examples of European vernacular writing that have come down to us are both official. The earliest examples of French are the Strassburg Oaths sworn in 842 by Charles and Louis against their brother, Emperor Lothair I, and the earliest examples of Italian are the *Placiti Cassinesi* of 960. Neither the Strassburg Oaths nor the *Placiti* represents the reduction to writing of extempore phrases from the vernacular. They are the first examples of chancellery usage. In each case, the judge prescribed the Latin formulas by which the witnesses swore in French or Italian. The witnesses knew the formulas in Latin and used the vernacular only for the sake of their audience.[17] Free, extempore composition in the vernacular by writers who had not been educated first in Latin was still several centuries in the future.

It is impossible to know how much of this sort of translation of official Latin into the vernacular has been lost from what Clanchey calls "the age of memory," but it is of no great importance since it represents the age of writing in dialect, not the beginning of standard language. So likewise does the first flowering of court poetry in Provence, Sicily, Galicia, and Germany between 1150 and 1250. For their tiny, homogeneous but sophisticated and widely travelled audiences, the trobars, troubadours, and minnesingers fashioned somewhat normalized written dialects of Provençal, Sicilian, Galician, and German, information which could be used to argue that the beginnings of the vernacular standards are not official but literary. The evidence of these writings, however, points in the opposite direction. None of these twelfth-century court dialects is the dialect from which the written standard eventually emerged. French court poetry began in *langue d'oc* whereas the standard emerged from *langue d'oil*. The best twelfth-century German poetry, written under the patronage of the Hohenstaufens, was in the Alemanic and Franconian dialects, but the standard language eventually emerged from Saxon and Thuringian. The poetry of the court of Frederick II was in Sicilian, but standard Italian originated in Tuscany. Until the end of the thirteenth century, Galician was the language favored for the court lyric in Spain, but the standard emerged from Castilian. The truth is that these courtly compositions were not really regarded as writing but as librettos, mnemonic devices to remind performers of their oral songs and stories.

Until after the Renaissance of the twelfth century, writing was Latin, and Latin was writing.[18] The period from the sixth through the twelfth centuries was known for the practice of *ars dictaminis*, when neither the author nor the receiver of a missive needed to be master of the techniques of writing; they were simply the "dictator" and the "auditor." An anonymous and invisible clerk, who alone maintained the integrity of the graphic code, linked the correspondents.[19] The regularization of government and resurgence of trade beginning in the twelfth century was what finally led to the development of official writing in the vernaculars.[20] In France, Spain, and England the resurgence of civic life was concomitant with the centralization of administration in a pivotal city. In spite of its lack of centralized political authority, Italy in the twelfth century witnessed the earliest resurgence of civic life and the earliest use of writing in the vernacular for business, especially in the Tuscan communes of the north. In Germany standardization was supported by the authority of the chancelleries of the Holy Roman Empire. Castilian Spanish began to be standardized in the thirteenth century, Parisian French in the fourteenth, London English in the fifteenth, and Saxon German in the sixteenth. These dates are approximate, but it is accurate to say that before 1100 virtually all official and commercial business in Europe was carried on either orally or in written Latin, and by 1600 virtually all of it was being carried on in the vernaculars. In each country the use of vernacular writing for government and business preceded the awakening of what Auerbach calls "vernacular human-ism," the development of the vernacular into a vehicle for literature and culture.[21] In some instances important literary works appear concomitant with the emergence of the vernacular standard: Dante's work in Italy, *Poema del Cid* in Spain, *Roman de la Rose* in France, and the poems of Chaucer in England. I believe, however, that these poems were not themselves creators of the literary languages but early examples of the use of the emerging official standards for literary purposes.

France and Spain

The archetypical evolutions of medieval written standards are in France and Spain, where the languages are aspects of the centrali-zation of government and the development of nationalism. The emergence of the Ile de France and Paris as the heart of the French nation is a familiar story. From the time the Capetians came to the throne in the eleventh century, the court was fixed in Paris. Whatever official writing the court did at this time was in Latin, and some of the earliest examples of literature, like the *Chanson de Roland* and the *Vie de Saint Alexis*, are in a mixture of Parisian and Norman dialect.[22] The royal chancellery in Paris was actually slower to begin using French than the provincial cities. The earliest French document in the archives of Tournai dates from 1197, whereas the first French document in the Chancellerie Royale is dated 1218.[23] The earliest documents in the provincial archives are in local dialects, but by 1250 the *français* of the Parisian chancellery began to appear in the local archives, and by 1300 local dialects disappear from official docu-ments.

From this time onward, Parisian French means the written standard of the royal chancellery. Like the Latin it replaced, this writing represented unity and authority in the face of diversity. The beginning of the growth of national spirit may be associated with the consolidation of administration under Louis IX, St. Louis (1214-70). His suppression of the great feudatories and his arbitration of borders with England and Aragon greatly enhanced the royal authority. His introduction of Roman law and the appellate jurisdiction of th crown throughout his territories and the regularization of the collection of taxes and administration increased the authority of the Chancellerie

Royale in Paris. A 1257 annotation attributed to the king indicates that correspondence with the chancellery was to be in French, even though the notation is, as usual, in Latin: "quod nos litteras maioris et juratorum Sancti Quintini in vir omandia in gallico scriptas vidimus."[24] Brunot details the manner in which regional secular and ecclesiastical cartularies began to follow the example of the Parisian chancellery. He concludes that by 1320 the French of the Chancellerie Royale had prevailed throughout the langue d'oil except in the north (modern Belgium), where dialect was written until the fifteenth century. Literature followed the same chronology with only one important author after 1320 writing in dialect. Froissart wrote his *Chronicles* in the dialect of his native Valence, perhaps conscious of his English audience and the growing overtones of nationalism associated with the French of Paris.

The situation in the south of France is more complex. The Albigensian wars, concluded by St. Louis in 1229, destroyed nearly all evidence of the unity of the Provençal culture that must have been the foundation for unity in the language. Perhaps as a result of the same continuity of the notarial tradition, Provence, like Italy, had begun to use the vernacular for administration a century before the north. Deeds and charters in langue d'oc date from 1034.[25] In 1178 when a mission was sent to Toulouse to combat heresy, two Cathari presented the document with a statement in occitan. When their audience invited them to speak Latin, the Cathari professed to know none, and the conference had to be carried on in Provençal. After the treaty of 1229, the assimilation of Provence into the administration of Paris brought to an end the official use of occitan. The royal seneschals who were appointed to govern the south used Parisian French for their administration, but the municipalities and local gentry insisted on using Latin. In order to reach the local populace, Parisian officials were forced to address them in Latin. Under Philip the Fair in 1317, it was decreed that the chancellery should write to "bonis villis gallicanis in gallico et occitanis in latino."[26] French began to replace Latin in the course of the reconquest of the south during the Hundred Years War with England, especially after Jean, duc de Berry, was invested with Aquitaine and established his court in Riom in 1360. By 1450 Parisian French had become the official written language throughout Provence, although the spoken dialect persisted, and indeed persists to this day.

By the middle of the fourteenth century in the north of France and by the middle of the fifteenth in the south, the writing of the Parisian chancellery had been accepted as standard for government and business and had a reasonably uniform lexicon, morphology, and syntax. In the sixteenth century, literary and other learned writers adopted this official standard, and uniform pronunciation began to be established in the seventeenth century. These movements take us beyond the period of our concern, but it is worth observing that the 1539 Ordinance of Villers-Cotterets legally established French as the language of administration and the law and was principally directed towards written language. In spite of a succession of attempts at reform, the traditional French chancellery spellings persisted.[27] In 1560 Mathieu explained, "Le gens qui proposent vne nouuelle maniere d'ecrire, ne iugent pas qu'ils entreprennent combat alencontre de la necessite. Telle necessite c'est la Chancellerie de France; sont cours du Parlement sont les iustices souueraines et ordinaires."[28] As education grew more general, competition arose between writing masters of the corporation of law clerks and teachers in the chantry schools over the privilege of teaching writing. As late as 1714, chantry school teachers were forbidden to put more than three lines of writing before their students as examples. The law clerks still controlled a monopoly on teaching writing and orthography.[29]

The movement in France towards fixing pronunciation is attributed to the court and salon society of the seventeenth century. Brunot says that printing and the speech of the salons combined to fix pronunciation.[30] What spelling reform occurred was influenced by the speech of the salons, but by the eighteenth century, "bon usage" came to mean speech imitating the decorum of written usage.[31] Because of the influence of the salons (themselves a kind of drama), French theater played a smaller part than the English and German theater in disseminating the standard pronunciation, but the theater was caught up in the eighteenth century movement to refine the language. Plays were censored to eradicate any sign of vulgar expression.

Like Parisian French, Castilian Spanish was standardized in the processes of national unification and the centralization of administration. The linguistic competition in Spain was less between the vernacular dialects and Latin than between the dialects and Arabic.

Spaniards in the parts of Spain under Arab domination never gave up their Romance dialects. Like English under the Normans, Spanish continued as the domestic language (called mozarabic because it was written in the Arabic alphabet), while Arabic was limited to administration and to the literature and learning of the small circle of rulers of Arab descent. The use of Arabic as an official language led to the decline of Latin to the point that in 1049 the canons of the Catholic Church had to be translated into Arabic to guarantee their preservation.[32] Spanish first emerged as an official language as the central plains were gradually recovered from the Arab rulers. The northwest coast and mountains were the only region in Spain subdued by neither the Visigoths nor the Arabs. Taking advantage of plague, drought, and revolt preoccupying the Caliphate, Alphonso I, Duke of Cantabria, created around 750 the Christian Kingdom of Galicia in the far northwestern corner of the peninsula. Other dukedoms soon asserted their independence, and by 900 these leaders had formed a loose federation designated as the Kingdom of Leon. The frontier between Leon and Moorish Spain comprised the dukedoms of Cantabria and Bardulia. The "castilla," or castles, scattered through the hills around Burgos, the major city of Cantabria, became the base from which the reconquest of the plains was achieved over the next hundred years. The dialect of the Castilians, as they came to be called, spread with their power, invading eastern Leon and pressing southward into the conquered portions of the Emirate of Toledo. Already in the tenth century legal documents, deeds, and church records in the Christian kingdoms were written in the vernacular dialects.[33] Galician was the preferred dialect for lyric poetry, but the military prowess of the Castilians led to the use of Castilian for the epic poems of the eleventh and twelfth centuries.

Castile completed the conquest of the Emirate of Toledo in 1085 under Alphonso VI, and Toledo remained the seat of the Castilian court until Philip II established the capital at Madrid in 1561. Alphonso VI moved his chancellery in Toledo into the mainstream of European scribal practice by replacing the Visigothic minuscule with the Caroline minuscule.[34] As Castilian influence spread, the hand and language of the chancellery in Toledo was adopted by the other chancelleries in Spain. Like King Alfred in England, Alphonso X (1252-84) is credited with taking a personal interest in establishing the Castilian standard.[35] In 1253 he decreed the usage of Toledo to be the standard for all official documents. Tradition holds that in 1276, Alphonso personally went through the *Book of the Eighth Sphere*, which had been written by his scholars, and eliminated irregularities in spelling and grammar and improved clumsy expression. In doing so, Alphonso thus established "castellano drecho," or correct Castilian. This standard corresponded to the usage of Burgos, the administrative center of ancient Castile, but with concessions to the dialects of Leon and Toledo. Alphonso himself continued to write poetry in Galician, but his chancellery used Castilian for all official writing, and he had science, history, and other prose translated into Castilian.

There is no need to trace the gradual domination of Castilian over Aragonese and Catalan and the eighteenth-century establishment of a separate Portuguese standard.[36] The spread of Castilian reaffirms the connection between political power and the establishment of standard language. It also reaffirms that the concept of a standard applies largely to the written form of a language. Even today, only a minority of the people in Spain, and no one in Spanish America, speaks Castilian Spanish as a native vernacular.[37] Educated people write *español correcto* and speak it following the usage of the written language, but it is nearly always a divergent from their normal colloquials. Antonio de Nebrija, himself an Andalusian, in the earliest vernacular grammar in Europe (1492), asserted that he was establishing a written standard for use throughout the Spanish empire because Spanish people were so colloquial in their usage.[38]

England

Historians of the English language have been tardy in acknowledging the influence of government in establishing conventions of the standard language, but the history of English parallels that of French and Spanish. The difference in England was the Norman Conquest, which brought to an end the Alfredian movement toward establishing an Anglo-Saxon standard. William the Conqueror issued documents in both Latin and Anglo-Saxon Standard, but Anglo-Saxon Standard disappeared by the beginning of the twelfth century. With the exception of the 1258 proclamation of Henry III, there are no official documents in English until the Petition of the Mercers to Parliament in 1386 and the coronation pledges of Henry IV in 1399. These documents, however, are atypical. Chancery Standard did not begin to develop until the reign of Henry V.[39] All of Henry's correspondence was in French until he invaded France for the second time in 1417, and from that point, all of the correspondence written by his signet clerks was in English and was modeled on his own usage. We have collected in *An Anthology of Chancery English* such letters, written between 1417 and 1422 by some thirteen different clerks.[40] The letters are remarkably uniform in their grammar and orthography and clearly provided the model for the English written by Privy Seal, Chancery, and parliament in the decades that followed. Like the standard of the Castilian chancellery that made concessions to the dialects of Toledo and Leon and the standard of the Saxon chancellery that made concessions to the usages of Prague and Vienna, English Chancery Standard is an amalgam of the midland Wycliffite standard and the southern London standard. From southern usage, Chancery Standard takes third person *th* (*sayeth*, *hath*), *yive* and *ayenst* with the semivowel, and *be/ben* instead of *are*. From northern dialects it takes *they, them, their; ly* for use with adverbs; loss of the *y* prefix on the past participle; and loss of the *en* inflection on the infinitive. By 1450 Chancery Standard was being used throughout England. In the Paston and Stonor papers it is easy to distinguish writers who had been trained in Chancery usage from those who still spelled by ear.[41] Chancery Standard served as the model for Caxton and the early printers and became the basis for the English prose styles that developed in the sixteenth century. These styles, as discussed in the introduction, made few changes in Chancery morphology and orthography, and their techniques of subordination and parallelism are sophisticated developments of structures borrowed by Chancery Standard from its Latin and French antecedents.

Like the Parisian and Castilian standards, Chancery Standard in England developed as a written convention. English pronunciation was not fixed until the end of the eighteenth century.[42] The English court did not have the sort of influence on the establishment of English pronunciation that the Spanish and French courts did on Castilian and French. In England, the preferred pronunciations were legislated by actors and politicians (who were sometimes the same).

Thomas Sheridan, father of the playwright, who began his own career as an actor, published the first dictionary of pronunciation in 1780 and urged that elocution in English become part of the school curriculum. His son, Richard Brinsley Sheridan, along with Edmund Burke, Charles Fox, and the two William Pitts exemplified his theories and made the last quarter of the eighteenth century the golden age of English oratory. Their pronunciation was disseminated by the actors at the end of the century and set the style for public school pronunciation in the nineteenth century, which later grew into the British Received Pronunciation. But this emphasis on the standardization of spoken English was not until four hundred years after the Chancery clerks had begun to standardize the written language.[43]

German and Italian

In neither Germany nor Italy was the standardization of the written language associated with the establishment of a strong central administration. In both it was largely commercial, although it did mark the emergence of a sense of nationhood. In Germany the centralized power of the Emperor began to disintegrate in the thirteenth century, and some of the earliest documents in German are the 2500 "Urkunden" from before 1299 (2200 of them are from the High German area), documents that arbitrated differences between the newly independent dukes and counts.[44] These were all in regional dialects. In the meantime, the cities of the Hanseatic League created a Low German commercial language, not unlike Dutch, from which a large body of contracts and commercial correspondence survives.[45] But as power moved to central Germany, the influence of the Hanseatic *koine* died. Standard written High German evolved from three successive Imperial chancelleries.[46] When the Luxembourg kings became emperors after 1308, their chancellery in Prague attempted to promulgate a written standard. After 1438 when the Hapsburgs became emperors, their chancellery in Vienna promoted a written standard adapted from Prague usage. Meanwhile the Electorate of Saxony (which had provided the first emperor for the Holy Roman empire)[47] was advancing to the leadership of Germany because of its central location and the wealth of its industrial cities such as Meissen, Dresden, Wittenberg, and Leipzig. After the accession of Ernest and Albert as electors in 1464, Saxony became the most influential state in Germany and the cradle of the Reformation. Its chancellery, with branches in Meissen, Dresden, and Wittenberg, developed a standard language based on those of Prague and Vienna. The Saxon Chancery language was adopted by the episcopal chancery in Mainz and was used for recording church diets and promulgating episcopal edicts, thereby adding religious to secular prestige. By the end of the fifteenth century the Geschaftsprach of the Hansa had given way to the Gemeinsdeutsch of the Viennese chancery and the Ostmitteldeutsch of the Saxon chancery. Historians of the German language give Martin Luther credit for tipping the scales in favor of Saxon. Himself a Thuringian under the protection of Elector Frederick III of Saxony (in whose castle he began his translation of the Bible), Luther wrote in his *Tischreden*: "I have no certain, special language of my own in Germany, but make use of the common German language so that both those in the south and those in the north may understand me. I speak according to the Saxon chancery, which is followed by all princes and kings in Germany. . . . Hence it is also the commonest German language. Emperor Maximilian and Elector Frederick, Duke of Saxony, have in the Holy Roman Empire, therefore, drawn together the German languages into a certain language."[48] Luther was wrong about the uniformity of German in his day, but his assertion indicates that his enormously influential Bibeldeutsch was based on the official language of the Saxon chancery.

The spread of the Ostmitteldeutsch standard was gradual over the next three centuries. Waterman indicates that it prevailed in Protestant Swabia by 1650, in Switzerland by 1700, in Vienna by 1750, but not until after 1800 in Catholic Bavaria and the Rhineland.[49] We are again speaking, of course, of a written standard. Little progress was made towards establishing a spoken standard until the nineteenth century. In 1612 Wolfgang Ratichius mounted a campaign to have German taught in the elementary schools in order to enhance the national spirit. This led to the production of handbooks, that of Justus George Schottel being one of the most influential. Schottel's prescriptive grammar, based on the literary norm, asserted that the spoken language was nothing but unregulated dialect unless it imitated the written language of learned men. Handbooks in the eighteenth century asserted this idea, and all authorities, like

Berthold Brocks in 1721, advised "Man muss sprechen, wie man schreibt."[50] Wilfred Voge devoted a book to the controversy over the pronunciation of German in the eighteenth century, and Werner Leopold could in 1959 still write an article discussing the decline of regional dialects as a result of World War II.[51] As in England, the stage was called on to disseminate correct pronunciation in the nineteenth century. Goethe and others stressed that this "Buhnensprache" was an ideal too mannered for general use.[52]

In Italy, the movement to vernacular writing began earlier than in any other European country (if we except the abortive attempt with Anglo-Saxon), but the historical and sociolinguistic developments of Italian are the most complex. There is no great problem in understanding the priority or continuity of Italian writing. Civic life persisted more tenaciously in Italy through the Dark Ages than in other parts of Europe, and guilds and trading companies continued to use administrative and language practices carried over from Roman civilization.[53] In 825 guilds were formally revived in the cities of Bologna, Cremona, Ivrea, Milan, Padua, Turin, Venice, and Florence by the Emperor Lothair I.[54] At this time there was no conscious gap between Latin and the vernacular. Latin was still regarded simply as the correct way of writing both Italian and French.[55] But as indicated by the edicts of Frankfurt and Tours, the Strassburg Oaths, and the *Placiti Cassinesi*, government officials finally began to concede during the ninth and tenth centuries that lay people could not understand Latin. Throughout much of Europe this was of no immediate concern, since government by the Germanic tribesmen was primarily oral. However, business in the Italian communes had been carried on in writing with no appreciable break, and the writing was, of course, Latin until the tenth century when the first translations of the Latin formulae into Italian began to appear.

Business and civic life in Italy was based on the notarial contract.[56] In England this would be called an indenture. The important difference, however, is that while in England, France, Spain, and Germany such indentures began as contracts drawn by chancery clerks and enrolled in the royal or ducal chancellery, in the Italian cities notaries were private practitioners (although nominally appointed by the Emperor) who were legally charged with drawing up contracts and preserving them in their private cartularies. Until after the thirteenth century, most Italian notarial documents are in Latin, but it is evident that business was conducted in the vernacular and that Latin was merely the language of record. There are glossaries of vernacular legal terms and vernacular formularies used in connection with legal education at Bologna dating from 1055, and the 1246 Statutes of Bologna specify that notaries must be able to read their documents in both Latin and the vernacular. In their matriculation examinations, notaries were asked first to explain the terms of the contract in the vernacular and then in the technical Latin.[57] One of the earliest examples of the use of the vernacular is two sheets of parchment dated 1211 from the account book of a Florentine bank. The language is so precise and expressive that Migliorini believes it indicates that a tradition of business writing in the vernacular was already well established.[58]

It is not difficult to guess why this development began in Tuscany. While middle and southern Italy were still being administered in the Latin of the papal curia or the Arabic, Catalan, or French of a succession of foreign rulers, the Tuscan communes had entered into their period of independence and increasing prosperity by the end of the eleventh century. The reason for the linguistic preeminence of Florence is less clear. Historians of the Italian language cite Florence's cultural importance, and particularly the influence of the "three crowns" of Florence, Dante, Boccaccio, and Petrarch, as one of the reasons for the city's linguistic dominance. I suspect, however, that this is a matter of *post hoc ergo propter hoc*. Like Luther, these three men wrote in the official language of their city. Dante was a city official between 1295 and 1300; Petrarch was the son of a Florentine notary; and Boccaccio, wherever he was born, was evidently the son of a Florentine merchant and was educated and for six years apprenticed to a merchant in Florence. These poets undoubtedly helped to establish the prestige of the Florentine dialect, but they were exponents of a written language already preeminent in northern Italy. In *De vulqare eloquentia*, Dante expressed his irritation at his fellow citizens' sense of linguistic superiority, and Boccaccio declared that his aim was to write the *Decameron* "in fiorentin vulgare."[59]

The linguistic preeminence of Florentine Italian rested partially upon the influence of the great Florentine banking and trading companies, and their use of vernacular writing while those in Venice, Bologna, Milan, and other cities were still keeping records in Latin. By 1115 Florence had thrown off the rule of the German emperor and established its merchant oligarchy. By 1200 merchants from Rome and other cities were turning to Florence for capital.[60] The Florentine trading and banking houses established offices throughout Italy and eventually throughout Europe. By 1233 these businesses had been authorized to collect the papal revenues. Florence's central location and economic prestige gave it the advantages of a capital city. What the royal chancelleries of Toledo, Paris, Westminster, and Saxony did for their languages, the chancelleries of the great Florentine houses of Bardi, Strozzi, Medici, and others did for Italian. By the seventeenth century, Florentine Tuscan had became the written standard accepted throughout Italy, although speech continued in dialects. Migliorini observes that writers outside of Tuscany objected when Florentine writers used colloquial Florentine and that formal Italian today still follows the conventions of the written language.[61]

Let me now summarize. First, it is apparent that the European languages were standardized first in writing and only later, if ever, in speech. Second, standard written forms appeared first in official government and business documents. These served as the basis for the usage of scribes and printers and eventually of handbooks and dictionaries created for teaching the standard written language. In *Literary Language and its Public*, Erich Auerbach remarks that he is concerned with the "style" that makes a language literary, not "merely with phonetics and morphology."[62] But without a uniform morphology and orthography, there can be no style. The relationship between oral style (what we today refer to as the individual "voice" of the author) and written style (the conventions of the language) is one of the more interesting areas of literary criticism. I shall go no further than to observe that unless there is a norm, there can be no variation. The question as to whether this norm is an internal force present in a group of socially related speakers—the "Sprachgefuhl" of August Sleicher and Jacob Grimm—or merely the conventions of the written language is moot. Since Grimm and other nineteenth century philologists deduced principles of linguistic variation, Sprachgefuhl has been in the ascendant and writing has been regarded merely as a subsidiary representation of speech. My study of the history of writing indicates that this is simply not true. Change lies in the nature of speech, and continuity lies in the nature of writing. Every enduring civilization has had a writing system and archives. Like those of the Roman Empire and Medieval Europe, the writing systems of all of the ancient civilizations (Mesopotamia, Egypt, China, and Central America) were the products of official secretariats striving for uniformity and continuity. Lest you believe that things are different now, let me conclude with an anecdote (the full account is available in Volume III of Mark Sullivan's *Our Times*).[63]

Supported by $250,000 of Andrew Carnegie's money, the Simplified Spelling Board in the early 1900s undertook to revise English spelling (which it so badly needs). The idea appealed to President Theodore Roosevelt. As an enlightened man, Roosevelt saw the need and by executive order instructed the White House staff and the Government Printing Office to use the simplified forms. The outcry in both England and the United States was instantaneous. The London *Times* huffed that the U.S. President ought to have consulted the British government on a matter so important to the country of the mother tongue. The British need not have worried, however. Congress would have none of it. Without a dissenting vote, Congress resolved that "Executive departments, their bureaus and branches, and independent offices of the government [and] the Government Printing Office must observe and adhere to the standard orthography prescribed in generally accepted dictionaries of the English language."

So there is no ambiguity as to what standard language is today. It is the official language of government, the judiciary, and business. And so it always has been. Since the advent of printing, popular education, and the mass media, the standard language appears to have moved out from under the aegis of government bureaucracy. Indeed, there is much criticism today of bureaucratese and legalese. But make no mistake, standard language is still anchored as firmly in the seats of power as it has been since the dawn of writing. When there have been efforts at spelling or lexical reform, as there were by the academies of Italy, Spain, and France, they have been government sponsored and supported and, one might add, not notably successful. Scholars and writers have had less influence on the shape of the standard language than the nameless bureaucrats and clerks in government offices.

Except for the moments in history during which they were in

the process of codification, written languages have always differed markedly from their spoken counterparts. Under the influence of handbooks and education, written languages have become more standard as the years progress. Other than in the growth of the lexicon, this standardization has reflected relatively little influence from the spoken stratum. After they have been codified, written languages have more influence upon the structure and pronunciation of the spoken than do the spoken on the structure and orthography of the written. The progressive drift towards the uniformity of spoken languages in America, Europe, and Asia is occurring under the aegis of expanding literacy—that is, under the influence of the written language. The emergence of the written standards from the chancellery languages of Europe between the twelfth and sixteenth centuries is no exception to this rule but rather an important chapter in the history of the relations between speech and writing, with continuing implications for the way we look upon language today.

V

ANIMADVERSIONS ON THE
TEXT OF CHAUCER

In this essay I would like to sum up where we stand on the text of
Chaucer, particularly the text of *The Canterbury Tales*. It is nearly
600 years since Chaucer began compiling the collection—the putative date of the gathering at the Tabard Inn is 17 April 1387.[1] It is
nearly a hundred years since Frederick Furnivall and Walter W.
Skeat chose the Ellesmere manuscript as the best copy text (the
death of Henry Bradshaw in 1886 left to Skeat the editing of the
Oxford Chaucer).[2] We are now in the throes of change in our views
of the texts of both *Troylus and Criseyde* and *The Canterbury Tales* that
may bring into question much of the criticism since 1900.

The first important fact to bear in mind is that we have no
authoritative text for any of Chaucer's writings. Strikingly, neither of
the first two fathers of English literature left official texts. Both
obviously felt that performance was more important than publication. No authoritative manuscripts of any of Shakespeare's plays
survive. He may have concerned himself with printing *Venus and
Adonis* and *The Rape of Lucrece*, but his plays belonged to the company.
Only after his death did his colleagues, John Hemings and Henry

Condell, collect the prompt copies, players' scripts, and pirated quartos to cobble together the First Folio. The problem of the text of Shakespeare's plays has preoccupied scholars ever since.[3]

The situation with Chaucer is very nearly the same. Except for the enigmatic manuscript of *The Equatorie of the Planetis*, there is no manuscript of any of Chaucer's works that can be reliably dated before his death in 1400. The problem of Chaucer holographs is especially puzzling. He was for some twenty-five years an important civil servant. His appointment as controller of customs in the port of London in 1374 specified "quod idem Galfridus rotulos suos dicta officia tangentes manu sua propria scribat et continue moretur ibidem et omnia que ad officia illa pertinent in propria persona sua et non per substitutum suum faciat et exequatur" (that the said Geoffrey shall write with his own hand his rolls pertaining to the same office, and shall constantly guard the same [rolls] and execute everything that pertains to that office in his own person and not through a substitute).[4] The oath he took on accepting his appointment has not been found, but an oath for the controller of petty customs recorded in 1376, which specified, "Vous jurrez qe vous frez continuele demeure en le porte de Loundres" (you swear that you will live continuously in the port of London), has an interlineation in a different hand that reads "en propre persone ou par suffisante depute qi vous vuillez respondre" (in your own person or by a sufficient deputy for whom you will answer). This addition led J.M. Manly to conclude that Chaucer may not have had to be present or keep the records in his own hand after all.[5] Nevertheless, the editors of *Chaucer Life-Records* insist that the original conditions were operative.[6] In spite of these conditions of appointment, not a document survives in the Public Record Office that can be reliably identified as from Chaucer's hand. This absence of documents led Furnivall to conclude in 1873 that "Every single original document drawn up or signed by Chaucer has disappeared from its proper place. Someone who knew the Records thoroughly has systematically picked out—probably scores or hundreds of years ago—all Chaucer's work from every set of Records, and either stolen them or tied them up in some bundle which may be among the unindexed Miscellaneous Records."[7] If so, they have not turned up in the extensive classifying and calendaring that has gone on in the Public Record Office since 1873, nor in the exhaustive combing of the Record Office, Guildhall, and other archives that Lilian J. Redstone and her assistants carried out for Manly and Rickert. R.E.G. Kirk proposed that six miscellaneous records were possibly in Chaucer's hand, and Manly and Redstone note one document whose hand and signature Derek Price found very similar to the hand and name "Chaucer" in the Peterhouse manuscript of *The Equatorie of the Planetis*.[8] But even if the Peterhouse manuscript might be a Chaucer holograph, which many Chaucerians doubt, the absence of holograph documents and signatures from Chaucer's official life remains a mystery.

The absence of any pre-1400 manuscripts of his literary works is equally mysterious. Although absence of authorial involvement in publication in the Middle Ages is not unusual, in the case of Chaucer it is unusual. Chaucer was not an anonymous provincial or proletarian, like the authors of the *Pearl* or *Piers Plowman*, but a member of the royal household from which he received grants throughout his lifetime. In the era before printing, presentation to a patron was the customary way to publish and to receive remuneration for one's writings.[9] There are presentation manuscripts from most of Chaucer's contemporaries, Machaut, Deschamps, Froissart, Gower, Hoccleve, and Lydgate.[10] Internal evidence indicates that several of Chaucer's poems were produced for royal patrons: *The Book of the Duchess* for John of Gaunt, identified at its conclusion, "Be Seynt Johan, on a ryche hille" (*BD* 1319), referring to John, Earl of Richmond, Gaunt's title before he married Blanche of Lancaster; *The Legend of Good Women* for Queen Anne: "And whall this book ys maad, yive it the quene, / On my byhalf, at Eltham or at Sheene" (*LGW* 496); and begging balades to King Richard and King Henry.[11] Yet we have no presentation manuscript of any work supervised by Chaucer himself. The Morgan Library manuscript of *Troylus and Criseyde*, which has on the first page the arms of Henry V when he was Prince of Wales, was written after 1400. The Ellesmere manuscript of *The Canterbury Tales*, whose opulence bespeaks a wealthy patron (about whose identity I will conjecture in a moment), was likewise written after Chaucer's death.

Chaucer's friend John Gower took pains during the 1390s to produce fine copies of collections of his English and Latin poems and to present them to wealthy patrons and establishments where they would be preserved.[12] In his fascinating autobiographical poem *Voir Dit*, Chaucer's early model Guillaume de Machaut describes "le livre ou je met toutes mes choses" that he was having copied for "one of my lords."[13] How can it be that an author immersed in this presentation culture, patronized by royalty, recognized by his contemporaries as one of the "premier poetes of this nacion," an "erthely god" who "the lond fulfild / Of Ditees and of Songes glade,"[14] would not have supervised the creation of at least one handsome copy of one of his poems for presentation to a patron?

Critics sometimes use the explanation that Chaucer was, like Shakespeare, concerned only with performance. We assume that Chaucer must have read his poems to the royal court and the Inns of Court, but again the evidence is exasperatingly tenuous. The poems contain frequent references to his audiences' "hearing" or "reading" (which are practically homologous since before the advent of printing nearly all reading was aloud), but recent studies interpret these references less as evidence of the performance than as devices by which Chaucer was inviting an "implied" or "fictional" audience to participate in the creative process.[15] The most interesting nearly contemporary testimony is the frontispiece to the Corpus manuscript of *Troylus and Criseyde*, which purports to show Chaucer reading to the court. But the speaker in the picture stands in a pulpit and addresses the audience without a manuscript before him, paralleling the iconography of sermon literature, and therefore this illustration offers no certain evidence that Chaucer read his poems aloud.[16]

Furthermore, there is internal evidence that Chaucer viewed his creations as written documents.[17] In the catalog of his works in *The Legend of Good Women*, he says that "He made the book that hight the *Hous of Fame*" and "in prose translated *Boece*" (*LGW* 417, 425). The list of his works in the *Retraccioun* at the end of *The Canterbury Tales* prays "to hem alle that herkne this litel tretys or rede" (*CT* 10.1081). Most direct is the famous charge at the end of *Troylus and Criseyde*:

> Go litel bok, go litel myn tragedye,
> Ther God thi makere yet, er that he dye,
> So sende myght to make yn som comedye.
> But litel bok, no makyng thow n'envye,
> And subgit be to alle poesye,
> And kys the steppes where as thow seest pace
> Virgile, Ovyde, Omer, Lukan, and Stace.

And for ther is so gret dyversite
In Englyssh and yn wrytyng of oure tonge,
So prey I God that noon myswryte the,
Ne the mysmetre for default of tonge.
And red wherso thow be, or elles songe,
That thow be understonde, God I beseche—
                                        (*TC* 5.1786-99)

Finally, there is the famous injunction to his scribe:

Adam scryveyn, if ever it thee byfalle
Boece or *Troylus* for to wryten newe,
Under thy long lokkes thow most have the scalle
But after my makyng thow wryte more trewe!
So ofte a daye I mot thy werk renewe
It to corecte and eke to rubbe and scrape;
And al is thorugh thy neglygence and rape!
                        ("To Adam Scryven")

How could the poet who wrote these lines not have superintended
the preservation of a single one of his poems? There is a mystery here
either in the psychology of the creator or in the fortune of his
manuscripts. Given his standing in court circles, which would have
led to the preservation of his manuscripts, we must assume that the
explanation is psychological. Again as with Shakespeare, no life
record ever mentions Chaucer's poetry or Chaucer as a poet. As far
as the documents are concerned, the poet and the controller of
customs could have been different people. We must suppose that in
his day Chaucer was thought of, and thought of himself, as a civil
servant, a man of affairs, and not as a writer. Would T.S. Eliot,
Wallace Stevens, or William Carlos Williams be thought of as poets
today had they not assiduously overseen publication of their poems?
The fact that Chaucer did not think of himself as an author must have
contributed to his difficulty in finishing his pieces. The *Parlement of
Foules*, *Boece*, and *Troylus and Criseyde* are complete (although, as I
shall note, the evidence of the manuscripts is that *Troylus*, at least,
was never considered "finished"), but *The House of Fame*, *The Legend
of Good Women*, *The Canterbury Tales*, the *Treatise on the Astrolabe*, and
(if it is by Chaucer) *The Equatorie of the Planetis* are all incomplete.
The right to adapt was the medieval author's defense against losing

control over his material.[18] Chaucer evidently felt that he had little to gain from formal presentation or publication of any kind, and he was loath during his lifetime to lose control of his materials.

Chaucerians are fairly well agreed as to the nature of the manuscripts Chaucer left behind. Unlike Machaut, who in *Voir Dit* describes how he dictated his poems to a secretary so constantly in attendance that he could assist in his master's dalliance with his lady Peronne, we have little evidence of Chaucer's method of composition. If the putative *The Equatorie of the Planetis* is really a Chaucer holograph, it indicates that he composed in vellum fascicles, crossing out, scraping off, rewriting, and interpolating words and sections as he went along. The poem to Adam scryven implies that once "endighted," the draft would be handed to a scribe who made a fair copy.[19] This copy was likewise on sturdy vellum, and Chaucer's corrections and revisions continued for the rest of his life. He would read from the velum as occasion demanded, but he would revise, rearrange, and add to a work over the years so that by the time he died in 1400, the scribe's fair copy would have been transformed into the poet's "foul papers." The manuscript, like the *Equatorie* manuscript, would have been filled with interlinear and marginal revisions, passages marked for rearrangement or elimination, and with additional interleaved sheets or (in the case of *The Canterbury Tales*) quires of additions that characterized a first draft in the era before microprocessors.[20] The most controversial question with regard to Chaucer's texts is the nature and accessibility of these foul papers.

Before the advent of printing, the most common way for a literary work to be disseminated was for a friend or associate to make a transcript from the author's personal copy.[21] The presumption would be that Chaucer's works were disseminated in this way. In the 1898 Globe Chaucer, William McCormick proposed that the different versions of *Troylus and Criseyde* represented copies made from Chaucer's official text in three stages of revision, which McCormick designated alpha, beta, and gamma. This hypothesis was further developed by Robert K. Root, and the doctrine of alpha, beta, and gamma as authorial versions of *Troylus and Criseyde* remained standard until this decade. In the most recent edition of the poem, however, Barry Windeatt argues that the differences in the versions do not appear to be authorial but rather "localized [that is, scribal] impositions on an established text."[22] He accepts that some of the variants may be authorial, but he interprets these as scribal choices from among the variant readings found in the foul papers. The omission of Troylus's song in Book Three (1744-71), his predestination soliloquy in Book Four (953-1085), and his ascent to the spheres in Book Five (1807-27) (which Root had taken as indications of earlier versions of the poem) do indicate that in the foul papers these passages may have been on inserted sheets,[23] but Windeatt finds no indication of a text that could read coherently without them. The conclusion from this analysis, which has been well received, is that all extant manuscripts of *Troylus and Criseyde* stem ultimately from a single copy text, the foul papers, as interpreted by three or more scribes after Chaucer's death.

This latest textual understanding of *Troylus and Criseyde* may be even more convincingly applied to the text of *The Canterbury Tales*. Manly and Rickert began their collation of the eighty-three manuscripts of the *Tales* in the heyday of the genetic method, hoping that by a mechanical process of recension they could get back to the archetype from which all of the manuscripts derived.[24] They failed in this objective. The manuscripts could not be classified into a stemma, and even manuscript versions of individual tales jumped from one group to another as they progressed. It is moving to think of Manly and Rickert having to explain, after fifteen years of nearly unlimited support, that:

> The classification as presented in the pages that follow must produce so great an impression of complication and variability as to raise the question as to whether it can be correct. . . . [Its] causes lie in these facts: the number of MSS of the *CT* is very large, and they were written over a period of about a century; they do not go back to a single archetype derived from a completed MS of Chaucer's, with tales arranged, linked, and subjected to his corrections and changes, but rather to a body of incomplete material, in different stages of composition and only in part put in order and corrected; many MSS have supplied from other sources parts missing in their exemplars. (2:41)

Manly and Rickert do not here treat the possibility of multiple copy texts representing different stages of composition, but earlier they had observed "that at Chaucer's death more than one copy of some of the tales—copies differing slightly in wording and in contents—

may have been in the hands of some of his friends seems not improbable" (2:36), and they provide a short list of possible authorial revisions (2:39). In a series of articles written later, Germaine Dempster emphasized that it was Manly's belief that the variations in the manuscripts derived from multiple copy texts representing different stages of composition and revision.[25] However, in the collations (which remain invaluable, whatever we may think about the principles of classification), Manly and Rickert did not take the problem of multiple copy texts into account and listed variants with a minimum of comment; they printed "the text established by the process of recension with all the faults which may have crept into the archetype and [left] for the critical notes comments upon archetypal errors and opinions as to the acceptability of emendations early and late" (2:40). It would appear that, to the end, Manly and Rickert had never fully made up their minds about multiple copy texts.

But from the publication of Manly and Rickert's eight volumes in 1940 to the discussions of this decade, the text of *The Canterbury Tales* has been based on the assumption that copies of the individual tales circulated among Chaucer's associates prior to his death, during which time Chaucer was still in the process of adding to and revising his personal manuscripts. Additionally, scholars have assumed that the individual lines of textual transmission derive from these multiple copy texts.[26] Most discussion of the "evolution" of *The Canterbury Tales* is based on study of the textual variations as representative of various stages of authorial composition. The conclusion that these variations are scribal rather than authorial would throw into question more than half a century of Chaucer criticism.

It must be borne in mind for *The Canterbury Tales*, as for *Troylus and Criseyde*, that not one of these independently circulated texts is extant. McCormick lists and Manly and Rickert describe in detail the twenty-eight manuscripts containing individual tales or groups of tales.[27] Of these, only the Merthyr fragment of the Monk-Nun's Priest link is early (ca. 1400). All of the others are late. Six fragments (including Merthyr) are only a leaf or two and could be from either single pieces or the whole collection, and thirteen are pious or moralistic pieces in religious miscellanies. Only two fragments, dating from ca. 1460 and 1483 (Si, Ra[4]), are independent fascicles of two or three tales.[28] So there is no manuscript evidence for the existence of individual tales copied during Chaucer's lifetime.

Again as with *Troylus*, the view of the text of *The Canterbury Tales* has shifted in the last decade to a renewed interest in the hypothesis of the foul papers. This has led to—or resulted from—a growing recognition of the excellence of the text of the Hengwrt manuscript in comparison with that of the Ellesmere, which dominated Chaucer scholarship for a century after Skeat chose it as the copy text for his historic Oxford edition. The excellence of the Hengwrt was confirmed when the recension process of Manly and Rickert, which began with Skeat's Ellesmere-based *Student's Chaucer*, produced a text closer to Hengwrt than to Ellesmere.[29] My own experience in editing *The Wife of Bath's Tale* for the Variorum Chaucer may be used as an example. According to Variorum procedure, I used Hengwrt as the copy text and collated it with the other seven pre-1410 manuscripts and Caxton's first edition. In the 1,264 lines of the prologue and tale, I made only twenty-nine alterations in the Hengwrt text, all but two corrections of manifest errors in transcription. Of the two, one was an emendation of a nonsense line probably found in the archetype and the other the correction of a form probably in the archetype, but whose rhyme and etymology indicate that it was an error: "Proverte is thyng althogh it seme elenge / Possession that no wight wol chalenge" (*CT* 3.1 199-200). The spelling *elenge* is found in seven of the eight pre-1410 texts, including both Hengwrt and Ellesmere, but its root is Anglo-Saxon *aelenge* ("tiresome"), which would normally develop into *alenge*, which rhymes with *chalenge*. Accordingly, *elenge* appears to be an error in the archetype.

My experience confirms both the correctness of the Hengwrt text and the elegance of its expression. In comparison, the Ellesmere, which is nearly as correct, sometimes seems stodgy. A summary discussion is no place to argue this point, but let me cite three examples from the first thirty lines of *The Wife of Bath's Prologue*. At line 7 Hengwrt's "If I so ofte myght han wedded be" is rendered by Ellesmere as "For I so ofte have ywedded bee." The revision is factually accurate, but it loses the Wife's taunt against the church fathers' strictures on remarriage. At line 12 Hengwrt's "That by the same ensample taughte he me" is rendered by Ellesmere as "By the same ensample thoughte me." Again the revised line is lucid, but it takes the edge off by shifting responsibility from masculine authority (in this case Christ himself) to the Wife. At line 29, Hengwrt's "That gentil text kan I wel vnderstonde" is rendered by Ellesmere "That

gentil text kan I vnderstonde." The line means the same thing, but
omitting "wel" again softens the blow. A pattern of this kind of small
stylistic revisions is what led Manly and Rickert to characterize
Ellesmere as an edited text. But who is to say whether such revisions
are authorial or scribal? Whoever made these changes knew the poem
intimately and displayed a consistent interest in changing its tone.
Indeed, the changes in the Ellesmere manuscript resemble the
changes made by the Romantic artists, both musical and literary, as
described by Charles Rosen:

> With Romantic artists, we reach a generation often disconcerted
> by the implications or intentions of their own works. When this
> happens, the revisions become a betrayal of the work when they
> are not a form of tinkering. We might say that the writer has
> ceased being an author and has turned into an interfering editor
> of his own work. With a number of works—"The Rime of the
> Ancyent Marinere," "The Ruined Cottage," Holderlin's "Pat-
> mos," Liszt's *Petrarch Sonnets*—the [modern] editor is forced to
> consider which revisions are developments of the intention, and
> at what point the changes begin to betray rather than to enrich.[30]

Some of the verbal changes between Hengwrt and Ellesmere may
represent this sort of tinkering as preserved in the foul papers and
treated differently by the original editors and scribes. The same
procedure could account for the greater regularity of the Ellesmere
meter. Hengwrt's meter is much less regular, which has been taken
by recent commentators as evidence that Chaucer's own verse was
more staccato and colloquial and that the scribes made Ellesmere
more regular. But could it not have been the author himself who, as
he grew older and worked over the lines, made them both milder in
tone and more regular in rhythm?

Hengwrt has the worst tale order of any of the pre-1410 manuscripts and omits *The Canon's Yeoman's Prologue* and *Tale* and about 100
more lines that seem very Chaucerian, 1,028 lines in all. The question
of how this came about has led Norman Blake back to the hypothesis
propounded by Aage Brusendorff and J.S.P. Tatlock that lapsed after
the publication of the Manly and Rickert edition. Blake argued that
no transcript of *The Canterbury Tales* was made from the foul papers
before Chaucer's death and that the pre-1410 manuscripts from

Hengwrt to Ellesmere are successively dependent efforts on the part of editors and scribes to arrive at a satisfactory order and veneer of completeness for materials left in a state of disarray. What makes it impossible to create a stemma of the manuscripts is that each successive scribe consulted not only the foul papers, which Dempster and Blake envisage as continuing in existence "perhaps as late as the second quarter of the fifteenth century,"[31] but also the previous manuscripts.

The bad tale order of Hengwrt and the variations in order of the other pre-1410 manuscripts indicate that what we now call the Ellesmere order of the tales is not Chaucerian but editorial.[32] Blake offers a plausible scenario for the development of the order through Corpus and Harley 7334, and scribes continued to work with the order of the tales until the order finally achieved in Cambridge Dd was adopted in Cambridge Gg and Ellesmere.[33] Although Vance Ramsey has called it into question, most scholars agree that Hengwrt, the first manuscript of this period of evolution, and Ellesmere, the last, are by the same scribe.[34] This systematic production of a series of manuscripts, each putting the text of *The Canterbury Tales* in more complete and more systematic form, bespeaks some sort of continuing direction. One might hazard that the other seven of the pre-1410 manuscripts were also undertaken to arrive at the stage where the Ellesmere could be produced. Furthermore, when the text had become defined as well as it could be, the expert scribe who had been called on to produce the earliest working draft was called on again to produce the sumptuous final version.

We have no evidence as to the identity of the supervisor of this editorial process nor of the patron who commissioned and paid for the sumptuous Ellesmere manuscript, but from the signatures and scrimshaw in the manuscript, Manly and Rickert traced it back to Thomas Chaucer who, they argue, "is logically the person to have had made what was clearly intended as an authoritative text" (1:159). Thomas Chaucer, chief butler to four successive kings beginning with Henry IV in 1402, was one of the richest magnates in the kingdom in the first half of the fifteenth century[35] and could have had both opportunity and motive for commissioning a group of scribes to sift through his father's (or his stepfather's, if he was really the natural son of John of Gaunt) *Nachlass* to create a presentation copy of *Troylus and Criseyde* for the crown prince and the most orderly text possible of *The Canterbury Tales*.

Current opinion tends towards the acceptance of the hypothesis that the copy texts for both *Troylus* and *The Canterbury Tales* were bundles of vellum fascicles interlarded with marginal and interlinear emendations and inserted leaves from which different scribes elicited different readings after Chaucer's death. I do not mean to imply that this opinion is universal; several scholars still support the multiple copy text hypothesis in one form or another.[36] But it appears to me that the single copy-text hypothesis is gaining ground. This hypothesis means that for neither poem is there an "authorized" manuscript. In such a situation both the genetic and the "best-text" methods of editing are meaningless. Rather the text must be established by studying the manuscript readings and affiliations to try to deduce by meaning, style, and scribal practice which readings are authorial and which are scribal, very much the process George Kane and Talbot Donaldson used in establishing a text for *Piers Plowman*.[37]

Let me give three examples of the variations among the manuscripts. Hengwrt (*WBP* 3.115-17) reads "Telle me also to what conclusioun / Were membres maad of generacioun / And of so parfit wys a wight yroght," while the Ellesmere and Cambridge Gg manuscripts read "And for what profite was a wight yroght," which answers the question that the Hengwrt reading merely prolongs. If the Ellesmere is here again found less tart, at 3.188 Ellesmere reads "Gladly sires sith it may yow like," which is less flat than the Hengwrt "Gladly quod she syn it may you lyke." At 3.474-75 where both Hengwrt and Ellesmere read "But age allas that al wole envenyme / Hath me biraft my beautee and my pith," Cambridge Gg, another of the pre-1410 manuscripts, reads "But age allas that al wole undermyne." The Cambridge Gg reading accords better than "envenyme" with "hath me biraft my beautee and my pith." So the most appropriate readings are not always to be found in either Hengwrt or Ellesmere. All of the texts of *The Canterbury* Tales since that of Thomas Wright (1847-51), except for Manly and Rickert's, are best-text editions corrected largely from other best texts, usually Ellesmere by Hengwrt or Hengwrt by Ellesmere. The entire text and all the variations have yet to be subjected to detailed consideration of *usus scribendi* unhampered by best-text or genetic presuppositions.[38]

The mystique emerging about the "Chaucerian" quality of the

Hengwrt text could, to my mind, do real damage to our appreciation of *The Canterbury Tales*. My instinct is best expressed by an editorial in the 17 September 1987 London *Times* headed "Whose Armada?" It complains that the plans for celebrating the four-hundredth anniversary of the Spanish Armada reject the traditional view that the battle was a signal victory by Sir Francis Drake and for the causes of England, Protestantism, and liberty on the grounds that scientific history now believes the Spanish fleet was dispersed by bad weather and the incompetence of the Spanish leaders. The *Times* argues that there are two kinds of history, one that is scientifically tested and literally accurate, and the other that has less to do with what happened but is essential to the maintenance of the nation's spirit. This second is myth, in the proper, philosophical sense of the word, "a presentation designed to symbolize profound convictions and elevate the human mind." The myth may not illuminate the past, but it tells us much that is significant about the present and our aspirations for the future.

I leave it to the theorists to debate the value of inspirational myth versus iconoclastic science. But I do sense that the present favor of the Hengwrt text lies less in its own merits than in the deconstructive temper of modern criticism. In a 1962 essay on the philosophy of criticism, Northrop Frye wrote that "the primary understanding of any work of literature has to be based on the assumption of unity. However mistaken such an assumption may eventually prove to be, nothing can be done unless we start with it as a heuristic principle." Later in the same essay, Frye writes, "The primary axiom of critical procedure is: Go for the structure, not the content." This was the foundation of the New Criticism, and of structuralism, but in a 1981 reply to Frye, Lawrence Lipking asserts that for the modernist critic, "the principle of unity pertains more to our way of seeing than to anything inherent in the object to be seen." Instead of looking for a pattern, "the proper task of criticism is to unsettle; not to yearn for an end to interpretation, but to emphasize and take pleasure in the contradictory and self-canceling notions that an unbound text inflicts on the reader."[39]

In content and arrangement, Hengwrt is certainly a much less bound text than Ellesmere, and it is possible, as Blake has shown, to explain nearly all of the changes and additions between Hengwrt and Ellesmere as products of the scribal desire for unity and pattern.

Hence, when unity and pattern are regarded as important, Ellesmere is the better text, but when deconstruction of unity and pattern is elevated to a critical principle, Hengwrt becomes the more interesting text.[40]

The important thing is not to load the dice by discussing Hengwrt as the Chaucerian version and Ellesmere as the edited version. Choice and arrangement of words and content are just as scribal and arbitrary in Hengwrt as in Ellesmere. The difference is in the principles of composition. The undramatic tale order of Hengwrt has no more authority than the dramatic tale order of Ellesmere, and it seems to me to inhibit our delight in the poem as it obviously inhibited the delight of the first readers. There may be orders more satisfactory than Ellesmere's. From the time of Skeat's 1892 edition until F.N. Robinson's in 1933, the Chaucer Society order prevailed, and some scholars still prefer it,[41] and recent critics have suggested other orders based on theme and genre.[42] But the important thing is that until the present decade, the editing and explication of *The Canterbury Tales* have been informed by the vision of pattern and completeness. Only now when pattern and unity are being denied as aesthetic principles is there movement towards the unsatisfactory Hengwrt. This is bad scholarship and worse criticism. It may be that the regularizing and elucidating tendencies of the scribes grew too free between Hengwrt and Ellesmere, and perhaps we should return to Hengwrt as a starting point for a text based on *usus scribendi*. But this we cannot judge until we undertake a variant-by-variant study of all the early texts. We cannot lose the 1,028 lines not preserved in Hengwrt, and we must protest with the London *Times* that science not be allowed to destroy myth.

Pattern must be recognized as desirable. A dramatic pattern of contrasts is implied at the beginning of the Canterbury collection by the "quitting" controversy in the Miller's Headlink. The Ellesmere order provides a very satisfactory pattern of contrasts. There may be others, but they must be, like the Ellesmere and Chaucer Society orders, grounded in some sort of dramatic evidence. They cannot be arrangements to suit thematic and stylistic abstractions. The scholarly mistake is privileging the Hengwrt text as most Chaucerian; the critical mistake is denying any pattern at all and treating *The Canterbury Tales* merely as a collection of stories. Six centuries of readers have delighted in the myth of the Canterbury pilgrimage. The myth will live because it symbolizes profound convictions and elevates the human mind. To deny or denigrate the myth is just as unsatisfactory to scholarship and criticism as it is to promulgate that myth naively.

VI

CHAUCER'S FRENCH: A METALINGUISTIC INQUIRY

Philologists believe that we think verbally, but behaviorist psychologists and linguists take a more cautious view. F.R. Englefield (130), for example, describes thinking as doing in the imagination what one has first learned to do with one's body, experiencing in the imagination what one has first experienced through the senses. According to this view, a person given to action will tend to think pictorially, and a person given to contemplation will tend to think symbolically. But concrete and abstract thoughts are both preserved in language. Even behaviorists recognize language as the chief storehouse of memory and as the vehicle for association and logic.

It follows that language and its written manifestation, literature, embody what Solzhenitsyn in his Nobel lecture termed "the soul" of a culture. Metalinguistics, first surveyed by Benjamin Lee Whorf in the 1940s, is an effort to get at the souls of cultures through their grammars and lexicons. Metalinguistics has not made much progress because the relations between culture and language are so uncertain. According to Whorf, the Hopi Indian language would be ideal for discussing relativity theory because it has no grammatical expression for time and its conception of space is metaphysical. But in point of fact, relativity was invented by speakers of German employing mathematical symbols.

Nonetheless, it is interesting to think about the soul of England between 1066 and 1400 in terms of its languages. At the beginning of this period there were two populations, a small (less than twenty thousand) French-speaking ascendancy, and a larger (perhaps four million) English-speaking populace. After 1066 all government, culture, and learning in England was carried on in the oral French and written Latin of the ascendancy. The rich Anglo-Saxon vocabulary for government, law, theology, poetry, and culture atrophied. For practical purposes, it ceased to exist. Yet the domestic language of the majority of the population remained English. What does this tell us about the cultural perceptions of the populace? Colin Morris (7) believes that "What cannot be verbalized can scarcely be thought." Did the disappearance of *mod-lufu, mod-sefa, mod-racu,* and all the other *mod* compounds, and the reduction of *mod* itself to the deprecatory sense of "mood" or "whim," betoken the loss of heart in the English population?

The period of the separation of the languages lasted until King John Lackland lost Normandy in 1204. After that the Anglo-Norman ascendancy had, perforce, to regard itself as English and the fusion of the languages began. Albert Baugh in his *History of the English Language* (177n) traces the bell curve of adoption of French words into English—very few before 1250, the high point between 1350 and 1400, and a slacking off after 1400. He categorizes the areas from which French words were adopted as government, law, the church, learning, warfare, chivalry, and high culture—the last an area commemorated by Sir Walter Scott's observation in *Ivanhoe* that pigs, sheep, and cows had English names in the field where Gurth herded them, but French names—pork, mutton, and beef—at the table where the Anglo-Norman lords consumed them.

The metalinguistics of late Middle English culture takes on a human face in the biography of Geoffrey Chaucer. It is interesting to speculate about what language Geoffrey grew up speaking. Presumably his family was originally of French extraction, to judge by his surname, from *chaussier*, French for shoemaker or hosier. The family had been in England for several generations. For at least three generations, they had been in wine merchandising and the royal service. The poet's father, grandfather, and stepgrandfather were all vintners—wholesale wine importers—and were from time to time employed in collecting the king's customs. They were all married to wives with English surnames, and presumably their domestic language was English. But their wine importing business and court connections must have kept them conversant in French. With Chaucer's own wife Philippa, the situation was different. Her father, Sir Paon de Roet, came to England from Hainault (today the French-speaking part of Belgium) in attendance upon Queen Philippa when she married Edward III in 1328. Sir Paon continued in her service, and his tomb in St. Paul's designates him as Guienne King at Arms. This means that he was charged with recording the genealogies of the noble families living in England's valuable properties in southern France. His court connections suggest that his domestic and professional language continued to be French. What language did his daughter Philippa grow up speaking, and what language did she and Geoffrey speak after they were married?

Whether Chaucer's domestic language was English or French, the languages of his education and professional service were French and Latin. London for the courtly and merchant classes in the fourteenth century must have been a good deal like Montreal or Brussels today, with a bilingual population but with French predominant in the administrative, economic, literary, and cultural spheres. The presence of French royalty as hostages in England until 1367 and the intermarriage of English aristocracy with the French made England a prime source of patronage for French court poets like Machaut, Froissart, and Otan de Granson. The libraries of the English contained exclusively French and Latin literature (Salter).

Chaucer's audacious innovation was to compose in English, for this Anglo-Norman audience, lyrics, romances, and pious tales for which French was considered the only appropriate language. We know that linguistic nationalism was rearing its head from the repeated warnings to parliament that a French victory in the Hundred Years War would annihilate the English language. We also know that Anglo-Norman French was beginning to be regarded as provincial from remarks such as Chaucer's about the Prioress's French and Gower's and others' apologies about their imperfect French. Still, the decision to write in English an elegy upon the death of Blanche, Duchess of Lancaster and wife to the third son of the king, was audacious. It could have been interpreted as a calculated insult. On the contrary, its success paved the way for other courtly poems in English by Chaucer and other authors, and eventually for a literary tradition in English.

This tradition was made possible by naturalizing not only a French vocabulary but also the perceptions which that vocabulary comprehended. The poverty of pre-Chaucerian English is suggested by the descriptions of the hero in the Anglo-Norman *Romance of Horn* and the Middle English *King Horn*. In the French:

> D'eskermir en tuz sens n'est a li cummunal
> Nul ki vest' el pais u burel u cendal;
> Nul ne seit envers lui bien mener un cheval,
> Nul si porter escu od bucle de cristal.
> Forte bel le fist Deus, li sire esperital,
> Ne mais tiel n'iert truve nul home charnal.
> Od tut çoe si est mut e humbles e leal,
> Qu'il ne freit de sun cors huniement vergundal
> Pur tut l'or ki onc fust trove en un jornal.

> (In every kind of swordplay no man in the country, dressed in coarse wool or fine silk, could equal him; none knew how to handle a horse compared with him, nor to carry a crystal-bossed shield. God, the heavenly father, made him strong and handsome; never had a man of flesh and bones seen one like him. In addition, he was so humble and loyal that he would never do himself any shameful dishonor, not for all the gold one could find in a day.) (Crane 31)

Against this very specific portrait we may set the generalization in *King Horn*:

> Fairer ne miʒte non beo born.
> Ne no rein vpon birine,
> Ne sunne vpon bischine:
> Fairer nis non þane he was,

He was briȝt so þe glas,
He was whit so þe flur,
Rose red was his colur.
In none kinge riche
Nas non his iliche.

(Fairer than him might no man be born, nor rain rain upon nor
sun shine upon. No one is more handsome than he was. He was
bright as glass, fairer than a flower. His complexion was red.
There was none in the kingdom equal to him.) (Crane 31)

The English is simply a series of hyperboles without a single specific
detail. The English *King Horn* is in no sense a translation but a much
condensed retelling. I would submit that the bareness of the English
version represents not only the more limited talent of the minstrel
but also the more limited resources of a language reduced for two
centuries to a peasant patois. The capacity to represent poetic speci-
ficity had disappeared from English, along with the Anglo-Saxon
warriors, priests, and bards who had nurtured the poetic vocabulary.
The English language knew *burel* (coarse wool) but lacked a native
contrast like *cendal* (fine silk). It lacked both the concepts and
language to *mener un cheval* or *porter escu*. Recovering the power of
poetic observation was concomitant with recovering the power of
poetic expression. This was a metalinguistic situation. Political and
economic conditions had to first produce an English-speaking
courtly and merchant class enjoying an affluent, chivalric, cultivated
lifestyle. Once such a population had developed, it would create a
language capable of exploring and expressing the subtleties of its
experiences.

How did this transformation take place? Let me deconstruct the
first two lines of *The Wife of Bath's Prologue* as a way into the question:
"Experience though noon auctoritee / Were in this world is right
ynogh for me." What interests me is that both *experience* and *auctoritee*
are French words for which there are no modern equivalents from
Old English. The earliest citations for *experience* in the *OED* are from
Wycliffe, Chaucer, Gower, and Langland, all dated about 1380.
Surely Old English had a term for this concept, but I don't know what
it was. Perhaps *snyttru* and its adjectival forms *snottor, snottorliche*
come closest, although these meant wisdom rather than experience,

and the last *OED* citation of the term is about 1200 in the *Ormulum*. By Chaucer's time the verb *snite* had come to mean to wipe the nose, and *snot* referred to mucus of the nose or the burnt part of a candlewick; neither alternative is terribly attractive. The most viable native equivalent of *experience*, knowledge acquired by performance, might be the nominal form of *do, doing*, for example, "I learned by experience" equals "I learned by doing." But for Chaucer and his contemporaries, as for us today, the concept *experience* is of French origin. Indeed, there is not a single Old English noun in any of the *OED* definitions for *experience*: the *action* of putting to *test*; a *tentative procedure*; *proof* by *actual trial*; *observation* of *facts* or *events*; a *state* or *con-dition* viewed subjectively; and so on. We are dealing here with what Baugh identified as the learned dimension of the language. It is hard to believe that in 1350 there was no native term for the concept, but it does appear to have been formulated, or reformulated, under the influence of the French word.

Old English did have a perfectly good word for authority—*dom*. But by 1350 this had been restricted to the notion of fate or destiny, as in "the day of doom," and the concepts of power had been taken over by French words like power, decision, judgment, authority. Again, the concept had been reformulated under the influence of the French vocabulary. Instead of writing: "Doing though noon at al of dom / Were in this world is right ynogh for som," Chaucer wrote: "Experience though noon auctoritee / Were in this world is ryght ynogh for me." On the metalinguistic level, this represents the introduction into English consciousness not only of French words but of the classic philosophical distinction between theory and practice. The Duenna in *Roman de la Rose* expressed this distinction through the terms *theoretique* and *practique*:

> n'onc ne fui d'Amors escole
> ou l'en leust la theoretique,
> mes je sei tout par la practique.
> Experiment m'en fet sage.

> (I had not studied Love in school, where one learns the theory, but I knew everything by practice. Experiment had made me wise.) (Lecoy 12771-74)

Experiment and *experience* were synonyms in the fourteenth century. About 1382 Wycliffe wrote, "Now y schal take experyment of ʒou," which around 1388 was changed to "take experience of ʒou." (It is interesting that in six manuscripts, the first line of *The Wife of Bath's Prologue* reads "Experiment though noon auctoritee.") The *Roman's* distinction between practice and theory underlies the Wife's distinction between experience and authority and provides an earthy context for the Wife's aphorism, which is made specific when the Pardoner bids the Wife to "teche us yonge men of your praktike" (3.187).

Although *experiment* is a more specific term than *experience*, both refer to abstract, philosophical concepts. But the learned was not the only dimension being reformulated under French influence. Let us consider a more specific passage. When the Wife of Bath slips her leash in Lent while her husband was in London, she recalls:

> Therefore I made my visitaciouns
> To vigiles and to processiouns,
> To prechyng eek, and to thise pilgrimages,
> To pleyes of myracles, and to marriages. (3.555-58)

Again, Chaucer had the *Roman* in his ear:

> Sovant aille a la mestre iglise
> et face visitacions
> a noces, a processions,
> a geus, a festes, a queroles.   (13487-90)

Chaucer retains *visitacions* and *processions*; the visit to *la mestre iglise* is made more specific by the use of *vigiles*, *prechyng*, and *pilgrimages*, all French words. *Noces* is rendered by another French word, *marriages*. *Geus* and *festes* are rendered logically by *pleyes of miracles* since the mystery cycles were performed on feast days. Only *queroles* is not adopted, although the word itself is preserved in the English term *carols*. In Chaucer's passage only the word *pleyes* is of native origin. It is first recorded meaning "dramatic performances" in the Old English *Orosius* (ca. 893): "Wearþ eft Godes wracu Romanum, þa hie aet hiora theatrum waeron mid hior plegan" (God's vengeance was inflicted on the Romans when they were in their theaters at their plays) (*OED* III.14). Interestingly, while the *OED* cites this as the earliest example of this sense of *play*, it does not cite it as the earliest example of *theater*. Evidently the editors felt that the Orosian translator had no native equivalent for *theatrum* and simply used the Latin word, but the translator converted Latin *ludus* into its native equivalent *play*. There is no evidence whether *play* had earlier included the meaning "dramatic performance" or whether the usage persisted, since the next *OED* citations designate use in the fourteenth century, the first around 1325, again in a learned context: "Hii ben degised as turmentours that come from clerkis plei." (They are dressed as torturers that appear in clerks' plays.) The first citation for *theater* comes from Chaucer's translation of Boethius: "Comune strumpets of swich place þat men clepyn the theatre" (*Boece* 1.1.25-30).

It would appear, then, that the concepts of dramatic plays and theaters were formed under the influence of Latin, but Chaucer's collocation "pleyes of miracles" again shows the influence of the French. I do not suggest that the English had no preaching or processions or marriages or miracle plays independent of the Anglo-Norman experience. Old English *wedding* is at least as common a term as the Anglo-Norman *marriage*. But the acculturation of the Anglo-Norman terms indicates an enrichment of the English experience as well as of the English vocabulary. This enrichment represents a trickle-down from the privileged segment of the population to the less privileged.

Chaucer's own practice gives some indication of this process. Table Four in the first appendix of Joseph Mersand's *Chaucer's Romance Vocabulary* (153) indicates that his early poems, those most directly dependent upon French sources, contain fewer French words than most of the Canterbury tales: *The Book of The Duchess*, seven percent French; *Troylus and Criseyde*, eight and a half percent; *The Legend of Good Women*, nine percent; and *The House of Fame*, eleven percent (I have rounded off the figures). Nearly all the tales contain twelve percent or more French, up to fifteen percent for *The Parson's Tale*. Four tales, for stylistic purposes, use less than twelve percent: *The Reeve's Tale*, seven percent; *The Miller's Tale*, eight and a half percent; *The Wife of Bath's Prologue*, ten percent (a tour de force considering the heavy dependence of this piece on French and Latin); and *The Nun's Priest's Tale*, eleven percent.

But why do Chaucer's early poems, even including *Troylus and*

Criseyde, contain fewer romance words than most of the Canterbury tales? I think that the best explanation is Ernst Windisch's theory about mixed languages as adumbrated in Otto Jespersen's *Growth and Structure of the English Language* (38). Windisch observed that it is not the foreign language an author uses that becomes mixed under foreign influence but his own native language. One example Windisch cited was taken from eighteenth-century Germany. It was then the height of fashion to imitate anything French, and Frederick the Great prided himself on speaking and writing good French. In his French writings, one finds not a single German word, but whenever he wrote German, French words and phrases abound in the middle of German sentences. F.W. Maitland (I.xviii) points out exactly the same phenomenon with regard to Law French. In Chaucer's time it was still remarkably pure; virtually no English words were used. But by the time of Henry VIII, it had become riddled with English words. Mersand's statistics suggest that when Chaucer first began to write English verse after the French fashion, he was very sensitive to the distinctions between the languages and attempted consciously or subconsciously to use as purely native a vocabulary as possible. This linguistic self-consciousness limited the conceptual scope and depth of his early poetry. As he progressed, his poetry grew more complex, and the complexity was made possible by reduction of his linguistic self-consciousness and the use of more and more words from the administrative, learned, and cultural French with which both he and his audience were so familiar. Counting all the words (i.e., every *the* and *it* as a separate word), *The Canterbury Tales* have a French vocabulary of 51.8 percent, nearly the proportion we have in Modern English.

In his *Speculum* article "Curial Prose in England," J.D. Burnley demonstrates how the lexicon, syntax, and style of official prose in the fifteenth century were derived from French. Most of the awkwardness of Chaucer's own prose is that it is essentially translation prose. The word order of the opening lines of *Melibee*, "A yong man called Melibeus, myghty and riche, begat upon his wyf," is that of his French source: "Uns jouvenceaulx appelez Melibee, puisans et riches, ot une femme." Later in the tale Chaucer's "Thre of his olde foes han it espeyed, and setten laddres to the walles of his hous, and by the wyndowes been entred" is in the French, "Trois des ses anciens enemis appuyerent eschielles aus murs de sa maison et par fenestres enterend dedens."

The miracle is that Chaucer's verse is never translation English; the idiom and word order are always natural. The idiomacy of Chaucer's verse is in contrast to the French texture of its vocabulary. As Chaucer, Gower, Wycliffe, and other sophisticated writers at the end of the fourteenth century fashioned a more expressive English, their process was to take from French any expression that was not immediately available in English. This same process is deplored by the French today, and we can observe it working in the opposite direction as Law French disintegrated in the seventeenth century. Maitland's example (68) has been frequently reproduced: "Richardson, Justice de Banc al Assises at Salesbury in summer 1631, fuit assault per prisoner. La condemne pur felony que puis son condemnation ject un Brickbat a la dit Justice que narrowly mist, I pur ceo immediately fuit indictment drawn per Roy envers la prisoner & son dexter manus ampute & fix al Gibbet sur que lui mesme immediatment hange in presence de Court." We call this terrible French, but the psycholinguistic process that produced it is identical with that which produced the language of *The Canterbury Tales*, which any purist in 1400 would have deplored as terrible English. But there were no purists in 1400. The bilingualism of the society made it so easy to merge the languages that when Sir John Cheke ventured a purism in 1561, "I am of the opinion that our own tung shold be written cleane and pure, unmixt and unmangled with borrowing from other tunges" (Baugh 216), he did not realize that *tung* and *borrowing* were the only function words of native origin in the clause—*opinion, cleane, pure, unmixt,* and *unmangled* were all from French. The political and social situation of English between 1290 and 1400 produced this fusion, instead of encouraging the languages to remain separate as they have remained in Belgium and Quebec. Most of us would testify to the expressiveness and flexibility of the final product, and we can be very grateful for the unselfconsciousness that governed, and continues to govern, the expansion of the English vocabulary.

VII

Piers Plowman AND CHANCERY TRADITION

I should now like to examine the relationship between the Chancery hand and language and the *Piers Plowman* manuscripts.[1] I will not deal with Langland's own orthography and morphology, as George Kane has in hand a fourth volume of the Athlone edition of *Piers Plowman* in which he will provide an analytic glossary and a study of the language. In their introduction to the edition of the B version, Kane and E.T. Donaldson have already discussed the poet's system of versification[2] and concluded that "much of his language accords with London English of his time" (215n). We will learn more about the poet's individual practice when Kane's fourth volume appears.

My interest is in the way in which the *Piers Plowman* manuscripts increasingly reflect Chancery practice and in the information they disclose about the methods of manuscript production. A definitive study would call for a detailed examination of the hands and spellings of all fifty-two manuscripts—a task beyond the reward that might be expected. I have based my study on the superb manuscript descriptions and textual analyses in Kane and in Kane and Donaldson and on photocopies of the first five pages of each of the B-version manuscripts, which Professor Kane has kindly made available to me. These materials reveal the growing normalization of the manuscripts and something of the process by which they came into existence.

Evidently, as with the Chaucer manuscripts, none of the *Piers Plowman* manuscripts dates from the author's lifetime.[3] Only four are dated from the fourteenth century (Table A). Thirty-eight manuscripts date from the first half of the fifteenth century, seven from the second half of the fifteenth century, and three (and the Crowley imprint) from the sixteenth century. The sixteen manuscripts of the B version (counting R^1 and R^2 as one, and omitting the Crowley)[4] give us an adequate spread over the century in which English was being regularized; four date from the turn of the century (Bm, Bo, C, W); three from the early fifteenth century (Hm, L, R); six from the first half of the century (C^2 Cot, F, M, O, Y); one from the second half of the century (H^3); and two from the sixteenth century (G, S). I will note the increasing appearance of forms in the manuscripts and consider whether this reflects the effect of a standard on the accidentals in the text.

The first influence of Chancery is on the script. Laying the photocopies of the opening pages of the B manuscripts side by side, one can observe the changes which support the dating. The seven before 1410 (Bm, Bo, C, W, Hm, L, R) are all in book hands designated by Kane and Donaldson as *anglicana formata*. Those that date after 1410 are in more cursive hands designated *anglicana*. The two manuscripts from the sixteenth century, in even more cursive hands, are designated "secretary." These designations follow M.B. Parkes,[5] whose analysis does not seem to me to make sufficient allowance for the hands used in the signet and Chancery offices, which I have called Chancery hand.[6] Parkes renames as *anglicana* the traditional business script previously called "court hand" after the guild of *scriptores litere curiales* first mentioned in London in 1357.[7] In the second half of the fourteenth century, this court or *anglicana* hand was modified by certain shapes adopted from the Chancellerie Royale in Paris, notably the single compartment *a* (vs. *anglicana* double compartment *a*), single compartment *g* (vs. *anglicana* double compartment *g*), short *r* (vs. *anglicana* long *r*), and modern *s* (vs. *anglicana* *s* with a large, closed lower compartment extending below the line).[8] It has been suggested that these characters were imported by the

TABLE A

Manuscript dates and abbreviations compiled from the descriptions by Kane and Donaldson. Italic, A version; large caps, B version; small caps, C version. I have converted N.R. Ker's system, used by Kane–Donaldson, for dating manuscripts.

1. ca. 1350–90 (XIV2) G (Camb. U. Dd.3.13)

2. ca. 1390 (XIV.ex) *E* (Bodley Laud misc. 656); K (BL Digby 171); V (Dublin, Trinity Coll. 212)

3. ca. 1400 (XIV/XV) *T* (Camb., Trinity Coll. R.3.14); *V*(Bodley, Vernon MS); Bm (BL Add. 10574); Bo (Bodley 814); C (Camb. U. Dd.1.17); W (Camb., Trinity Coll. B.15.17); N (John Holloway); M (BL Cotton Vespasian B.XVI); U (BL Add. 35157); X (Hungtington HM 143); Z (Bodley 851)

4. ca. 1400–10 (XV.in) *L* (Lincoln's Inn 150); *M* (Soc. of antiquaries 687); N^1 (Natl. Library of Wales 733B); *U* (Oxford, Univ. Coll. 45); *Ch* (Liverpool U., Chaderton F.4.8); Hm (Hungtington HM 128); L (Bodley Laud Misc. 581); R^1 (BL Landsdowne 398); R^2 (Rawlinson 38); J (London U. S.L.V. 88); P (Huntington HM 137); P^2 (BL Add. 34779); Q (Camb. U. Add. 4325)

5. ca 1410–50 (XV1) *H*^{2} (BL Harley 6041); K (Bodley, Digby 145); C^2 (Camb. U. L1.4.14); Cot (BL Cotton Caligula A.XI); F (Oxford, Corpus Christi Coll. 201); M (BL Add. 35287); O (Oxford, Oriel Coll.); Y (Camb., Newnham Coll. Yates-Thompson); A (London U. S.L.V. 17); Ca (Camb., Gonville and Caius Coll. 669/646); D (Bodley, Douce 1041); F (Camb. U. Ff.5.35); S (Camb., Corpus Christi Coll. 293); Y (Bodley, Digby 102); N^2 (BL Harley 2376)

6. ca. 1450 (XV) *F* (Morgan M818); *R* (Bodley, Rawlinson 137)

7. 1450–90 (XV2) *A* (Bodley, Ashmole 1468); *D* (Bodley, Douce 323); *E* (Dublin, Trinity Coll. *D*.4.12); *H* (BL Harley 875); *W* (Duke of Westminster); H^3 (BL Harley 3954)

8. After 1500 (XVI) G (Camb. U. Gg.4.31); Cr (Crowley imprints); S (Sion Coll. Arc. L. 40 2/E); R (BL Royal 18B)

scribes of the Privy Seal office of the Black Prince.[9] They are first found in the episcopal chancelleries of York, London, and Canterbury and in the royal Chancery.[10] All of the signet letters of Henry V, written by some thirteen different scribes, use these forms, which were gradually adopted by other government clerks and then by clerks of the guilds and private households and by independent scriveners. By the end of the century, they had become the normal forms in Tudor secretary.[11]

The principal difference between *anglicana* and Tudor secretary was the more fluent duct and greater legation of letters in the latter. Until the advent of printing, formal documents were published in the set hands designated respectively as *anglicana*, court, Chancery, and bastard. But as printing assumed the burden of formal publication, handwriting was reduced to a medium for private memoranda and communication, and scripts became increasingly free and personal.[12] Between the set *anglicana* of the fourteenth century and the cursive secretary of the sixteenth was a set hand much like *anglicana* but with increasingly freer duct and with the continental letter shapes enumerated above which lent themselves to a more cursive script: single compartment *a*, single compartment *g*, short *r*, and modern *s*. This intermediary hand is what I designate in *An Anthology of Chancery English* as Chancery hand.[13]

It is interesting to observe how the B-version manuscripts of *Piers Plowman* illustrate the fifteenth-century developments towards the Chancery hand. In the first place, the manuscripts illustrate the inconsistency of the script. Changes in language can be perceived over long periods of time, but at any given moment, all we can see is variety. Table B illustrates the adoption of the new letter forms by the scribes of the B manuscripts. The left column of the table presents the B manuscripts, listed according to the Kane and Donaldson sigils and arranged by date of writing. As indicated in the table, the development of the single compartment *a* form in manuscripts does not show the expected drift. By the time we reach the sixteenth century, both manuscripts have this *a*, but until that time, all but manuscript C² have *anglicana a*. Single compartment *g* is more regular. Until 1410 all manuscripts have *anglicana g*; after 1410, five of nine manuscripts have single compartment *g*; after 1450 all three manuscripts have single compartment *g*. The movement towards short *r* is even more regular; scribes nearly always used long *r* until 1410 and nearly always short *r* after that time. The forms of *s* are as inconclusive as those of *a*. The two earliest manuscripts have the *anglicana* form regularly but only the relatively early Hm manuscript shows the modern *s* form regularly. In the latest two, the *anglicana* form has disappeared, but the only short *s* is final and a very cursive stroke. Through most of the manuscripts the *anglicana s* is initial and the modern form final; often initially, and nearly always medially, the modern *s* form is long.

The introduction of the Chancery forms into the scripts raises questions about the method of manuscript production. After Laura Hibbard Loomis's article on the Auchinleck manuscript, it was customary to associate the production of large literary codices with the emergence of commercial bookshops[14] where a master scrivener supervised the work of a number of clerks on a regular basis. Recently, however, Ian Doyle and Malcolm Parkes have questioned the existence of such shops on the grounds that they would constitute too great a capital investment and that no evidence has been found to indicate the existence of such a commercial scriptorium. Doyle and Parkes adopt instead Graham Pollard's suggestion that books and other documents were produced only to order. A public scrivener, the *stationarius*, might accept an order for a large project and do some of the copying himself, but he would subcontract sections of the book to independent scribes who would carry them off to their own quarters for simultaneous copying.[15] The existence of manuscripts in multiple hands offers a clue to the nature of such book production. Doyle and Parkes base their argument on the identification of five different hands in Trinity College, Cambridge, MS R.3.2 of Gower's *Confessio Amantis* and other manuscripts copied in the same hands. Scribe B copied both the Hengwrt and Ellesmere manuscripts of *The Canterbury Tales*. Scribe D copied six manuscripts of the *Confessio Amantis*, two of *The Canterbury Tales*, one of Trevisa, and the *Piers Plowman* section of MS J (see Table A). Scribe E, Thomas Hoccleve, copied collections of his own works as well as documents in the Privy Seal. Timothy Shonk has recently produced a convincing description of the way the Auchinleck manuscript could have been put together by a principal scribe who did some of the copying and who put together and numbered sections copied by five other scribes. His analysis provides a better explanation for the awkward transitions in the manuscript than any other that has been put forward.[16]

TABLE B

R regular
r *forms*: or=short r after o
s *forms*: i initial (usually long); f final; x only long s initially, very cursive stroke finally

FORMS	anglicana	single compartment	anglicana	single compartment	long	short	anglicana	modern
	a	a	g	g	r	r	s	s
MSS								
ca. 1400								
Bm	R		R		R	or[1]	R	
Bo	R		R		R	or	R	
C	R		R		R	or	i	f
W	R		R		R	or	i	f
1400-10								
Hm	R		R			R		R
L	R		R		R	or	i	f
R	R		R		R	or	i	f
1410-50								
C²	R	R	R		R	or	R	
Cot	R			R		R	i	f
F	R		R			R	R	
M	R		R		[mixed]		i	
O	R		[mixed]			R	i	f
Y	R		R		R	or	i	f
1450-90								
H³	R			R		R		f
after 1500								
G		R		R		R		x
S		R		R		R		x

[1] Also short r after e, Passus 1.1.

As Kane and his associates describe, eight of the *Piers Plowman* manuscripts show multiple hands. Three (H, Bo, Z) have different hands in different quires in a manner that would have permitted simultaneous copying. Three others (J, Yates-Thompson, Digby 102) show enough variation to be perhaps by different hands. Manuscripts C^2 and U show different hands, but the *Piers Plowman* portion of each is in a single hand. The other forty-four *Piers* texts are in single hands. Several of these hands must have belonged to scribes working in Westminster and Chancery during the fifteenth century. The Inns of Chancery provided the training for most of these clerks,[17] and Chancery hands have been identified in the teams described by both Shonk (Scribe III) and Doyle and Parkes (scribes C and E/Hoccleve). At least five of the sixteen B manuscripts are in Chancery hands: Hm, Cot, and Yates-Thompson, which Kane and Donaldson describe as "*anglicana* with secretary forms"; C^2, described as "small *anglicana* tending to currency"; and F, which is quite plainly Chancery.

There seems no possibility that Langland himself was one of this scribal cohort. In the most thorough examination of the possibility, E.T. Donaldson points out that Langland never mentions such occupation and that all of his autobiographical references support the notion that he was "a married clerk, of an order certainly no higher than an acolyte, who made his living in an irregular fashion by saying prayers for the dead and for the living who supported him."[18] So it would appear that the characteristics in the manuscripts are all due to later copyists rather than to the author himself.

English orthography and morphology were gradually being regularized in the fifteenth century by the cohort of Chancery and Chancery-trained scribes. M.L. Samuels has discerned three stages in the development of a written standard.[19] The first stage is represented by the Wycliffite/Lollard manuscripts produced towards the end of the fourteenth century in the north Midlands. Samuels finds this writing to be much more standard than the London manuscripts of the same period. Not until after 1417, when government began to be carried on in English by the secretariat of Henry V, was there any significant movement towards the standardization of London book hands. By 1430, however, the drift towards Chancery script both within and outside the government was well under way.[20]

The movement of the orthography of the B-version manuscripts towards Chancery Standard is revealed by Table C. As in

Table B, the left column of this table presents the B manuscripts, listed according to the Kane and Donaldson sigils and arranged by date of writing. The other columns present the results of comparing selected orthographic features with the analytical glossary in *An Anthology of Chancery English*. I have chosen twelve items for comparison. Two items provide multiple instances in the pages examined (the first five for each manuscript): the first person pronoun *I* and the unstressed vowel before *s* in plural and past tense inflections. The remaining ten items are individual words. If, in any given manuscript, the target word does not occur (due to textual variation or loss), I have substituted another word with the same phonetic characteristics, indicating the line from which it comes. Arabic numbers following words in the table are line references to Kane and Donaldson's prologue unless otherwise indicated.

The first person pronoun was quickly restricted to *I* in Chancery Standard; *y* appears only five times in early documents as compared with *I* 154 times. *Y* is regular (R) in the opening lines of the pre-1410 *Piers* manuscripts and in two later manuscripts, although even in these it is interesting to see *I* in line 2. However, as the first two columns in Table C indicate, the drift was clearly towards *I*.

Spelling of the unstressed vowel in plural and past tense inflections developed steadily towards *e* in Chancery Standard,[21] and so it did in the B manuscripts. As indicated in the third and fourth columns of Table C, only the early Bm has *i/y* regularly. The later F and H[3] frequently use *i/y* with *s* (*hillis, wawys*) and *e* with *d* (*leuede, lokede*). But in general, the *e* spellings conform to Chancery.

The preservation of the *gh* spelling for the gutteral as it died out in pronunciation is one of the most distinctive features of Chancery usage. The *gh/h* spelling is found in the Midlands and London from early Middle English, but forms with 3 are favored in most provincial dialects (see Samuels, Fig. 2). We can see the drift towards *gh* in the B manuscripts with the words *thought* (Table C, column 5) and *high* (column 6). For *thought*, *gh* appears in the Chancery glossary eight times, *thowte* once, and 3 not at all. In the B manuscripts, 3 appears in five of the seven manuscripts before 1450 and four of the nine manuscripts after 1450. Chancery *gh* appears in one manuscript before 1450 and three after 1450.

For *high* the drift is more pronounced. In the *Anthology* glossary, *gh* appears forty-seven times, the *hie/hye* form eighteen times, and 3

TABLE C

FORMS	1 I	2 Y	3 i/y	4 e	5 poȝte 6	6 heiȝ 13	7 seiȝ 14	8 plouȝ 20	9 noȝt 9	10 chosen 31	11 swiche 32	TOTAL OF CHANCERY FORMS
					+ Chancery forms		**R regular**		**U usual**			
MSS ca. 1400												
Bm	2	R	R		fouȝten 42	eȝen 74	say	+ plough	+ not	chesen	+ suche	3
Bo	2	R		[even]	fouȝten 42	eiȝen 74	say	+ plough	+ not	chesen	+ suche	3
C	+R			+R	+ thoughte	+ heighe	seigh	+ plowth	+ nouȝt	chesen	swilkee	5
W	+R			+R	poȝte	heiȝ	seiȝ	plouȝ	noȝt	+ chosen	swiche	3
1400-10												
Hm		R		+R	thougthe	+ hye	+ saw	+ plough	nouȝt	chesen	+ suche	6
L	+R			+R	thouȝte	hieȝ	seigh	+ plow	+ nought	+ chosen	+ suche	6
R*	+R			+R	wrouȝte 1.13	miȝt 156	seiȝ 218	bouȝ 205	nouȝt 152	X	+ swiche 5.152	2
1410-50												
C²	+R			[even]	thouȝt	+ hie	+ sauȝt	+ plow	+ not	schoysn	swyche	5
Cot	+R				thorgh 1081	myȝte 38	sey	+ plough	+ nat	chesen	+ such	5
F	2,6	R	i/ys	ed	thowhte	heyȝ	seyȝ	plowh	nowht	+ chosen	swiche	1
M	+R			+R	thouȝte	heiȝgh	say	+ plow	nowȝt	+ chosen	+ suche	5
O	+R			[even]	pouȝte	hyȝ	+ sawȝ	+ plow	+ not	+ chosen	swiche	5
Y	+R			+R	+ thoughte	+ heigh	seigh	+ plowe	+ nought	+ chosen	swich	7
1450-90												
H³	+R		i/ys	e/yd	thouthe	hey	+ saw	+ plow	nout	+ chose	sweche	4
after 1500												
G	+R			+R	thougt	+ heygh	seyghe	+ plogh	+ noght	+ chose	+ such	7
S*	+R			[even]	+caught 107	+ highe 128	se 218	+ plow 119	+ not 152	X	X	5

* R and S are defective at the beginning; R starts with Prologue 125, S with Prologue 73.

1 thorgh = through.

not at all. In the B manuscripts, *gh* appears once before 1450 and five times after 1450; 3 appears six times before 1450 and four times afterwards; and *i/y* appears once before 1540 and twice afterwards.

Plough/plow offers another sort of problem. The word lost the gutteral in the south of England early enough to develop the *w* spelling (the earliest *MED* example is 1150/1250), but the gutteral was preserved in the Midlands and the North much later (it is still preserved in Scots). Hence the word has come into Modern Standard English with variant spellings. It appears in the *Anthology* glossary three times as *plogh*, once as *plough*, and not at all with *w* or 3. The drift in the B manuscripts is towards *w*: before 1450 3 appears four times, *gh* three, and *w* twice. After 1450 *w* appears seven times, *gh* twice, and 3 not at all. It would appear that modern usage was taking shape; pronunciation used the southern *w* while the spelling variations between *w* and *gh* persisted.

Not has two forms in Modern Standard English: the negative particle spelled *not* and the substantive spelled *naught*. These distinctions had begun to appear in Chancery usage. The *Anthology* glossary has only *gh* forms for the substantive and non-*gh* forms for most negative particles (189 times *nat/not*; thirty-two with *gh/h*, fifteen with 3). The form in column 9 of Table C is the particle ("Coueiten no3t in contree to [cairen] aboute" [1.29]). It appears twice without *gh* before 1450 and five times after 1450, six times with 3 before 1450 and once afterwards; and once with *gh* before 1450 and three times afterwards.

The preterit of *see* (Table C, column 7) appears three times as *sawe* in the *Anthology* glossary, once as *sye*, and never with *gh/h/3*. The B-version manuscripts show no clear drift. *Saw* appears only once before 1450 and once afterwards. Vocalized forms with something approaching the vowel of the present appear twice before 1450 and three times afterwards. But forms with *gh* and 3 appear in both periods, occurring in five of eight manuscripts before 1450 and five of nine after 1450.

The infinitive and present subjunctive of *choose* in the *Anthology* glossary is always *chese*, but the past participle is always *chose/chosen*. The drift in the B manuscripts (Table C, column 10) is normal: *o* forms twice in the pre-1450 manuscripts and *e* forms four times; *o* forms six times in the post-1450 manuscripts and the *e* form once.

The *such* forms show devolution. The *u* was the preferred

Chancery form (185 times compared to seventeen with *wi/wy*), but *u* appears in four of the eight pre-1450 B manuscripts and in only three out of eight in the post-1450 (Table C, column 11).

This sort of comparison could go on infinitely, but enough has been presented to indicate the drift of both the hand and the spelling of the B version manuscripts of *Piers Plowman* in the direction of Chancery usage. In Table C Chancery forms have been marked with a plus (+), and the numbers in the final column indicate the number of Chancery forms among those noted in each manuscript. Although there is variation, the totals in the post-1450 manuscripts are generally greater than in the pre-1450 manuscripts.

Table C indicates also that in choosing W as their base manuscript for the edition of the B version, Kane and Donaldson chose the most archaic of the three that might have served (see Kane and Donaldson 214-15). In Table C manuscript W shows only three Chancery forms, compared with six for L and seven for Y. In manuscript L, ʒ alternates with *gh*, while in Y, ʒ has disappeared completely. Appearance of the ʒ gives the Kane and Donaldson text a more archaic flavor than that of modern editions of Chaucer and Gower. Samuels cites manuscript W and the Ellesmere manuscript of *The Canterbury Tales* as especially representative of London English at the beginning of the fifteenth century.[22] But it is noteworthy that both the Hengwrt and Ellesmere use *gh/h*, as does the Fairfax (Macaulay's copy text for his edition of the *Confessio Amantis*). Thus, the choice of *Piers Plowman* manuscript W over L, which nearly always uses *gh*, sets the edition less in the mainstream of linguistic development. The prevalence of ʒ forms in the early manuscripts of the B version may suggest that this was Langland's own usage. But manuscript W creates a different impression of Langland's language from that which Hengwrt and Ellesmere create of Chaucer's language. Samuels suggests that the *thorw* form of *The Equatorie of the Planetis* may be Chaucer's own spelling,[23] but we read him with the *thurgh* of the Hengwrt and Ellesmere.

The literary manuscripts of the fifteenth century all show in some ways Chancery coloring in both hand and language. It is the responsibility of the editor to sort through the variations and arrive as nearly as possible at the author's ideolect and ideograph. But inconsistency in this process conveys to the modern reader greater differences than may actually have existed in the authorial forms. To the historian of the language, there is an intrinsic interest in observing the process by which the ideolect is absorbed into the language. The B-version manuscripts of *Piers Plowman* provide a tangible example of this evolution in process, just as the editorial methods of Kane and Donaldson provide a methodology for recovering the ideograph.

VIII

Caxton and Chancery English

In the previous essays I have discussed the part played by the English civil service in helping to create and disseminate a standard written English in the fifteenth century. Before Henry V, official writing in England was in Latin and French. Writing in English, always unofficial and intended for local audiences, was essentially the phonetic transcription of regional dialects. The characteristic that sets a standard language apart from a dialect is the degree of its uniformity throughout a society, and this uniformity is more nearly achieved in written than in spoken language. M.L. Samuels has indicated that the first movement toward the creation of an English written standard can be found in the sermons and tracts by Wycliffe and his followers in the North Midlands in the last quarter of the fourteenth century.[1] This Wycliffite standard was spread throughout England by the Lollard preachers. Eventually it came to be used for secular works, and this standard continued to appear throughout the fifteenth century.

Concurrently with the Wycliffite writers, the government and merchant classes in London began to turn to English. Their writings are not as uniform as the Wycliffite. The language of the court poetry and of the texts printed by Chambers and Daunt reveals no metropolitan standard but is rather a bundle of related dialects reflecting in different ratios the southern substratum of London speech and the overlays of midland and western dialects imposed by immigrant clerks.[2]

An official written standard came into existence in August 1417 when Henry V embarked upon his second invasion of France. Until that time, all of his correspondence had been in Latin and French, but from August 1417 until his death in August 1422 Henry communicated in English with the officers of his government, the London municipal corporation and other municipalities, guilds, abbeys, individuals, and institutions. Although written by more than a dozen different scribes, his Signet letters are remarkably uniform in style and language, without any trace of regional dialect and with orthography and syntax that point the way toward Modern English. Two extant holograph letters indicate that this Signet usage was based on Henry's personal style. As Malcolm Richardson has shown,[3] the English of Henry's Signet letters served as the model for the English of documents written in the other offices of government, which together were designated as "Chancery." Although few in number and diverse in style before 1422, from 1422 onward documents in English in the files of the privy seal, Chancery, and parliament increase in number and by 1430 had evolved the fairly standard forms and expression that M.L. Samuels designated "Chancery Standard." Malcolm Richardson, Jane Fisher, and I have prepared an anthology of the 103 original Signet letters of Henry V and 138 other documents from the privy seal and Chancery collections in the Public Record Office in London illustrating the evolution of Chancery Standard to 1455. This essay will make some comparisons between Caxton's language and the language of these Chancery documents.

The spread of Chancery Standard outside of government is only now beginning to be explored. Its influence is acknowledged in the statement of 1422 quoted in the second essay, explaining why the Brewer's Guild changed its recordkeeping from Latin and French to English.[4] The original of this statement, by William Porland, clerk of the Brewers' Guild, is in Latin; the translation is from the Brewers' abstract book. The passage nicely illustrates the complementary roles of Signet and Chancery. "Letters missive" are the Signet letters of Henry V; the "matters" of the "Lords and trusty Commons" are the proceedings of Commons and of the Court of Chancery, which were in the hands of the Chancery clerks. Susan Hughes has compared the English of the London Guildhall records with Chancery English before 1422.[5] She concluded that the Guildhall clerks assimilated the Signet usage more rapidly than did the Chancery clerks. We know that Henry wrote directly to the London corporation because eight of his English letters are preserved in the Guildhall letter books, and it is noteworthy that the language of the letter books and other documents originating in the Guildhall more closely resembles Chancery Standard than does the language of the returns from the guilds and the parliamentary and Chancery proceedings before 1422.

Mary Relihan has studied the English of the Stonor Letters 1420-83. She finds that although nonstandard and dialectal forms persist throughout the correspondence, "there is no letter in any classification which does not have several of the characteristics of Chancery Standard," and, not surprisingly, the most standard usage appears in letters written by professional scribes who might be presumed to have had formal training.[6]

Although he was not studying it in the light of Chancery Standard, Norman Davis has shown how the language of John Paston II and III began to move in the direction of Chancery Standard after 1460.[7] Many years ago H.C. Wyld in *A History of Modern Colloquial English* remarked that the letters of John Shillingford (1447-50) and the writings of Reginald Pekok and John Fortescue (ca. 1450) reveal a movement in the second half of the fifteenth century toward a common form of English.[8] Most recently, Ian Doyle and Malcolm Parkes have shown that Hoccleve, himself a clerk in Privy Seal, joined four other clerks (all of whom wrote in Chancery script) in copying a manuscript of the *Confessio Amantis*.[9] One of these four scribes was the copyist of the Hengwrt and Ellesmere manuscripts of Chaucer's *The Canterbury Tales*. This evidence that Chancery clerks, or clerks with Chancery training, took part in the London book trade shows how Chancery usage could influence more general writing.

It should be made explicit that what I describe as a movement beginning in the Signet of Henry V and moving outward from Chancery to the municipalities, guilds, and bookshops, Wyld, Davis, A.C. Baugh, E.J. Dobson, and other historians of the English language regard simply as a linguistic consensus emerging among the literate classes in the London metropolis.[10] M.L. Samuels descriptive term "Chancery Standard" was introduced without any implication as to the direction of influence. Like Wyld and Dobson, Samuels saw the growing uniformity of the written language reflecting a growing uniformity in speech. I argue, on the other hand, that since a principal characteristic of any standard language is its divorce from regional pronunciation, lexicon, and syntax (a Scot and an Englishman write the same, no matter how they speak), the most important development in the writing of English in the fifteenth century was the beginning of its emancipation from speech—the beginning of an ideographic rather than a phonetic code (as in the spellings of *rite* and *right*, *rowed* and *rode*, *bow* and *bough*; the signals of capitalization and punctuation; and so forth).[11] This development has never been absolute, and some of the orthographic changes in the seventeenth and eighteenth centuries continue to reflect developments in pronunciation (such as the distinction between *ee* and *ea*). To a large extent, however, the vocabulary, syntax, and orthography of writing, fixed upon in the fifteenth and sixteenth centuries, have come down as a system independent of developments in speech (for example, the *r*'s in *here* and *there* have been preserved in the writing of those who have lost them in pronunciation, and writing is full of locutions like "have not" and "it is I" that are no longer characteristic of speech).

The part played by Caxton in the creation of the written standard is still subject to debate. No one denies the eventual influence of printing upon the standardization of the language. Marshall McLuhan made a profession of the typographic fracture between head and heart.[12] Margaret Shaklee speaks for what Caxton ought to have done for the standardizing of the language: "Caxton may have influenced the direction in which the language grew more than any other man, for he set himself up as the editor of the texts he printed and tried to settle the variant forms both of spelling and grammar that came across his desk. . . . Caxton probably adopted the current Chancery standard when he began to print in 1476, since he set up his press in Westminster instead of London and since Chancery standard had become the written language in which most businessmen (Caxton included) were schooled."[13] But Norman Blake in *Caxton and His World* categorically denies that Caxton had any direct influence upon modernizing or standardizing the language.[14] He allows that various groups of scribes before Caxton had begun to develop standardized "house styles" (what I would describe as the usage of Chancery and Chancery-related offices). Blake says, however, that Caxton himself was not a professional scribe and therefore had no interest in the development of uniform usage. In an earlier study of the printed editions of *Reynard the Fox*, Blake discerns an unsystematic and unself-conscious drift toward a standard orthography,[15] but he would place the influence of printing much later, after the emergence of handbooks and dictionaries.

Helmut Wiencke in *Die Sprache Caxtons* is more affirmative than Blake about the development of Caxton's language.[16] In a study of four of Caxton's editions, *Recuyell of the Histories of Troye* (ca. 1474), *History of Jason* (ca. 1477), *Fables of Aesop* (ca. 1484), and *Eneydos* (ca. 1490), Wiencke discerns a drift toward normalization and modernization. However, both Blake and Wiencke base their discussions upon the recurrence of isolated words—mostly nouns and verbs—in various parts of the text. Although this method makes possible Blake's valid generalizations about the influence of Caxton's sources on his spelling and about the poverty of the vocabulary of Caxton's prefaces in comparison to his translations, it fails to convey the texture of Caxton's writing.[17] This texture is created by the form words (articles, prepositions, auxiliary verbs, and pronouns) even more than it is by the substance words (nouns, verbs, and adjectives).

In order to examine the similarity between Caxton's usage and Chancery Standard, I have chosen the four passages, each of about two hundred words, printed in Appendix 2[18]: the prologue to the *Recuyell of the Histories of Troye*, ca. 1474; a paragraph from the *Mirrour of the World*, translated in 1480; the end of Caxton's prologue to *Eneydos*, ca. 1490; and a paragraph from *Eneydos*, translated in 1490. These passages yielded 264 different words, omitting proper nouns, listed in the table of forms in Appendix 1, along with the parallel forms from the glossary of *An Anthology of Chancery English*. Of these 264, 48 are not found in the Chancery documents, which leaves 216 for comparison. The same poverty of vocabulary that Blake has noted in Caxton's prefaces and epilogues can be seen in the Chancery documents, whose 70,000 morphs yield only some 4,000 different words.

This limitation of vocabulary can be interpreted as evidence of the paucity of content in these administrative missives, but it can also be recognized as evidence of the legalistic urge to confine the vocabulary to terms and formulas that mean as nearly as possible the same thing on every occasion. Linguistic variation may be the soul of poetry, but it is anathema to laws or contracts, where words must have exact denotations established by precedent and legal decision.[19] Blake's description of Caxton's personal vocabulary as "limited and generally of a prosaic, practical nature"[20] is an accurate characterization of the vocabulary of the Chancery documents (one of which I print, as an example, at the end of Appendix 2).

The number of times a word occurs in the Caxton selections and the Chancery documents is noted in the table of forms. Chancery never achieved anything like absolute uniformity in its orthography. What can be documented from 1422 to 1455., though, is a gradual drift toward normalization and modernization. In most cases, the forms that have passed into Modern English (MnE) are the majority forms in Chancery. The orthographic variations that Blake found persisting longest in the fifteenth-century printed editions of *Reynard the Fox* are likewise characteristic of Chancery. The interchanges between *i/y*, *i/j*, *u/v*, *u/w*, and *ȝy/gh* were essentially graphemic, just as we today use different shapes for *s*, *t*, *f*, or other letters in our handwriting. Interchanges between sibilant *c* and *s* were products of the conflict between French and English usage. Interchange between *a/o* and *a/au* before nasals, *er/ar*, and *o/ou* and the inconsistent doubling of vowels and consonants may have originated in different pronunciations but were in the process of becoming regularized.

In the face of these variations, the remarkable thing is the extent of the similarity between the forms in the Caxton selections and the favorite forms in the *Anthology* glossary. Of the 216 parallels, 186 (86 percent) are identical or nearly identical in Caxton and Chancery (Appendix 1, Tables B-I). Only 42 (19 percent) are different (Tables J-L). (These and other totals add up to more than 100 percent because some forms are listed more than once, as in Tables C and D.) Of the 186 equivalents, 76 (41 percent) are MnE forms; 24 (13 percent) are MnE forms except for final *e*; 26 (14 percent) are MnE forms except for *i/y*; nine (5 percent) are MnE forms except for *u/v*. If these essentially graphemic distinctions are ignored, 135 (73 percent) of the 186 parallels are close to Modern English. This 73 percent may be taken as an index of the degree of modernity of Chancery orthography as it appears in these Caxton selections. Even more significant as evidence of the influence of Chancery Standard upon Caxton and his compositors are the 51 parallels (27 percent, Tables F-I) that do not represent Modern English forms. Of these, 43 (23 percent, Table F) are exact parallels; five are the same except for *i/y*; two are the same except for final *e*. These parallels suggest that we are not dealing merely with a generalized drift toward modernity but with similar Middle English spellings that persisted in both Chancery and in Caxton.

Not surprisingly, 59 of the 186 parallel items are form words (Table M), since it is in syntax and accidence that standardization occurs first. Only five of Caxton's form words are not favorite Chancery forms (Table N): *ony* (no. 152), *than* (adv. no. 208), *therin* (no. 212), *them* (no. 213), and *thise* (no. 218). All of these are variant forms in the Chancery documents. Caxton's *them*, where the Chancery favorite is *theym*, is the one instance where Caxton's form is more modern than the Chancery favorite. Among the 42 instances where Caxton's forms are different from the Chancery favorites (Tables J-L), Caxton's forms are more modern in 11 instances (Table L) and Chancery's more modern in 15 instances (Table K). This ratio of 11:15 provides an index to the conservatism of Caxton's orthography.

This comparison does not support Helmut Wiencke's conclusion about the movement of Caxton's language:

> Die Caxtonsche Drucksprache—Sprache in orthographischer, phonetischer und morphologischer Hinsicht—repräsentiert nicht ein starres, "zuständisches" Gebilde; sei is in dauerndem Wandel begriffen. Welcher Art dieser klar erkennbare Um-bildungsprozess sei, is mit dem einen Satz gesagt: Die Caxton-sche Drucksprache schlägt gleichsam die Brücke von der mittel zur neuenglischen Sprachwelt—anders formuliert: aus an-fänglichem Polymorphismus, wie er fürs Mittelalter charakter-istischist, erwächst allmählich die sprachlich Einheit.[21]

> (The Caxton print language—with respect to orthography, phonetics, and morphology—did not represent a fixed, unified picture represented in continuous usage. The Caxton print language appears as a bridge leading from Middle to Modern English, whose chief medieval characteristic is its gradual movement towards linguistic unity.)

Wiencke gives lists showing how nonstandard forms in the *History of Troye and the History of Jason* appear as more standard forms in *Aesop* and *Eneydos*. The problem is that his lists are eclectic. As it turns out, there are only 50 overlapping words in the four passages I have chosen for comparison. In 36 instances (Table O), there is no difference between the early and later texts, and in eight instances (Table P) there is movement forward of the sort indicated by Wiencke. But set against these, there are the same number of instances of movement backward (Table Q).

In sum, the orthography and morphology of these selections would appear to indicate that Caxton employed, and therefore transmitted, essentially Chancery forms from the time that he began to publish until the end of his career, with no perceptible drift toward more modern or more regular forms. A more complete analysis might alter this conclusion, but not eclectic studies like those of Blake and Wiencke. It would be surprising if Caxton's practice shifted much through the sixteen years of his publishing career. He was some fifty-three years of age in 1474. For thirty-seven years, since being apprenticed to the Mercers' Guild in 1437, he had been exposed to Chancery Standard as it was employed in English government and business. There is every reason to suppose that his own writing habits were well established. It is likely, as Norman Blake has indicated, that Caxton was inclined to preserve some spellings and locutions from his copy texts, but even here the evidence is clouded. Arthur Sandved in *Studies in the Language of Caxton's Malory* concludes that there are many forms in the Winchester manuscript that are different from Caxton's own forms as recorded by Wiencke.[22] Among the ten verbs treated by Sandved that are found in my table of forms, Caxton's *Malory* parallels the Winchester usage in five instances (Appendix 3, A). In three instances, the manuscript has Chancery forms not found in Caxton's *Malory* (Appendix 3, B). In two instances Caxton's *Malory* uses Chancery forms not found in the manuscript. This evidence does not disprove Sandved's conclusion, but it is too slight to warrant any independent judgment.

Analysis of this kind could be carried on *ad infinitum*, but it would, I believe, lead to essentially the same conclusion. From the beginning of his printing career until the end, Caxton and his compositors used a preponderance of Chancery forms and spellings. He was influenced by his sources in the spellings of substance words, but his form words and inflections are essentially Chancery. In my examples Caxton shows as much variation in 1490 as in 1474, and it is very nearly the same sort and same amount of variation as in the Chancery documents themselves.

Caxton's place in the history of the development of standard written English must be regarded as that of a transmitter rather than an innovator. He should be thanked for supporting the foundation of a written standard by employing 86 percent of the time the favorite forms of Chancery Standard, but he is also responsible for perpetuating the variations and archaisms of Chancery Standard to which much of the irregularity and irrationality of Modern English spelling must be attributed. Some of these variations have been ironed out by printers, lexicographers, and grammarians in succeeding centuries, but modern written Standard English continues to bear the imprint of Caxton's heterogeneous practice.

Appendix 1
Table of Forms

A: Caxton's prologue to *The Recuyell of the Historyes of Troye*, 1475
B: From Caxton's translation of the *Mirrour of the World*, 1480
C: From Caxton's prologue to *Eneydos*, 1490
D: From Caxton's translation of *Eneydos*, 1490

Caxton's Forms	Chancery Forms
(Numbers represent the number of occurrences.)	
1. a 2A 4D	The usual form before consonants
2. abreggyng (abridging) 1 B	
3. after 1 C	after 126, aftir 31, aftur 10, aftre 9
4. alle 1B 2C	all 207, alle 120, al 94
5. alayaunce (alliance)1D	alliaunces 1
6. almyghty 1C	almyghty 4, almighty 1
7. also 1D	also 163, alsoo 4, al soe 2
8. am (1st sing.) 1C	Usual Form
9. and 13A 11B 8C 7D 7 5C 1D	*and* usual form; 7 never used; & common
10. arryued 1D	arriued 1, arived 1, aryved 1
11. as 1B	as 811, als 17
12. assayed 1D	
13. at 1A 1B, att 1B	at 352, atte 86, att 7
14. away 1B	away(e) 6, awey 4
15. be (inf.) 1B 1C, (3rd subj. sing.) 1C	be 814, bee 23
16. ben (3rd pl. = are) 2B	ben = are 46, ben = past part. 20
17a. bere (bear) 1B	bere 8, beer 1
17b. bare (past t. = bore) 1D	bare 1, bere 1
17c. born (born) 1C	born 4, boryn 1, bore 1
18a. begynncth 1A	begynn + 4
18b. begonne 1A 2D	begonne 1, bigonne 1, bygonnen 1
19. begoten 1C	
20. besoughte 1D	
21. body 1B	
22. bookes 1A, boke 2C	bokes 4, bok 1, buke 1
23. braunches 1D	braunches 1
24. but 2B 1D	but 121, bot 1, buth 1
25. by 4A 1B 2C 1D	by 792, bi 11
26. byseching 1C	*bi* forms 16, *be* forms 5, *by* forms 3
27. chapelayn 1A	chapeleyn 3, chapellain 2, chaplein 1, chapelyn 1

28. called 1D — called 29, callid 7, callidde 1, callyd 1
29. can 1B — can 25, kan 10
30. castell 1D — castel(1) 62, castil 1, chastel 1
31. cause 1B — cause 38
32. coffres 1B — coffors 2, coffres 1
33. comaundement 1A, commaundemente 1D — commaundement 17, comaundement 13, com(m)andement 11

34a. come 1B 1C — come 31, com 3
34b. cometh 1B — comeþ 1, commeth 1
34c. came 1D — com(e) 14, c(k)am 6
35. composed 1A
36. correctyon 1C — coreccione 1, correcte 1
37. counseilled 1B — counseilled 1, conseled 1
38. countre 1A, contrey 1 — contre(e) 12, cuntre(e) 7, contray 6, countre 1

39. creatour (creator) 1B — creature (creature) 2
40. crysten 1C — cristen(e) 5, crysten 1, cristian 1
41. cyte 2A 2D — citee 38, cite 28, cyte 5
42. dampned 1B
43. day 2A, dayes 2B — day 292, daie 6, daye 2
44. deed (dead) 1B — ded 2, dede 2, deed 1
45. delyte 1B
46. deth (death) 1B — deth(e) 14, ded(e) 4, deþ 1
47. disordinat 1B
48. doctrynes 1B — doctrine 1
49. dommage 1D — damage 3
50. doo 2D — doo 6, do 2, doe 2
51. dradde 1C — dradde 1, dred 1
52. drawen (past part.) 2A — drawen 1, draw 1
53. duc 1C — duc 33, duke 9
54. duchesse 1A
55. dye (die) 2B — deyde 5, died 2
56. dyuerce 1A, dyuerse 1D — diuerse(e) 39, dyuers(e) 16, diuerce 1

57. dwelle 1D — *dw* forms 15, *du* forms 5
58. egal 1C — egalli 1
59. encreasyng 1C — encresyng 12, encreses 1, encresced 1
60. ended 1A — end(e) (noun) 30, eend 1
61. englisshe 1A — englyssh 1, Englissman 1

62.	enleuen (eleven) 1A	
63.	enterprysed 1D	enterprise 1
64.	erle 1C	erle 31, erl 13
65.	euerlastynge 1C	*eu* forms 36, *ev* forms 3
66.	eyghte 1A	
67.	feest 1D	fest(e) 53, feest 1
68.	folke 1D	folk(e) 14
69.	fonde 1D	
70.	for 1B 1C 6D	for 821, ffor 33, fore 8
71.	fortresse 1D	forteresses 1
72.	foure (four) 5A	four(e) 3
73.	frenshe 1A, frensshe 1A	
74.	fro 2C, from 1D	fro 70, from 29, froo 2
75.	fynysshid IA	finisshed 7
76.	fyrst 1A 1C	first(e) 17, furst 9, ferst(e) 4, fyrst 1
77.	garlandes 1D	
78.	glad 1C, gladly 1C	gladde 2, gladly 1, gladnesse 1
79.	gloryous 1A	glorious 2
80.	god (God) 4A 3C, goddes (pl.) 1D	god 241, godde 6, gode 1
81.	grace 1A 3C	grace 78
82.	grete (great) 2B 1D	grete 211, greet 37, gret 19
83.	greue (grieve) 1B	greved 2
84.	greuaunce 1D	greuaunce 1
85.	grounde 1D	ground 3, grounde 2, grond 4
86.	handes 1D	handes 31, hondes 6
87a.	haue 3B	haue 428, haf(e) 6, han 2
87b.	had 2D	hadd(e) 59, had(e) 48, hed 1
88.	he 2C 4D	he 382
89a.	his 1A 4C, hys 1A	his 553, hus 15, hys 5
89b.	hym 1D	hym 287, him 113
90.	hedes (heads) 1D	hed 1, hede 1
91.	helpe 1B	help 2, helpe 1
92.	here (here) 1A	here 57, her 15, heere 4
93.	herte 1B	hert(e) 10
94.	heuen 1C	
95.	heyer (heir) 1C	heir(e) 5, heyr 1, eyres 3
96.	historyes 1A	
97.	holy 1A	holy 23, holi 1, hooly 1
98.	honderd 3A, hondred 1D	
99.	humble 1C	humble 21
100.	hurte 1D	hurt 18, hurte 9

101. hye 1A 1C	high 30, total *gh* forms 47, hye 9, heye 5, hie 4
102. I 4C	I 154, y 5
103. yf 1B 2C	if 77, yf 26, yif 18, other *y/ʒ* forms 12
104. in 7A 4B 4C 5D	in 1683, yn 199
105. Incarnacion 2A	
106. intituled 1A	
107. is 1C	is 347, ys 42
108. it 1C	it 213, hit 161
109. kepe 1B	kepe 16, keep 1
110. kynge 2C, kyng 2D	kyng(e) 307, king(e) 68
111. lady 1A	lady 19
112. latyn 1A	
113. lette 1D	lette 3
114. londe 1D	land(e) 30, lond(e) 27
115. longe 1D	long 22, longe 17, lang(e) 2
116. lord 3A 2C, lorde 1C	lord 301, lorde 72
117. loste 1C	lost 6, loste 1
118. loue 1D	loue 18, love 11, luf 1
119. lyf 2B 2C, lyfe 1C	lif 8, lyf 7, lyfe 7, life 1
120. lyke 1C	like 29, lyk(e) 21, liche 3
121. lyue (live) 1B 1C	
122. lyttyl 1D	litil(l) 4, litel 1, lytyll 1, lytle 1
123. made 2D	made 6
124. make 1D	make 47, maake 6
125. maker 1B	makers 1
126. man 1A, men 2D	man 49, manne 1, men 65, mene 1
127. manere 1B	maner 90, manere 51, maniere 3
128. mangeries (managements) 1C	
129. many 1C	many 32, meny 3
130. march (March) 1A	March 12
131. may 2B 2C	may 152, maye 3
132. me 1C	me 55
133. mercer 1A	mercer 4
134. messagers (messengers) 1D	
135. more 1C	more 90, mo(o) 7, moore 5, mor 4
136. moste 1B 1C, most 3C	most 60, moste 15
137. mouth 1B	
138. muste 2B	most(e) 2, must 1
139. my 2C	my 158
140. myghty 2A	myghty 5, mighty 1, myghti 1

141. named 1A	named 3, nempned 1
142. nature 1B	nature 1
143. naturall 1C, naturell 1C	naturell 1
144a. ne 2B	ne 77
144b. nor 2D	nor 43, ner 21
145a. nede (noun) 2B	nede 14
145b. nedes (adv.) 3B	nedes 1
146. noble 1A 2C	noble 61, nobill 3
147. not 4C 2D	not 158, nat 28, noght 1
148. noye (annoy) 1B	
149. of 22A SB 9C 10D	of 4416
150. olyue (olive) 1D	
151. ones (once) 1C	ones 1, onys 1
152. ony 1C 2D	any 130, eny 104, ony 16
153. or 1B	or 376, vre 1
154. ooste (host) 1D	hoost 28, oost 5, ost 1
155. other 1B	other 155, oþer 59, othir 33
156. otherwyse 1C	oþerwise 2, otherwyse 1, other-wise 1
157. ouermoche 1B	
158. our 3A 1B 1C	oure 893, our 263, owr 21, owre 4
159. out 2A	oute 49, out 31, owte 11, owt 3
160. peas 2D	pees 39, peas(e) 6
161. persone 1A	persone 49, person 15, personne 4
162. peryllis 1B	periles 1
163. possyble 1C	possible 4
164. praye 1C	pray 17, praye 5, prey 3
165. preest 1A	prest 7, preest 6, priestes 1
166. present 1C, presente 1D	present 76
167. prynce 1A 1C	prince 17, prynce 5
168. pryncesse 1A	princesse 1, princes 1
169. procede 1B	procede 10
170. progenytours 1C	progenitours 6, progenitoures 2
171. prosperous 1C	
172. proued 1D	proued 3, provid 1, preued 1
173. receyue 1C	resceyve 6, receyue 3, receiue 3
174. recuyell (collection) 1A	
175. redoubtyd (respected) 1A	redoubted 1
176. rendre 1B	
177. rentes 2B	rentes 14, rentis 2
178. requyre 1D	requere 3, requir 1
179. rest 1D	reste 6, rest 3, reest 1

180. reteyne (retain) 1B	
181. renommed (renowned) 1C	
182. right 1A, ryght 2A	right 124, ryght 18
183. royame 1D	reaume 25, roialme 3, royaume 5
184. ryche 1D	riche 2
185. same 1D	same 329
186. said 1A, sayd 2A 3C	seid 710, said 695, sayd 42
187. sciences 1B	science(s) 3
188. self 1B	self 15, selfe 6, selue 1
189. sende 1D	sende 5, send 3
190. septembre 1A	
191. seruaunt 1C	seruant 40, seruaunt 4
192. shall 1C	shall 89, shal 89
193. shortyng 1B	
194. sixty 3A	
195. so 1B 1C, soo 1D	so 200, soo 18
196. sonner (sooner) 1B	sonner 3, soner-1, souner 1
197. sone (son) 1A	sonne 6, sone 2, son 1
198. souerayn 2C	soueraigne 41, souerayn(e) 30, souuerain 2
199. soule 1B	soule 9, sowle 4
200. streyngthes 1D	*streng* forms 5, *streyng* forms 1, *stren* forms 1
201. studyed 1B	
202. subget 1C	subgit 4, subget 1
203. submytte 1C	
204. suche 2B	suche 113, such 72, *sw* forms 9, *si/y* forms 7
205. susteyne 2B	
206. sygnyfieth 1D	signifie 3
207. take 1B	take 40, taake 1
208. than (adv. then) 1B	then(ne) 60, than(ne) 29
209. thank 1C	thanke 3, thankke 1, þank(k)e 3
210. that 6B 2C 9D	that 799, þat 842
211. the 17A 6B 5C 8D, ye 1A	the 3512, þe 1988, ye 156
212. therin 1C	þerinne 4, therin 3, therein 2
213. them SB, theym 1D	theym(e) 32, them 21, þaim 13
214. they 7B 3C, theye 1B	they 132, thei 48, *ai/ay* forms 44
215. their 11B, theyr 1B 1C 4D	their 45, þeire 19, theyre 2
216. thinge (pl.) 1B	*ing* forms 30, *yng* forms 24
217. this 1B 2C 1D	this 251, þis 154, thys 19
218. thise (pl.) 1B	thes(e) 39, this(e) 10, thees(e) 37

219. thousand 3A	
220. thus 1B	thus 10
221. to 2A 1B 4C 12D	to 2520, too 7
222. tocomynge (future) 1C	
223. towarde 1D	toward 11
224. towne 1D	towne 65, town 33, towen 1 *ou* forms 69
225. transitorye 1C	
226. translacion 1A	translacion 3
227. translated 1A	
228. tree 1D	tree 2
229. tresours 1B	
230. tyme 1A	tyme 301, time 19
231. vnderstode 1B	vnderstande 16, vnderstanden 7, vnderstonden 1
232. vnderstondyng 1B	vnderstondyng 1, vundreston-dyng 1, vnderstandyng 1
233. vnto 1A 3C	vnto 338, unto 1
234. vpon 2D	vpon 94, vppon 45, opon 6, upon 4
235. vsed 1B	vsed 18, vsyd 1
236. venerable 1A	
237. vertue 1C	vertue 9, virtue 3
238. vertuouse 1A	
239. volume 1A	volumes 1
240. was 1A 2D	was 197, woṣ 1
241. we 1C	we 462, wee 3
242. wel 2B, well 1C	wel 114, well 22
243. wente 1D	went 1, wentte 1, wende 1
244. were 1D	were 106, wer 17
245. werke 1A	*er* forms 5, *ir* forms 2, *or* forms 1
246. whan 2B 1D	whan 12, whanne 7, when 9, whenne 3
247. where 1D	where 65, wher 29, whar 1
248. wherin 1B	
249. wherof 1B	wherof 10, whereof 6
250. whiche 1A 1B 1C	whiche 206, which 149, wiche 13
251. whom 1B	whom 22, whome 5, whoom(e) 3, wham 1
252. wolde 1B 1D, wold 1B	wolde 36, wold 20, would 1, wuld 1
253. worde 1B 1C	worde 7, word 3, woord 2
254. worshipfull 1A	worshipful 94, worshipfull 8
255. wyse 1B	wyse 53, wise 15

256.	wyses (ways) 1D	
257.	wysest 1D	wysest 2
258.	wysedom 1D	*is* forms 9, *ys* forms 2
259.	wyth 1C 2D	with 346, wyth 24
260.	wythin 1D	*wi* forms 55, *wy* forms 28
261.	wythoute 2D	*wi* forms 50, *wy* forms 5
262.	wytte 2C	wittes 1
263.	yere 3A	yere 99, yer 25
264.	yonge 1D	yonge 2

Table A
Forms Not in the Chancery Glossary

2B 12D 19C 20D 21B 35A 42B 45B 47B 54A 62A 66A 69D 73A 77D 94C 96A 98AD 105A 106A 112A 121BC 128C 134D 137B 148B 150D 157B 171C 174A 176B 180B 181C 190A 193B 194A 201B 203C 205B 219A 222C 225C 227A 229B 236A 238A 248B 256D (Total: 48)

Table B
MnE Forms in Both Caxton and Chancery

1AD 3C 7D 8C 9ABDC 11B 13AB 14B 15BC 17cC 24BD 25ABCD 28D 29B 31B 34aBC 34bB 43A 60A 70BCD 78C 80AC 81AC 88CD 89aAC 92A 97A 99C 102C 104ABCD 107C 108C 111A 116AC 123D 124D 125B 126A 129C 130A 131BC 132C 133A 135C 136C 139C 141A 142B 144bD 146AC 147CD 149ABCD 153B 155B 166C 182A 185D 187B 188B 192C 195BC 207B 210BCD 211ABCD 214BC 215B 217BCD 220B 221ABCD 228D 239A 240AD 241C 244D 247D 251B (Total: 76)

Table C
MnE Forms except Final *e*

4BC 57D 68D 72A 85D 91B 100D 115D 117C 161A 164C 189D 199B 204B 216B 223D 224D 243D 250ABC 253BC (Total: 20)

Table D
MnE Forms except *i/y*

6C 10D 18aA 48B 56D 63D 76AC 79A 89bD 103BC 110CD 120C 140A 156C 163C 167AC 168A 173C 184C 206D 230A 255B 257D 259CD 260D 261D (Total: 26)

Table E
MnE Forms except *u/v*

10D 56D 65C 87aB 118D 172D 233AC 234D 235B (Total: 9)

Table F
Non-MnE Parallel Forms in Caxton and Chancery

16B 17aB 17bD 18bAD 23D 30D 33A 37B 46B 50D 51C 52A 53C 58C 64C
74C 82BD 84D 86D 90D 93B 109B 113D 143C 144aB 145aB 145bB 151C
154D 169B 177B 196B 226A 232B 237C 242B 24SA 246BD 249B 252BD
263A 264D (Total: 42)

Table G
Non-MnE Parallels except Final *e*

127B (Total: 1)

Table H
Non-MnE Parallels except *i/y*

26C 61A 119BC 170C 262C (Total: 5)

Table I
Non-MnE Parallels except *u/v*

83B (Total: 1)

Table J
Differences between Caxton and Chancery

SD alayaunce/alliaunces 32B coffres/coffors 34CD came/com(e) 36C correctyon/correccione 38AD countre, contrey/contre, cuntre 41D cyte/citee 44B deed/ded(e) 55B dyc/deyde 67D feest/fest(e) 75A fynysshid/finisshed 122D lyttyl/litil 160D peas/pees 165A preest/prest 183D royame/reaume 186 AC said/seid 202C subget/subgit (Total: 16)

Table K
Chancery Form nearest to MnE

40C crysten/cristen(e), cristian 49D dommage/damage 95C heyer/heir(e) 101AC hye/high 114D londe/lande 152CD ony/any 162B peryllis/periles

175A redoubtyd/redoubted 191C seruaunt/seruant 198C souerayn/soueraigne 200D stryngthes/strengthes 208B than/then 218B thise/these 254A worshipfull/worshipful 258D wysedom/wisdom (Total: 15)

Table L
Caxton Form nearest to MnE

22AC bookes/bokes 59C encreasyng/encresyng 71D fortresse/forteresses 78C glad/gladde 87bD had/hadd(e) 138B muste/moste 178D requyre/requere 197A sone/sonne 212C therin/perinne 213A them/theym 231B vunderstode/vnderstande (Total: 11)

Table M
Form Words the Same in Caxton and Chancery
(Those in Italic Not the MnE Form)

1 3 7 8 9 11 13 14 15 *16* 24 25 29 70 *74* 87a 88 89a *89b* 104 107 108 131 132 139 *144a* 144b 147 149 185 188 192 195 *204* 210 211 214 215 217 220 221 *233* *234* 240 241 244 *246* 247 *249* *250* 251 *252* (Total: 52)

Table N
Form Words different in Caxton and Chancery

152 208 212 213 218 (Total: 5)

Table O
No Change between Early and Late Texts

1 a 4 alle 9 and 15 be 18b begonne 24 but 25 by 34a come 41 cyte 70 for 76 fyrst 80 god 81 grace 82 grete 88 he 89a his 101 hye 103 yf 104 in 119 lyf/lyfe 131 may 146 noble 147 not 149 of 152 ony 158 our 210 that 211 the 217 this 221 to 233 vnto 240 was 246 whan 250 whiche 253 worde 259 wyth (Total: 36)

Table P
Movement Forward

33AD comaundement/commaundement 56AD dyuerce/ dyuerse 74CD fro/from 98AD honderd/hondred 110CD kynge/kyng 136BC moste/most 144BD ne/nor 242BC wel/well (Total: 8)

Table Q
Movement Backward

13AB at/att 22AC bookes/bokes 116AC lord/lorde 186AC said/sayd 195BCD so/soo 213BD them/theym 215BCD their/theyr 252BD wold/wolde (Total: 8)

Appendix 2

Selection A. Caxton's prologue to *The Recuyell of the Historyes of Troye*, printed 1475, ed. W. J. B. Crotch, Early English Text Society, OS 176 (London, 1928) 2.

Here begynneth the volume intituled and named the recuyell of the historyes of Troye / composed and drawen out of dyuerce bookes of latyn in to frensshe by the ryght venerable persone and worshipfull man. Raoul le ffeure. preest and chapelayn vnto the ryght noble gloryous and myghty prynce in his tyme Phelip duc of Bourgoyne of Braband etc In the yere of the Incarnacion of our lord god a thousand foure honderd sixty and foure / and translated and drawen out of frenshe in to englisshe by Willyam Caxton mercer of ye cyte of London / at the commaundement of the righht hye and myghty and vertuouse Pryncesse hys redoubtyd lady. Margarete by the grace of god. Duchesse of Bourgoyne of Lotryk of Braband etc / Whiche sayd translacion and werke was begonne in Brugis in the Countre of Flaundres the fyrst day of marche the yere in the Incarnacion of our said lord god a thousand foure honderd sixty and eyghte / And ended and fynysshid in the holy cyte of Colen the .xix. day of septembre the yere of our sayd lord god a thousand foure honderd and sixty and eneleuen etc.

Selection B. From Caxton's *Mirrour of the World*, translated 1480, ed. Oliver H. Prior, Early English Text Society, ES 110 (London, 1913) 21.

Yf the men in thise dayes vnderstode wel this worde, they wolde reteyne more gladly the doctrynes that procede and come fro the mouth of our creatour and maker. But the grete rentes that they haue, and the grete tresours of their coffres be cause of shortyng and abreggyng of their dayes, by their disordinat mangeries that ouermoche noye and greue them, so that nature may not wel bere ne susteyne, wherof they muste nedes the sonner rendre their soule and dye. Thus their Rentes, their tresours or other thinge wherin they delyte them, take a waye theyr lyf, their herte and their wytte alle att ones, in suche wyse than whan deth cometh and muste nedes dye, they haue loste wytte and vnderstondyng; of whom many been deed and dampned, whiche at their nede may not be counseilled ne can not helpe them self whan they haue most nede.

They lyue not lyke them that, for to kepe them fro peryllis, studyed in sciences and vsed their lyf in suche manere that they wold but systeyne their body only as . . .

Section C. From Caxton's prologue to *Eneydos*, printed in 1490, ed. W. J. B. Crotch, Early English Text Society, OS 176 (London, 1928) 110.

[For I haue but folowed my copye in frenshe as nygh as me] is possyble / And yf ony worde be sayd therin well / I am glad. and yf otherwyse I submytte my sayd boke to theyr correctyon / Whiche boke I presente vnto the hye born. my tocomynge naturell 7 souerayn lord Arthur by the grace of god Prynce of Walys Duc of Cornewayll. 7 Erle of Chestre fyrst bygoten sone and heyer vnto our most dradde naturall 7 souerayn lorde 7 most crysten kynge/ Henry the vij. by the grace of god kynge of Englonde and of Fraunce 7 lord of Jrelonde / byseching his noble grace to receyue it in thanke of me his moste humble subget 7 seruaunt / And I shall praye vnto almyghty god for his prosperous encreasyng in vertue / wysedom / and humanyte that he may be egal wyth the most renommed of alle his noble progenytours. And so to lyue in this present lyf / that after this transitorye lyfe he and we alle may come to euerlastynge lyf in heuen / Amen:

Selection D. From Caxton's *Eneydos*, translated 1490, ed. W. T. Culley and F. J. Furnivall, Early English Text Society, ES 57 (London, 1890) 123.

Whan Eneas had begonne his fortresse / he called to hym a hondred of the wysest men that were in his ooste / for to sende theym towarde kyng Latynus, in his cyte of Laurence, for to requyre hym of peas 7 alayaunce; and that he was not arryued in his londe for to doo to hym, nor to the contrey, ony dommage / but besoughte hym that he wolde not lette hym of that he had enterprysed to make a castell vpon his grounde that was begonne / For he made this for to rest hym and his folke / and for to dwell wythin his royame, by the commaundemente of the goddes, wythoute to doo hym ony hurte nor greuaunce. The messagers wente soo longe wyth theyr ryche presente that they bare from Eneas / to kyng Latynus, and wyth garlandes vpon theyr hedes, made of olyue tree / and also in theyr handes, braunches of the same / that peas and loue sygnyfieth / that they came to tbe cyte of Laurence, where they fonde, a lityll wythoute the towne, a grete feest of yonge men / that proued and assayed theyr stryngthes in dyuerse wyses/ . . .

Selection E. Example from a petition to the Chancellor by Thomas Bodyn, PRO Ancient Proceedings C1/19/492, 1450-54 (no. 220 in the Fisher and Richardson *Anthology of Chancery English*).

And often tymes in the bigynnyng of the same terme and mony tymes sithon: the said Thomas with his frendes hath prayed and required the said

Robert to putt and fynd hym to scole in fourme aforsaid after the effecte of the said covenaunt and accorde. the which to doo the said Robert wolnot. but that to doo at all tymes vtturly hath refused to the grete hurte harme and losse of the said Thomas. Please hit your good and graciouce lordship to consider the premisses and that the said Thomas therof may haue no remedy by the course of the comen lawe of this lande / And theruppon to graunt a write to be direct to the said Robert to appere by fore the kyng in his Chauncerie at a certeyn day and vppon a notable payne by your gracious lordship to be lymyted there to answere and to doo resceyve of and in thise premisses as by the Courte of the same Chauncerye thenne shall be ordeigned and he shall pray to god for you.

Appendix 3

Numbers refer to the Table of Forms, Appendix 1.

A. Forms in Caxton's *Malory* possibly influenced by the Winchester MS.

16. ben. Sandved finds the 3rd plural "are" in the majority in Winchester and the Caxton *Malory*. Wiencke finds "ben" the usual form in the early texts, "are" increasing in frequency in text D. Caxton may have been influenced by Winchester (Sandved 371).

17a. bere. Wiencke finds "bere" Caxton's usual form. Winchester and *Malory* have "beare" (Sandved 364).

28. called. The usual ending is *ed* but Winchester and *Malory* sometimes have *yd* (Sandved 335).

51. dradde. The 8 *a* forms in *Malory* correspond to 8 of the 16 *a* forms in Winchester, and 9 *e* forms correspond to *e*'s in Winchester. But 6 times *Malory* changes Winchester *e* to *a* (Sandved 349).

175. redoubtyd. Winchester has only "doute." *Malory* follows this three times. Wiencke finds *bt* the usual form (Sandved 322).

B. Chancery forms in Winchester not found in Caxton's *Malory*

34c. came. Winchester usually has "com"; *Malory* tends to change this to "cam(e)" (Sandved 353).

59. encresyng. Winchester regularly has *es*. Wiencke finds *es* in early Caxton, *eas* in late (Sandved 335).

186. said/seid. Winchester regularly has *ei/ey*, Caxton *ai/ay* (Sandved 351).

C. Chancery forms in Caxton's *Malory* not found in Winchester

10. arryued. Winchester regularly uses *r*, Caxton *rr* (Sandved 337).

50. doo. Winchester regularly has *do*. Wiencke finds *do* in early Caxton, *doo* in late (Sandved 373).

IX

THE HISTORY OF RECEIVED
PRONUNCIATION

The history of the evolution of Received Pronunciation (RP) has never been written. This is the pronunciation that distinguished the British ruling class until the end of the Second World War and is still taught around the world as "Standard British English."[1] By the end of the nineteenth century, this pronunciation came to be designated "Public School English" and "Oxford English," and from the advent of radio until the 1960s and 70s, it was also "BBC English." In recent years, as class has tended to be de-emphasized in British society, pronunciation in the schools and universities and on radio and television has become more varied; nevertheless, RP is still important to an English person's reception in society. Robert Burchfield, editor of the Supplement to the *Oxford English Dictionary*, observes in his book *The English Language* that "Rightly or wrongly, delicate judgements are made about a person's social acceptability or his level of education by the way in which the stress is placed on such words as *centrifugal, controversy, dispute* (noun), *exquisite, and kilometre.*"[2]

How did this class marker evolve? Language as a class marker

is indigenous in society.[3] In England it goes back at least to the
Norman Conquest. For some four hundred years after 1066, French
was the language of the court and commerce, and English was a
domestic patois.[4] In the fifteenth century, beginning with the reign
of Henry V (1413-22), written English began to resume its place as
the language of government and business, but French continued as
the language of prestige in aristocratic circles. As late as 1460, Sir John
Fortescue observed that the English aristocracy still used French in
government, business, and recreation.[5] All those who spoke English
spoke in regional dialects that carried no particular social distinctions
except that even for Chaucer and the author of the *Second Shepherds'
Play*, southern dialect seemed more prestigious than northern.[6] As
French disappeared from the court and bureaucracy, social distinctions began to be made in the pronunciation of English. The earliest
recorded judgment is John Hart's reference of 1570 to "the Court,
and London, where the flower of the English tongue is used."[7]
George Puttenham elaborated upon this idea in *The Arte of English
Poesie* (1589). A poet's language must, he said:

> be naturall, pure, and the most usuall of all his countrey; and for
> the same purpose rather that which is spoken in the kings Court,
> or in the good townes and Cities within the land. . . . Ye shall
> therfore take the usuall speach of the Court, and that of London
> and the shires lying about London within lx. myles, and not
> much above. I say not this but that in every shyre of England
> there be gentlemen and others that speake but specially write
> as good Southerne as we of Middlesex or Surrey do, but not the
> common people of every shire . . . but [in writing] we are already
> ruled by th'English Dictionaries and other bookes written by
> learned men.[8]

For Hart and Puttenham the most prestigious pronunciation
was that of the court and its affinity that lived in and around London.
This speech was as much a regional dialect as that of Yorkshire or
Worcestershire. It was assumed that educated people from the north
and west of England would write the standardized bureaucratic
English that had developed in Chancery and the London guilds but
that they would still speak with their local accents. We know that Sir
Walter Raleigh, who wrote beautiful court English, "spoke broade

Devonshire to his dyeing day."[9] In the next century, Dr. Johnson told Boswell that "when people watch me narrowly, and I do not watch myself, they will find me out to be of a particular county. In the same manner, Dunning may be found out to be a Devonshire man. So most Scotchmen may be found out."[10]

Until the end of the eighteenth century, everyone in England spoke a local dialect. Pronunciation was considered an inherited trait. Gentlefolk had different pronunciation from commoners, and in a society stratified by birth there was no more thought that commoners could assume gentle pronunciation then that they could assume gentle blood. It is noteworthy that from the time English dialects began to appear in eighteenth-century novels and plays (Fielding, Goldsmith), they have been used chiefly as class markers and seldom (except by Dickens) for comedy, whereas in America dialects have always been used primarily for comic effect.[11]

In the eighteenth century, English society began to shift from caste determined by birth to class determined by wealth and occupation.[12] There are no absolutes in this shift. Since the Middle Ages, exceptional individuals had moved upward in society by merit and luck, but heredity continued to play an important part in British culture.[13] In the eighteenth century systematic methods began to be introduced to assist upward mobility. Chief among these was education; one did not have to inherit polite culture, one could learn it. Until the eighteenth century, schools had been strictly vocational; they taught skill in reading, writing, and arithmetic for business, and knowledge of theology, law, and medicine for the appropriate professions. But in the eighteenth century, the emergence of the "bourgeoisie" prompted schools to take on the responsibility for cultivating gentility, and gentility, of course, meant money and position. Hugh Blair, in one of the first textbooks for the study of English, *Lectures on Rhetoric and Belles Lettres* (1783), makes this connection very clear:

> [I]n the education of youth, no object has in every age appeared more important to wise men, than to tincture [young people] early with a relish for the entertainments of taste. The transition is commonly made with ease from these to the discharge of the higher and more important duties of life. Good hopes may be entertained of those whose minds have this liberal and elegant

turn. It is favourable to many virtues. Whereas, to be entirely devoid of relish for eloquence, poetry, or any of the fine arts, is justly construed to be an unpromising symptom of youth; and raises suspicions of their being prone to low gratifications, or destined to drudge in the more vulgar and illiberal pursuits of life.[14]

Dr. Johnson's *Dictionary* (1747) and eighteenth-century grammars were the vehicles for developing cultural literacy and disciplining students against barbarisms (regionalisms) and vulgarisms (working class usages) in their writing.[15] But Johnson and the grammarians did not undertake to refine and ascertain the spoken language. In the Plan for his dictionary, Johnson promised "a dictionary by which the pronunciation of our language may be fixed," but he did not fulfill this promise. He went only so far as to mark accents, explaining in the introduction to the *Dictionary* proper (1755) that "sounds are too volatile and subtle for legal restraints; to enchain syllables and to lash the wind, are equally the undertakings of pride, unwilling to measure its desires by its strengths." When Boswell protested this omission, Johnson explained that pronunciation was too diverse to be standardized: "When I published the Plan for my dictionary, Lord Chesterfield told me that the word *great* would be pronounced so as to rhyme with *state*, and Sir William Young sent me word that it should be pronounced so as to rhyme with *seat*, and that none but an Irishman would pronounce it *grait*. Now here were two men of the highest rank, the one the best speaker in the House of Lords, the other the best speaker in the House of Commons, differing so widely."[16]

But if Johnson was too modest to legislate pronunciation, others were quick to meet this felt need. Wordlists of pronunciations were produced by Kendrick (1773) and Perry (1775), but the first recognized authority was Thomas Sheridan, father of the dramatist. In his *Course of Lectures on Elocution* (1762), Sheridan distinguished between regional, vulgate, and genteel pronunciations:

Thus not only the Scotch, Irish, and Welsh, have each their own idioms, which uniformly prevail in those countries, but almost every county in England, has its peculiar dialect. Nay in the very metropolis [London] two different modes of pronunciation prevail, by which the inhabitants of one part of the town, are distinguished from those of the other. One is current in the city, and is called cockney; the other at the court-end, and is called the polite pronunciation. As amongst these various dialects, one must have the preference, and become fashionable, it will of course fall to the lot of that which prevails at court, the source of fashions of all kinds. All other dialects, are sure marks, either of a provincial, rustic, pedantic, or mechanic education; and therefore have some degree of disgrace annexed to them. And as the court pronunciation is no where methodically taught, and can be acquired only by conversing with people in polite life, it is a sort of proof that a person has kept good company, and on that account is sought after by all, who wish to be considered as fashionable people, or members of the beau monde.[17]

Sheridan brought out a version of Johnson's dictionary marked for pronunciation, *A Complete Dictionary of the English Language* (1780), in which he undertook to ascertain and fix pronunciation just as Johnson had ascertained and fixed spelling and meaning. The model for his pronunciation was "the age of Queen Anne," when "it is probable that English was spoken in its highest state of perfection."[18] Sheridan's claim to authority was that his grammar school master in Dublin had been a friend of Swift, "who had passed the great part of his life in a familiar intercourse with the most distinguished men of his age." Sheridan subsequently compared his own pronunciation with that of such distinguished personages as the Duke of Dorset and the Earl of Chesterfield. The feebleness of this claim is evident when set against Johnson's disparagement of the same authorities, and Sheridan himself was criticized for having an Irish accent. The *ipse dicta* of all prescriptivists are, however, dogmatic.[19]

The discussion of articulation in the Prosodical Grammar prefixed to Sheridan's *Dictionary* indicates that fashionable pronunciation had already begun to adopt the plosive intonation and suppression of secondary accents that distinguish RP from the more even accentuation of English regional dialects and American English. Sheridan criticizes the "too great precipitancy of utterance" that leads to indistinct articulation. "This fault is so general, that I would recommend it to all who are affected by it, to pronounce the unac-

cented syllables more fully than necessary, till they are cured of it"
(liv-lv).

Sheridan's *Dictionary* was soon superseded by John Walker's
Critical Pronouncing Dictionary and Expositor of the English Language
(1791), which provided the most influential authority for pronunciation in both Britain and America for the next half century.[20] It was
Walker who introduced the designation "received" for the prestige
accent. London pronunciation, he wrote, is "undoubtedly the best
. . . that is, not only the best by courtesy, and because it happens to
be the pronunciation of the capital, but best by a better title, that of
being more generally received" (xvi). "Received" in this sense
means "generally adopted" or "approved" (*OED* #1). Walker did not
comment on the plosive articulation of the fashionable dialect, but
he recognized the loss of *r* that came to distinguish RP from the
English regional dialects and General American. Sheridan had specified that "This letter is never silent" (*Dictionary* xxii) without further
comment. Walker repeats "This letter is never silent," but elabo-
rates:

> In England, and particularly in London, the *r* in *lard, bard, card,*
> *regard*, &c. is pronounced so much in the throat as to be little
> more than the middle or Italian *a*, lengthened into *baa, baad,*
> *caad, regaad*; while in Ireland the *r*, in these words, is pronounced
> with so strong a jar of the tongue against the foreplate of the
> palate, and accompanied with such an aspiration or strong
> breathing at the beginning of the letter, as to produce the
> harshness we call Irish accent. But if this letter is too harshly
> pronounced in Ireland, it is often too feebly sounded in England,
> and particularly in London, where it is sometimes entirely sunk
> . . . *Rome, river, rage*, may have the *r* as forcible as in Ireland, but
> *bar, card, hard*, &c. must have it as soft as in London.

When Walker and modern commentators speak of the "London" accent, they are referring to the fashionable court and bureaucratic accent identified by Puttenham and Sheridan. This had from
the beginning been a class accent, the pronunciation of the gentry.
Up to the eighteenth century, the London accent had likewise been
regional—the pronunciation of the gentry in the London area. But
as London grew in importance, it became necessary for the upwardly

mobile to assume the marks of the London gentry in clothes, manners, and especially in the fashions of speech. This imitation of the London gentry shaped the cultural history of Victorian England and was recorded by such writers as Austen, Thackeray, Dickens, Hardy, D.H. Lawrence and Nancy Mitford—not to mention Shaw's *Pygmalion*.[21]

Sheridan and Walker were simply the most prominent of a profession of "orthoepists" emerging at the end of the eighteenth century. Orthoepists were independent tutors, much like music teachers today, who coached provincials in fashionable articulation. After some success as an actor and manager in Dublin and London, Thomas Sheridan supported himself by giving private lessons in elocution. He wrote textbooks and articles in which he argued that English should be taught alongside Latin. He lectured on elocution at both Oxford and Cambridge and received honorary M.A. degrees from both institutions. He achieved sufficient reputation to be pensioned by the Earl of Bute. Even so, he was never able to get English into the public school or university curriculum.[22]

John Walker came from a dissenting family of the sort for whom the dissenting academies were created. After some success as an actor, he co-founded a school for Catholic youth who were not allowed to attend the public schools, where he taught for two years. Thereafter he supported himself, like Sheridan, by tutoring, lecturing, and publishing, but unlike Sheridan, he made enough from his lectures and publications to "amass a competent fortune."[23]

The pronunciation and intonation of the aristocratic circle in London was noticed by American commentators at the turn of the century. Noah Webster in 1789 denied that there was a standard English pronunciation and deplored the court pronunciation that was on its way to becoming RP: "[T]he English themselves have no standard pronunciation, nor can they ever have one on the plan they propose. The Authors who have attempted to give us a standard [i.e., Sheridan] make the practice of the court and stage in London the sole criterion of propriety in speaking. An attempt to establish a standard on this criterion is both *unjust* and *idle*."[24] Webster goes on to condemn the unsubstantiality of fixing pronunciation on the model of an idle aristocracy. Of Virginians, whose pronunciation was modeled so closely on that of the English aristocracy, he writes:

People of large fortunes, who pride themselves on family distinctions, possess a certain boldness, dignity and independence
in their manners, which give a corresponding air to their mode
of speaking. Those who are accustomed to command slaves,
form a habit of expressing themselves with a tone of authority
and decision.

In New England, where there are few slaves and servants,
and less family distinctions than in any other part of America,
the people are accustomed to address each other with that
diffidence, or attention to the opinion of others, which marks a
state of equality. Instead of commanding, they advise.[25]

With Webster's condemnation of a style that conveys "pride and a
consciousness of superiority" we may compare Matthew Arnold's
description of the style inculcated by the English public schools:

The aristocratic classes in England may, perhaps, be content to
rest satisfied with their Eton and Harrow. The State is not likely
to do better for them. Nay, the superior confidence, spirit, and
style, engendered by a training in the great public schools, constitute for these classes a real privilege, a real engine of command, which they might, if they were selfish, be sorry to lose by
the establishment of schools great enough to beget a like spirit
in the classes below them.[26]

I italicize the word "style" because it is style that most characterizes RP.

James Fenimore Cooper was likewise sensitive to the intonation patterns of the British aristocracy. In *Notions of the Americans*
(1828) he observed that though Americans pass for natives every day
in England, "it is next to impossible for an Englishman to escape
detection in America." There exists:

a slang of society in England which forms no part of the true
language. Most of those who escape the Patois adopt something
of the slang of the day. There is also a fashion of intonation in
the mother country which it is often thought vulgar to omit.
(Letter V).

That the better company of London must set the pronunciation of words in England, and, indeed, for the whole English
Empire is quite plain, for this very company comprises all those

whose manners, birth, fortune and political distinction make them objects of admiration. It becomes necessary to imitate their affectations whether of speech or of air, in order to create the impression that one belongs to their society. (Letter XXIV).[27]

Timothy Dwight observed *(Travels* [1796]) that the people of Boston "speak the English language in the English manner. . . [with] a pronunciation unusually rapid. . . . [T]he rapidity of their pronunciation contracts frequently two short syllables into one, and thus renders the language, itself too rough, still rougher. Dissyllables accented on the first and terminating on the last with a liquid, particularly *l, n,* or *m,* they pronounce in such a manner as to leave out the sound of the vowel. Thus *Sweden, Britain, garden, vessel,* are extensively pronounced *Swed'n, Brit'n, gard'n, vess'l.*"[28]

In 1779 Henry Van Schaack remarked that the New England dialect was "not more remarkable than that of almost any county in England. The Somersetshire is infinitely more uncouth."[29] Clearly, to him, London dialect already represented a standard. James Russell Lowell observed in the *Biglow Papers* (1885) that "No one is more painfully conscious than I of the contrast between the rifle-crack of an Englishman's yes and no, and the wet-fuse drawl of the same monosyllables in the mouths of my countrymen."[30]

Pronunciation that had at first characterized the court circle came to be inculcated in the schools for the gentry. Until the Education Act of 1870, English public schools and universities were open only to Anglicans, while in Scotland, common schools and universities were open to all classes. After the Restoration, "dissenting academies" began to be founded in England by dissenting clergymen to educate the children of the non-Anglican commercial classes. These schools laid great stress on English composition, and many of the most important grammars and anthologies were created for their use, but since neither their teachers nor their students were of the gentry, they had little influence on the development of RP.[31]

After 1800, RP was fostered in the English public schools that developed as incubators for the ruling class, which came to administer the expanding British empire.[32] These schools, intended to train leaders, were sharply differentiated from common schools and dissenting academies that were intended to train clerks and business people.[33] The public schools had no formal procedure for teaching English; their curriculum remained entirely Latin until nearly the end of the nineteenth century.[34] Most of their students, however, came from families that naturally spoke the court dialect, and the masters were likewise of the court affinity, so recitations and school intercourse were carried on exclusively in the court accent.

It was the pronunciation and intonation of the aristocratic circle in London, recorded by Sheridan and Walker, that developed during the nineteenth century into "Public School English." Interestingly, the first edition of the *OED* contains no entries for either "Public School English" or "Oxford English." These were added in the second (1939) edition. The earliest citation for "Oxford English" is 1904, and for "Public School English" 1931. But obviously these terms had begun to be used in the nineteenth century. In the eighteenth century, Oxford and Cambridge had been at a nadir. Between 1750-59, new entrants to Oxford averaged 180 a year and to Cambridge 150. These students were almost exclusively headed for divinity.[35] By 1820-29, new entrants to Oxford were up to 440 and Cambridge to 400, and some were headed towards politics and the foreign service. But the first institutions to train leaders for the empire as it began to stretch overseas were the public schools. This term, as defined in the *OED*, stretches back to the Roman Empire as the designation for fee-charging schools under public management and open to the public, in contrast to the private tutors who educated most of the aristocracy and gentry. But in the nineteenth century, the term "public school" came to be applied especially "to such of the old endowed grammar schools as have developed into large boarding schools, drawing from the well-to-do classes of all parts of the country or the empire, pupils who in the higher forms are prepared mainly for the ancient universities or public services, and some large modern schools established with similar aims" (*OED*, s.v. "Public School"). The principal function of the public schools was socialization and the transmission of culture.[36] An important dimension of this process of socialization was the inculcation of RP.

It must be understood that until the end of the nineteenth century, reading continued to be largely an oral exercise. This had been the method from classical times onward, which is why rhetoric was, until the present century, conceived of chiefly as an oral accomplishment. Children learning to read were taught to sound out the syllables and words, and they read aloud individually and in chorus. Students translating Latin stood and translated orally. Towards the end of the nineteenth century, educators in Europe and America began to discern that silent reading was more rapid and led to better comprehension than oral reading, and educational methodologists began to promote silent reading. As late as 1871, however, David B. Towne in his third reader asserted that "A just and distinct articulation is the first and most important requisite of good reading and speaking. . . . Correct articulation is the basis of this art [i.e., reading]."[37] So the public schools did not need to teach English language and literature to teach pronunciation; recitation, oral reading, and oral translation provided ample opportunity for drill and correction.

In the second half of the nineteenth century, Oxford and Cambridge began to improve in intellectual and political significance. The Oxford Debating Society, founded in 1789, became the Oxford Union in 1829. Under William Gladstone (elected secretary in 1830), the Union became the training ground for British political leaders,[38] and adoption of the "Oxford accent" became a *sine qua non* for acceptance into this circle (as exemplified by Margaret Thatcher, whose original accent was not RP). Since the Second World War, there has been some change. When Robert Graves returned to Oxford in 1961 to take up the Professorship of Poetry, The *Times* reported him saying that "Only the ordinary accent of the undergraduate has changed. In my day you very seldom heard anything but Oxford English; now there is a lot of north country and so on. In 1920 it was prophesied that the Oxford accent would overcome all others. But the regional speech proved stronger. A good thing."[39] Randolph Quirk observes that the extension of educational opportunity since World War II has created a situation in which an educated man may not belong to the upper class and may have in his speech many non-RP characteristics (as exemplified by Margaret Thatcher's successor, John Major). Nevertheless, if one seeks social advancement, he or she is still probably obliged to modify his or her accent in the direction of RP. Pronunciation remains a marker of position in society.[40]

Since World War II, the English ruling class has come to be called "the Establishment," and in an interesting series of essays edited by Hugh Thomas, the influence of this establishment is traced through the public schools and into the military, civil service,

City banks, Parliament, and the BBC. Of all the voices of the Establishment, says Henry Fairlie, the British Broadcasting Corporation is the most powerful. And the voice of the BBC is still RP.[41]

As English is taught abroad by the British Counsel and other agencies, the pronunciation is still Standard English, which means RP. O'Donnell and Todd observe that "In England the existence of a single dialectal basis for the standard language ensures a considerably higher degree of unification for its pronunciation norms. The so-called Southern English or Received Pronunciation (RP) is widespread among the educated population of the entire country, and, in contrast to the territorial dialects, does not have any local colouring. . . . The fact that in America there is no single pronunciation standard based, as in England, on some local type of pronunciation, is quite well known."[42]

NOTES

II A Language Policy for Lancastrian England

1. Pollock and Maitland summarize the history of English legal language (1:80-87). Fisher gives citations for the English records in the Rolls of Parliament and statistics on the increasing number of English entries in the Rolls; there was one entry in English in 1404 and fifteen in 1449 (see Essay III, note 37).

2. The date on the vellum is 13 October 1399, but Ferris shows that the grant was made in February 1400 and backdated to October 1399.

3. The 1416 proclamations and later English missives from Henry V in the London Corporation's Letter books are printed by Riley.

4. On Thomas Chaucer, see Ruud; Baugh; Roskell; and Crow and Olson 541-44. The *Dictionary of National Biography* gives a substantial listing of Thomas's many grants and offices, as do Wylie and Waugh, Appendix E, and McFarlane 96-101. On the close association between Thomas Chaucer and Henry Beaufort, see Harriss, *Cardinal* 20 and index.

5. Heller discusses the development of French as the official language in Montreal; Haugen the development of Norwegian Riksmal (ch. 6); and Misra the spread of Hindi. Grillo treats peripheral and prestige languages in Great Britain and France. Wardhaugh treats not only the rise to dominance of English in Great Britain and French in France but the competition of languages for dominance in Belgium, Switzerland, Canada, and African countries. Cooper devotes a whole volume to the politics of language change.

III Chancery and the Emergence of Standard Written English

1. A recent questioning of the nature and function of the written standard is the *Students' Right to Their Own Language*, with an accompanying

bibliography. In the preparation of this essay, I am pleased to acknowledge the assistance of a fellowship from the National Endowment for the Humanities and a grant from the Hodges Better English Fund of the English Department of the University of Tennessee.

2. Hubert Hall observed in *The Red Book of the Exchequer*, l:xx: "As far back as we can trace the issue of royal laws or royal missives, even back to the remote antiquity of oriental monarchy, we shall find the two essential conditions of their composition and preservation, a clerical staff and a repository." This observation was borne out by the discovery in Yunmeng province of a thousand bamboo slivers inscribed with the earliest laws of China from around 475 B.C. (*New York Times* 29 March 1976: C8).

3. On the uniformity of late West Saxon, see Kenneth Sisam, "Aelfric's Catholic Homilies" 12; F. Klaeber, *Beowulf* lxxxviii; C.L. Wrenn, *A Study of Old English Literature* 197ff.; and Mary Richards, "Elements of Written Standard in the Old English Laws." On the possibility of an Anglo-Saxon Chancery, see Hubert Hall, *Studies in English Official Documents* 175, 189; W.H. Stevenson, "An Old English Charter" 731-44; and Richard Drogereit, "Gab es eine angelsachsische Konigskanzlei?" 335-426.

4. The abrupt changes in twelfth-century English represent less actual changes in the language than the effort to represent colloquial dialects in writing; see H.C. Wyld, *A Short History of English* 82ff.

5. Wyld, *A Short History of English* ch. 7; A.C. Baugh, *A History of the English Language*, ch. 6; G.H. McKnight and B. Emsley, *The Making of Modern English* ch. 1; T.N. Toller, *Outlines of the History of the English Language* ch. 11.

6. H.C. Wyld, *A History of Modern Colloquial English* 4-5.

7. Lorenze Morsbach, *Uber den Ursprung der neuenglischen Schriftsprache.*

8. A.A. Prins, *French Influence on English Phrasing* 4.

9. R.W. Chambers and Marjorie Daunt, *A Book of London English* 1, 7-8.

10. T.F. Tout, *Chapters in Medieval Administrative History* 1:3; F. Palgrave, *An Essay Upon the Original Authority of the King's Council.*

11. Details of the origin of Chancery may be found in Tout, *Chapters in Administrative History* passim, but especially vol. I; Tout, "The English Civil Service in the Fourteenth Century" 185-214; Tout, "The Household of Chancery and Its Disintegration" 46-85; and H.C. Maxwell-Lyte, *Historical Notes on the Use of the Great Seal of England* 1ff.

12. In his "Early Modern Standard English" 25-54, E.J. Dobson discusses the movement towards establishing a standard pronunciation in the sixteenth and seventeenth centuries (the subject of the last essay in this collection).

13. Gower's apology is in *The Complete Works of John Gower*, 1:391, Balade XVIII.4. Examples of bad law French are quoted by F.W. Maitland, *The Year Books of Edward II* l:xliff.

14. Tout, "Household Of Chancery" 58-59 draws upon Rymer's *Foedera* 3:533-62.

15. The fullest history of the Rolls House is by H.C. Maxwell-Lyte in his *Fifty-seventh Report of the Deputy Keeper of Public Records*. In *Historical Notes on the Use of the Great Seal*, Maxwell-Lyte observes that the separation of the household of the chancellor from the household of the king began in 1260 when Henry III granted Nicholas, archdeacon of Ely, then chancellor, 400 marks a year for the maintenance of himself and the clerks of Chancery. See also W. Holdsworth, *A History of English Law* 1:419ff.; B. Wilkinson, *The Chancery Under Edward III* 57-59; and V.H. Galbraith, *An Introduction to the Use of the Public Records* 1ff.

16. Tout, *Chapters in Administrative History* 1:16, 2:305; Wilkinson, *Chancery Under Edward III* ch. 2, esp. 24-25; J.F. Baldwin, *The King's Council During the Middle Ages* 236 et passim; A.J. Otway-Ruthven, *The King's Secretary and the Signet Office in the Fifteenth Century*; Florence M.G. Hingham, "A Note on the Pre-Tudor Secretary" 361-62. Galbraith, *Introduction to the Use of the Public Records* 28, remarks that, although they were separate departments, Chancery, Privy Seal, and Signet "form a single, great administrative machine for the discharge of routine business [although] the precise way in which this complicated system worked is imperfectly known."

17. Pollock and Maitland, *The History of English Law Before the Time of Edward I* 1:194; Holdsworth, *History of English Law* I:396, 403; Wilkinson, *Chancery Under Edward III* 27.

18. Tout, *Chapters in Administrative History* 3:447-49. On the nature and function of Chancery's Register of Writs, see Palgrave, *Essay on the Original Authority of the King's Council* 16-19; Holdsworth, *History of English Law* 2:524.

19. Baldwin, in *The King's Council* 238ff., and, even more emphatically, A.R. Myers, "Parliamentary Petitions in the Fifteenth Century" 385-404, 590-613, argue that the original petitions to parliament were not drawn up by the Chancery clerks, but by scriveners and other unofficial scribes. However, Maxwell-Lyte, *Historical Notes* 155, 265; Wilkinson, *Chancery Under Edward III* 78-80; C.H. McIlwain, *The High Court of Parliament and Its Supremacy* 210; and W. Baildon, *Select Cases in Chancery, 1364-1471* xii, all agree that the great similarity in style, form, and physical appearance indicates that the Ancient Petitions in the Public Record Office (SC8) were drawn up by the Chancery clerks. This is borne out by the fact that from the time they began to appear in English (after 1420), these documents rarely show regional usages and are always written in Chancery Standard.

20. Harold F. Hutchinson, *King Henry V: A Biography* 95.

21. Tout, *Chapters in Administrative History* 3:447-49; Palgrave, *Essay on the King's Council* 23.

22. Various aspects of the duties of the clerks of parliament are treated by Tout, *Chapters in Administrative History* 3:447-48; W. Stubbs, *The Constitutional History of England* 3:451-60; A.F. Pollard, *The Evolution of Parliament* 58; W.H. Dunham, *The Fane Fragment of the 1461 Lords' Journal* 35-46; Stubbs,"Modus Tenendi Parliamentum" (ca. 1400) 504-6; and Hargrave, "A

Treatise of the Maisters of Chauncerie" (ca. 1596) 300-303. The *Rotuli Parliamentorum* (1423) IV.201 give detailed regulations as to how the Council and parliament are to receive and act on petitions.

23. Wilkinson, *Chancery under Edward III* ch. 3 et passim.

24. George W. Sanders, ed., *Orders of the High Court of Chancery* 1:1-7a, and see the discussions in Tout, *Chapters in Administrative History* 3:443-45, and Tout, "The Household of Chancery" 61ff.

25. Pollock and Maitland, *History of English Law* 1:82.

26. Hall, *Studies in English Official Documents* 210, gives examples of the way Norman scribes translated Old English writs "to bring them up to date," using such non-Latin constructions as "Salutat amicabiliter" for "Cret freondliche," "Ego demonstro vobis" for "Ic cythe eow," or "Dominus vos conservat" for "God eow gehealde."

27. R.E. Latham, "The Banishment of Latin from the Public Records" 169; Maxwell-Lyte, *Historical Notes on the Use of the Great Seal* 51, 258.

28. Pollock and Maitland, *History of English Law* 86. V.H. Galbraith, "The Literacy of Medieval English Kings" 30, speaks of French as the language of the king's private correspondence (by the fourteenth century, Privy Seal) and Latin as the language of public proclamations (Great Seal).

29. G.E. Woodbine, "The Language of English Law" 395-463. The proclamation of 1258 appears in both English and French in F. Mossé, *A Handbook of Middle English* 187-89.

30. Otway-Ruthven, *The King's Secretary* 21, 91ff. Margaret Sharp, in "The Administrative Chancery of the Black Prince Before 1362" in Tout, *Essays Presented to T.F. Tout* 323, observes that in the Chancery of the Black Prince "some of the letters are written in Latin; these include most letters of appointment, and other formal letters patent, most of the letters of ecclesiastical business, and, I think, all of the charters. The majority of the entries, however, are in French; even matters of some importance may be dealt with in that tongue. It is sometimes difficult to detect why one letter should be in one language and another in the other; but generally Latin seems to denote the maximum degree of formality."

31. On the re-establishment of English, the best summary remains ch. 6 in Baugh, *History of the English Language*. Richard's command to Gower is in *The Works of John Gower*, Unrevised Prologue, ll. 53-54.

32. *1295*: "[Rex Franciae] linguam Anglicam, si conceptae iniquitatis proposito detestabili potestas correspondeat, quod Deus avertat, omnino de terra delere proponit," W. Stubbs, *Select Charters* 480. *1340*: Sir Robert Sadington: "Et si est il en ferme purpos a ce que nostre seigneur le Roi et son Conseil ont entendu en certeyn, a destruire la langue Englys et de occuper la terre d'Engleterre ... " RP II.147b. *1344*: "& coment son dit Adversaire [the French King] s'afforce tant come il poet a destruire nostre ... dit Terres & Lieux, & la Lange d'Engleterre," RP II.158b. *1346*: "Et sur ce fu monstre une Ordenance faite par le dit Adversaire, & ascuns Grantz

de France & de Normandie, a destruire & anientier tote la Nation & la Lange Engleys," RP 11.158b. *1376*: "son dit Adversaire . . . s'afforce par toutes les voies q'il poet . . . a destruire nostre Seigneur le Roy & son Roialme d'Engleterre, & d'ouster de tout la Lange Engleys, que Dieu ne veulle," RP II.362b.

33. *1362*: "Primierement feust crie fait en la Sale de Westminster par . . . du Chanceller par cause que plousours Prelatz, Seigneurs & Communes, qui duissent venir a cest Parlement ne sont pas . . . preschein a venir. Au quel jour, esteantz nostre Seigneur le Roi, Prelatz, Countes, Barons, & les Communes en la Chambre de Peinte . . . monstre en Englois par . . . de Grene, Chief Justice le Roi, les Causes des Somons du Parlement," RP II.268; the omissions are illegible in the original Roll, C65/20/1. That the records were not kept in the language of oral discussion is clearly indicated by Statute I.C.15, 36 of Edward III, which directs that despite the use of English for oral pleading, court records are to be enrolled in Latin; see Pollock and Maitland, *History of English Law* 1:83n3 and note 37 following.

34. *1362*: "Et apres le Chanceller dit, coment les Prelatz, Ducs, Contes, Barons, & toute la Commune, avoient monstrez au Roi les grantz Meschiefs que sont avenuz as pluseurs du Roialme, de ce que les Lees, Custumes, & Estatutz de dit Roialme ne sont pas conuz comunement en ycel, par cause q'ils sont pledez, monstrez, & juggez en la lange Franceois, q'est trop desconu en la dit Roialme, issint que les gentz qui pledent, ou sont empledez, en les courtz le Roi & les Courtz d'autries, n'ont entendement ne conissance de ce q'est dit pur eux ne contre eux par lour Sergeantz & autres Pledours.

"Et par cela cause & pluseurs autres le Roi desirrant le bon government & tranquillite de son poeple, & de ouster les Meschiefs que sont & purront avenir cele partie, de l'assent des ditz Prelatz, Ducs, Contes, Barons, & Commune en cest present Parlement assemblez, voet que toutes Plees que serront a pleder en ses Courtz quelconques, devant quelconques ses Justices, ou en ses autres Places, ou devant ses autres Ministres quelconques, ou en les Courtz & Places des autres Seigneurs quelconques deinz son Roialme, soient pledez & monstrez en la lange Engleise . . . ," RP II.273b. As may be seen, this statute is broader than the law courts. It requires all the king's ministers, i.e., all departments of government, to conduct their oral inquisitions and discussions in English.

35. RP II.275a, II.283a, III.98a. In 1377 the Archbishop of York, then chancellor, specifies "j'ay dist sont tant a dire en Franceys" (RP III.3a). In 1384 and 1385 (RP III.184, III.203), the opening of parliament is recorded in Latin instead of the customary French; see note 37 following.

36. PRO SC8/20/997; Chambers and Daunt, *Book of London English* 33-37.

37. *1393*: RP III.524; *1404*: RP III.549; *1411*: RP III.650; *1414*: RP IV.22, 57; *1421*: RP IV.158, 159; *1422*: English 6 entries, French 35 entries,

Latin 5 entries, out of a total of 46 entries; *1423*: English 10, French 43, Latin 7 (total 60); *1425*: English 13, French 25, Latin 19 (total 51); *1426*: English 9, French 20, Latin 19 (total 38); *1427*: English 6, French 34, Latin 13 (total 46); *1429*: English 18, French 33, Latin 26 (total 70); *1430-31*: English 7, French 32, Latin 14 (total 46); *1432*: English 9, French 33, Latin 19 (total 52); *1433*: English 18, French 34, Latin 23 (total 69); *1435*: English 8, French 14, Latin 10 (total 29); *1436-37*: English 15, French 15, Latin 11 (total 38); *1439*: English 29, French 27, Latin 12 (total 63); *1441-42*: English 21, French 16, Latin 9 (total 39); *1444*: English 34, French 8, Latin 13 (total 51); *1447*: English 12, French 7, Latin 8 (total 25); *1449*: English 15, French 6, Latin 10 (total 25). The individual entries come to more than the total because when they are in two or three languages, they have been counted two or three times. After 1450 the only French entries are the lists of receivers and triers of petitions, which continued in French until at least 1503 (the end of the printed RP volumes) except that in 1491 and 1495 these lists are in Latin. Beginning in 1425, the opening of parliament, which had been customarily recorded in French, began to be recorded in Latin; Latin was used for the opening, for descriptive headings, and for a few entries at least until 1503. Some of the entries during the early part of the century again reveal that the discussion was in English. For example, no. 16 of 1426 (RP IV.298) has the exposition in Latin, but the lines spoken by the witnesses are in English. In no. 19 of 1432 (RP IV.393), the clerks of the Royal Chapel present a petition in Latin, but the introductory appeal to parliament is in English. The transition from French to English in the Statutes of the Realm came when the statutes began to be incorporated in the Rolls of Parliament during the reign of Richard III; see Pollock and Maitland, *History of English Law* 1:86n.

38. On the service of the Chancery clerks in parliament, see Stubbs, *Constitutional History of England* 3:451-52; Tout, *Chapters in Administrative History* 3:447-49; Holdsworth, *History of English Law* 1:403; and Hargrave, "A Treatise of the Maistres of Chauncerie" 308-9.

39. Both -*lich* and *y*-forms occur in Chaucer, but in limited and specialized context. Most editions of Chaucer and Middle English grammars summarize Chaucer's grammar and give information about the dialectal forms, but there is no satisfactory study of the variant forms and spellings in the different texts and manuscripts of Chaucer's work, which are, of course, all scribal.

40. Wyld, *History of Modern Colloquial English* 70. Wyld's observations about the "influence of the archaic system of spelling insisted upon by the early printers and their successors" does not take into account the conventions of the Chancery Standard from which the printers were working.

41. The monopoly of the Chancery clerks came to be concentrated in the office of the "six clerks," whose control of the flow of documents into and out from Chancery became a scandal by the eighteenth century, and the

practice was not terminated until 1842; see Holdsworth, *History of English Law* 1:421-23. A more sympathetic "insider's" view is T.W. Sraithwaite, *The "Six Clerks of Chancery," Their successors in Office, and the Houses They Lived In—A Reminiscence.*

42. As French became a "taught" language in England, its spelling grew more regular, although never as regular as Latin; see Maitland, *Year Books of Edward II* 1:xliii.

43. N. Denholm-Young observes in *Handwriting In England and Wales* 35, that "the special set Chancery hand became stereotyped in the reign of Henry VI." In discussing the breakup of this hand into the various departmental hands of the sixteenth century, H.F. Jenkinson, *Paleography and the Practical Study Court Hand* 1:15, says, "No doubt [this] development was at first unconscious, due to the recruiting of clerks in different departments by a system of apprenticeship." Apropos the larger question of the relationship between handwriting and the development of the language, Jenkinson points out in "Elizabethan Handwritings" 3-4, that the "fashions" in business hands "were largely set by the royal courts and other departments of public administration, and in developments which occurred in public administration from the thirteenth century downwards we find a very close connexion with those of writing, means of authentication of executive documents, the conventional form of these documents, the departments or functionaries which controlled and issued them, and even the language in which they were written—all these went through a series of changes closely parallel to each other and to those of handwriting."

44. As shown by the Year Books, French *tu* was never used in formal pleading (Maitland, *Year Books of Edward II*, 1:liii). But what remained official usage in French became familiar usage in English.

45. Eilert Ekwall in *Studies in the Population of Medieval London* shows the migration to London in the fourteenth century (especially from the northern Midlands) which was supposed to have influenced the dialect of the city. See also Wilkinson, *The Chancery Under Edward III* 178.

46. M.L. Samuels, "Some Applications of Middle English Dialectology" 81-94. In this article, Samuels for the first time identified and introduced the designation "Chancery Standard." His view is that this standard represents an amalgam of the language spoken by the various populations in Chancery.

47. T.F. Tout long ago pointed out that an appreciable portion of fourteenth-century English literature was produced by "civil servants of the state"; see "Literature and Learning in the English Civil Service in the Fourteenth Century" 365-89. Susan Hughes, "Guildhall and Chancery English," has discussed the difference between City and Chancery English.

48. The deficiencies of fifteenth-century English prose are detailed with many examples by S.K. Workman, *Fifteenth Century Translation.* The "tightening" of prose style that Workman attributes to translation, I would

attribute at least partly to the lucidity and coherence of the Latin and French official styles. This accounts for the "legal coloring" that critics have noted in the styles of Malory, the Pastons, etc.

49. On the influence of French style and idiom on the formation of Standard English, see Galbraith, "The Literacy of Medieval English Kings" 30; Prins, *French Influence on English Phrasing* 38-39 et passim; and Norman Davis, "Styles in English Prose of the Middle and Early Modern Period" 165-81.

50. Mary Dominica Legge, *Anglo-Norman Letters and Petitions from All Souls MS.182* 1.

51. The related files are Chancery Warrants (C81), which are mostly pleas like SC8, but converted into warrants by an annotation by the king or Council; Detached Early Proceedings (C4); and Placita in Chancellaria (C44), pleas on the common law side of Chancery, nearly all in Latin.

52. The related files are Ministers' Accounts (SC6), original accounts of bailiffs, reeves, receivers, etc., all in Latin; and Exchequer Accounts (E101), nearly all in Latin.

53. Palgrave, *Essay Upon the King's Council* 21; McIlwain, *The High Court of Parliament.*

54. A broad topic that we cannot pursue here is the political climate for the revival of English as the language of government. Such considerations would include the weakness of Henry IV as a usurper, which strengthened parliament; Henry V's need for the support of parliament in his French wars; Henry VI's ineffectuality throughout his long, nominal reign; and the culminating civil war between factions of the nobility. All of these factors contributed to the decline of the Anglo-Norman aristocracy and the rise of the native population. It seems no accident that the term and concept "gentleman" emerged during the same period that government and business were adopting English for official use; see B. Wilkinson, *Constitutional History of the Fifteenth Century* 1; T.B. Pugh, "The Magnates, Knights, and Gentry" 86-128.

55. See note 19.

56. For some discussion of these new procedures see A.D. Hargreaves, "Equity and the Latin Side of Chancery" 498.

57. See note 41.

58. Otway-Ruthven, *The King's Secretary* 76, 87 et passim.

59. That they were not trained in Chancery may be seen by the signatures of the bishops and magnates attached to the Household Ordinances of Henry VI in *A Collection of Ordinances and Regulations for the Government of the Royal Household* 24.

60. For example, PRO E28/57 and 97 are drafts of summons to arms, with spaces for names and dates; E28/55/48 is a sample letter of appointment for a priest with a list of addresses at the bottom; E28/56/33 is the draft of an order for bishops to assemble at Ely with instructions about copies.

61. For example, R. Davies, *Extracts from the Municipal Records of the City of York* 108, 111, and 115 refer to royal commands; letter from the king's secretary, 163; statement by the king's controller, 195. Also see H.T. Riley, *Memorials of London and London Life* 654, 657, 664, 674, letters from Henry V in Guildhall Letter Books. Mary Patricia Relihan in "The Language of the English Stonor Letters, 1420-1483" finds that writers who may have been trained in the Inns of Court have many more Chancery forms than university graduates.

62. The largest body of Council proceedings are in B.M. Cotton Cleopatra F. III and IV and Cotton Vespasian F. VII. These, supplemented from manuscripts in the PRO E28 files, have been edited by Sir Harris Nicholas, *Proceedings and Ordinances of the Privy Council of England*; Nicholas begins with 1389-90. The first English entry, instructions to an English diplomat, is 1410 (1:323-27); the second, advice from the peers on the French succession, is 1414 (2:140-42); in 1417 there is a letter in English from the bishops to the king (2:236) and the first Council minutes in English (2:237-39). Throughout the rest of Henry V's rule, the English is mostly letters, although two discussion papers (2:350-58, 2:363-67) suggest that the business of the Council was being carried on in English. Beginning with the conciliar rule in the name of the infant Henry VI, Council minutes in English begin to grow more frequent. In 1437, the year in which Henry VI assumed rule in his own name, the proceedings become nearly all English. We may observe in passing that Rymer's *Foedera* gives a quite erroneous impression of the rate at which English penetrated the administration, first because Rymer concentrated on foreign relations and charters and grants (documents in which French and Latin persisted longest) but also because of his own linguistic prejudices. Rymer included an English document only when he could not find one in French or Latin that told the same story.

63. Statutes of the Realm, 2 Inst. 405, quoted from L.O. Pike, "Common Law and Conscience in the Ancient Court of Chancery," *Law Quarterly Review* 1 (1885): 443-44: "And whensoever it shall happen from henceforth in the Chancery that in one case a writ is found, and that in like case falling under the same law and needing like remedy a writ is not found, let the Clerks of Chancery agree in making a writ, or adjourn complaints to the next Parliament. And let the cases where they cannot agree to be set forth in writing, and let the Clerks refer the cases to the next Parliament. And let the writ be made by agreement among men learned in the law, so that it happen not from henceforth that the Court of the Lord the King do fail complainants when seeking justice." See also Pollock and Maitland, *History of English Law* 1:195-96; and Baldwin, *King's Council During the Middle Ages* 237.

64. In the reign of Henry VI, it became customary for the clerks of the Privy Seal to write their names in the lower right-hand corners of writs that had been prepared by subordinates. In Chancery, the name of the cursitor

is found on the face of the instrument and that of his superior on the hack. There was a formal procedure of *inspeximus* testifying that an enrollment had been reviewed and approved; see Maxwell-Lyte, *Historical Notes on the Use of the Great Seal* 14, 34, 226; Otway-Ruthven, *The King's Secretary* 26.

65. Charles Duggan, in *Twelfth Century Decretal Collections and their Importance in English History*, finds similar influence exercised by a handful of clerics associated with Thomas à Becket in the formulation of decretal collections and the codification of papal authority in the twelfth century.

66. Tout, "The Household of Chancery," describes the original functions of the households of Chancery; Holdsworth, *History of English Law* 12:40ff., discusses the Inns of Chancery as preparatory schools for the Inns of Court.

67. Sanders, *Orders of the High Court of Chancery* 1:4; Tout, "The Household of Chancery," *Essays in History Presented to R.L. Poole* 67.

68. H. Rashdall, *The Universities of Europe in the Middle Ages* 3:162. The statute is printed by S. Gibson, *Statuta Antiqua Universitatis Oxoniensis* 240-41.

69. Sir John Fortescue, *De Laudibus Legum Anglie*, ed. and trans. S.B. Crimes, 115.

70. Ibid., 117.

71. A.F. Leach, *Schools in Medieval England* passim; C.L. Kingsford, *Prejudice and Promise in the XV Century* 35-39.

72. Tout, "Household of Chancery" 73.

73. Leach, *Schools in Medieval England* 235.

74. Kingsford, *Prejudice and Promise* 39.

75. K.B. McFarlane, *Lancastrian Kings and Lollard Knights* 115.

76. The petition asks that four parsons of London be authorized in their parishes to "sette a persone sufficiantly lerned in gramer, to hold and exercise a Scole in the same science of gramer, and it there to teche to all that will lerne" (RP V.137). See Kingsford, *Prejudice and Promise* 37-38.

77. Quoted from Baugh, *History of the English Language* 179; see also W.H. Stevenson, "The Introduction of English as a Vehicle of Instruction in English Schools" 421-29; Leach, *Schools in Medieval England* 23ff.

78. As H. Jenkinson put it in "The Teaching and Practice of Handwriting in England" 136: "Up to the beginning of the sixteenth century, school statutes did not contemplate any provision for subjects like writing or accounting in the school curriculum." T.F. Tout describes the training of the apprentice clerk in "Literature and Learning in the English Civil Service" 368.

79. Fortescue, *De Laudibus Legum Anglie* 119: "Because of [their] costliness, there are not many who learn the laws in the inns except the sons of nobles." C. Ogilvie, in *The King's Government and the Common Law, 1471-1641* 49, observes: "members of the Inns of Court were, as a general rule,

indistinguishable in education and social status from prosperous country gentry, to which most of them belonged."

80. Rolls Series, *Calendar of the Roll Proceedings of the King's Council in Ireland, 1392-93*, Appendix C1: "The [Irish] Chancery has but one Clerk and one Petty Clerk, and they are not capable of transacting the business of the court. A properly qualified Clerk of the Rolls should be speedily sent over. The Exchequer is in like case." Wilkinson, in *Chancery Under Edward III* 89-90, discusses the loaning of Chancery clerks to offices in various parts of England, where the clerks could introduce the practices of the central administration.

81. Margaret Deansley, "Vernacular Books in England in the Fourteenth and Fifteenth Centuries" 349-58, demonstrates the paucity of books of any kind, and particularly *belles lettres*. Writing bound as books was likely to be pious material; writing not bound as books (single sheets, rolls) was likely to be bureaucratic or commercial.

82. "And Lowis, yif so be that I shewe the in my lihte Englissh as trewe conclusiouns towcheng this matere, and nahwt only as trewe but as many and as subtil conclusiouns as ben shewed in Latyn in ani commune tretis of the astrelabie, kon me the more thank; and preye God save the King, that is lord of this langage, and alle that him feyth bereth and obeieth, everech in his degree, the more and the lasse," Chaucer, *Treatise on the Astrolabe*, in Fisher, *Chaucer's Poetry and Prose* 909.

83. See note 31.

84. Pollock and Maitland, *History of English Law*, 1:195.

85. For an instance in the Year Books in which a case turned on the correctness of Latin, and the "people in Chancery" are cited by the judge as authorities, see W.C. Bolland, *A Manual of Year Book Studies* 105. English was another matter. In a case in 1426, when objection was raised because Banester was written Benster, the judge ruled that words are pronounced differently in different parts of England "and one is just as good as the other" (Bolland 105).

86. C.L. Kingsford, *Prejudice and Promise* 30; Hall, *Studies in English Official Documents* 271. Hall observes, "The Paston, Stonor, and Cely letters are indeed merely survivals of a large class of everyday correspondence composed in the *stilus Anglicus*, which may be dated from or near the beginning of the fifteenth century. At the same time, it will be found that the essential formulas in these vernacular letters are practically versions of French and Latin phrases which are in turn derived from an early Chancery style."

87. Norman Davis, "The Language of the Pastons" 119-144, esp. 130-31.

88. Kingsford, *Prejudice and Promise* 35.

89. See Norman Davis, "The Language of the Pastons."

90. Tout, "Literature and Learning in the English Civil Service" 370-89.

91. The statement is quoted in the first three editions of Baugh, *History of the English Language* 183, with "lords" and "commons" lower case, which conceals the reference to parliament. These have been capitalized in the fourth edition.

IV European Chancelleries and the Rise of Standard Written Languages

1. The essays in Sections IV and VI in Joshua A. Fishman's *Readings in the Sociology of Language* are the most useful that I have found, but they, too, are focused largely on single languages.

2. J. Berry, "The Making of Alphabets," summarizes this point of view. On page 738n6, Berry gives a list of articles advancing the notion that writing is a visual system independent of the vocal-auditory process. My interest is less in the theoretical than in the historical relation between writing and speech.

3. V.V. Nalimov's recent *In the Labyrinths of Language: A Mathematician's Journey* is an interesting case in point. Nalimov appears to equate "language" with writing, as when he discusses the "structure" of $ds2=dx2+dy2+dz2-c2dt2$ (43).

4. Karl W. Deutsch, "The Trend of European Nationalism—The Language Aspect." Philippe Wolff, in *Western Languages* 139ff., deals far too generally with the convergence of dialects in Europe. How much they have actually converged on the colloquial level depends on one's point of view.

5. William J. Entwistle, *The Spanish Language* 118.

6. Wolff, *Western Languages* 38.

7. Erich Auerbach, *Literary Language and Its Public in Latin Antiquity and in the Middle Ages* 261-62.

8. M.T. Clanchey, *From Memory to Written Record* 18ff.

9. Elliot R. Goodman, "World State and World Language" 717-36.

10. Helmut Gneuss, "The Origin of Standard Old English and Aethelwold's School at Winchester," 63-83.

11. Wolff, *Western Languages* 88, 118, attributes this phrase to von Wartburg. On the linguistic activities of Charlemagne, see also John T. Waterman, *A History of the German Language* 76ff.

12. Giacomo Devoto, *The Languages of Italy* 210. For discussion of how the Reformation broke the hold of Latin, see W.B. Lockwood, *Informal History of the German Language* 130, etc.

13. M.L. Samuels, "Some Applications of Middle English Dialectology" 81-94.

· 14. Waterman, *History of the German Language* 146-47, shows how Luther's Bibeldeutsch spread along with the Reformation in Germany.

15. Ferdinand Brunot, *Histoire de la Langue Française* II.14.

16. Clanchey, *Memory to Written Record* 226.

17. On the *Placiti Cassinesi* see Bruno Migliorini, *The Italian Language* 61. The nature of the Strassburg Oaths is identical.

18. See Auerbach, *Literary Language* 119-21.

19. Clanchey, *Memory to Written Record* 23, 97, 219, has interesting things to say about the tension between warriors and clerks in the Germanic Middle Ages. See also Auerbach, *Literary Language* 281ff.

20. Goodman, "World State and World Language" 718, quotes Lenin to the effect that trade and not government is the basis for unification of language. In the Middle Ages in Europe, as in the Third World today, it was not easy to distinguish trade from government. The examples of Germany and Italy vs. France, Spain, and England could be discussed from this point of view.

21. Auerbach, *Literary Language* 319.

22. Brunot, *Histoire* I:326-29. The sketch that follows is heavily dependent on Brunot, vols. I-IV.

23. Brunot, *Histoire* I:361.

24. Brunot, *Histoire* I:362.

25. Wolff, *Western Languages* 146ff.; Brunot, *Histoire* I:367.

26. Brunot, *Histoire* I:370.

27. Brunot, *Histoire* II:21ff., IV:118.

28. Brunot, *Histoire* II:115. In this connection Brunot remarks (II.32) that the influences of official writing upon the development of French grammar and style are not sufficiently recognized.

29. Brunot, *Histoire* IV:127-28.

30. Brunot, *Histoire* IV:96ff.

31. Alfred Ewert, *The French Language* 18.

32. Entwistle, *Spanish Language* 106ff.

33. Robert K. Spaulding, *How Spanish Grew* 72ff. Wolff, *Western Languages* 175.

34. Entwistle, *Spanish Language* 152.

35. Wolff, *Western Languages* 178ff. Spaulding, *How Spanish Grew* 139; Entwistle, *Spanish Language* 107, 153, 170-73.

36. These topics are treated in detail by Entwistle, *Spanish Language* passim; Spaulding, *How Spanish Grew* 63-70; Wolff, *Western Languages* 213.

37. Entwistle, *Spanish Language* 247-48.

38. Entwistle, *Spanish Language* 197ff.; Spaulding, *How Spanish Grew* 137.

39. See Essay III.

40. The earliest official documents are collected in *An Anthology of Chancery English*, ed. John H. Fisher, Malcolm Richardson, and Jane Law Fisher.

41. See Norman Davis, "The Language of the Pastons" 119-44, esp. 130-31; Mary Relihan, "The English of the Stonor Letters."

42. See E.J. Dobson, "Early Modern Standard English" 25-54. Dobson writes, "The second feature in which the standard language of the

sixteenth and seventeenth centuries differed from ours was in the much greater variety of pronunciation which it permitted" (30); "The main period of orthographical influence on pronunciation is in the eighteenth century and after" (34). This topic is treated in the final essay in this collection.

43. The influence of the theater on English pronunciation awaits further study. It must be followed up in connection with Thomas Sheridan, father of the playwright, and his school of elocution.

44. Waterman, *History of the German Language* 112-13; Wolff, *Western Languages* 172.

45. W.B. Lockwood, *An Informal History* 79.

46. Waterman, *History of the German Language* 112ff.; Lockwood, *An Informal History* 90ff.

47. Saxon leadership begins with Otto I, Duke of Saxony, who after 936 established centralized authority in Germany for the first time since Charlemagne. In 962 he was crowned Emperor of the Holy Roman Empire; see Wolff, *Western Languages* 128.

48. Translated from Adolf Bach, *Geschichte der deutschen Sprache* 252.

49. Waterman, *History of the German Language* 146-47.

50. Ibid., 141-42.

51. Wilfred M. Voge, *The Pronunciation of German in the Eighteenth Century*; Werner F. Leopold, "The Decline of German Dialects" 340-63.

52. Theodor Siebs, *Deutsche Buhenanssprache*. This handbook has gone through some 18 editions.

53. Wolff, *Western Languages* 184-92.

54. Edgcumbe Staley, *The Guilds of Florence* ch. 2.

55. On Latin and Italian, see Devoto, *Languages of Italy* 190-91; on Latin and French, see F. Pollock and F.W. Maitland, *The History of English Law* 1:82.

56. There is a general discussion of the nature and importance of the notarial contract at the beginning of David Herlihy's *Pisa in the Early Renaissance* 1-10ff. See also David Abularia, *The Two Italies* 8ff.

57. Lauro Martinez, *Lawyers and Statecraft in Renaissance Italy* 35; Benjamin Z. Kedar, "The Genoese Notaries of 1382" 73-94. Devoto, *Languages of Italy* 48ff.: Migliorini, *Italian Language* 81-82.

58. Migliorini, *Italian Language* 69.

59. Migliorini, *Italian Language* 136-39.

60. Glenn Olsen, "Italian Merchants and the Performance of Banking Functions in the Early Thirteenth Century," *Economy, Society, and Government*, ed. Herlihy, 43-64. Robert Lopez, "Stars and Spices: The Earliest Italian Manual of Commercial Practice" 35-42, discusses eight manuals of merchant practice compiled in or near Florence between the late thirteenth and the fifteenth centuries. The documents printed by A. Sciaffini, *Testi Fiorentini del Dugento e dei premi del Trecento*, indicate the priority of Florence in the use of the vernacular in business. Christian Bec, in *Les marchands*

écrivains: affaires et humanisme a Florence, 1375-1434, associates Florence's cultural influence with its economic superiority, see esp. 24-25; see also Devoto, *Languages of Italy* 216ff.

61. Migliorini, *Italian Language* 286, 303.

62. Auerbach, *Literary Language* 328.

63. Mark Sullivan, *Our Times: The United States 1900-1925* 3:163ff.

V Animadversions on the Text of Chaucer

(This is a version of the presidential address delivered at the annual meeting of the Medieval Academy of America at the University of Pennsylvania on 9 April 1988.)

1. The fullest discussion of the dates is by W.W. Skeat in the Oxford Chaucer, 3:373-74.

2. A.S.G. Edwards, "Walter W. Skeat," in P. Ruggiers, ed., *Editing Chaucer* 174.

3. For a convenient summary, see ch. 7, "The Publication of Shakespeare's Works," in Stanley Wells, *Shakespeare: The Writer and His Works.*

4. Martin M. Crow and Clair C. Olson, eds., *Chaucer Life-Records* 148.

5. J.M. Manly, "Chaucer as Controller" 408. There is a good summary of the holograph situation in Derek J. Price, ed., *The Equatorie of the Planetis* 162-69.

6. Crow and Olson, *Life-Records* 151.

7. F.J. Furnivall, *The Athenaeum* 29 November 1873: 698; quoted in Price, ed., *Equatorie* 162.

8. R.E.G. Kirk, *Life Records of Chaucer* 233, 251n, 278n, 335n; Manly, "Chaucer as Controller"; Price, ed., *Equatorie* 163. M.L. Samuels, in "Chaucer's Spelling" 7-37, argues that the Peterhouse *Equatorie* manuscript probably preserves Chaucer's own spelling. Since the manuscript shows the process of composition, Price proposes that it may be a Chaucer holograph.

9. R.K. Root, "Publication before Printing" 417-31; Karl J. Holzknecht, *Literary Patronage in the Middle Ages* ch. 9, "Presentations."

10. Holzknecht, *Literary Patronage* s.v. index. Aage Brusendorff, in *The Chaucer Tradition* 113, tentatively identifies the manuscript Froissart presented to Richard II. There is a particularly nice frontispiece of Caxton presenting *The Receuyell of the Histories of Troy* to Margaret, Duchess of York, in Ruggiers, *Editing Chaucer*. Derek Pearsall, "The Troilus Frontispiece," 72n, cites five Lydgate and two Hoccleve manuscripts with presentation pictures and remarks on the lack of presentation pictures in both Chaucer and Gower manuscripts. Jeremy Griffiths, "*Confessio Amantis*: The Poem and Its Pictures" 163 and plates, cites author pictures in two Gower manuscripts, but neither of these implies a presentation.

11. Unless otherwise noted, quotations from Chaucer are from *The*

Complete Poetry and Prose of Geoffrey Chaucer, ed. John H. Fisher. The balades are short poems 16 and 18 in this edition.

12. Fisher, *John Gower* 116ff.

13. Sara Jane Williams, "An Author's Role in Fourteenth-Century Book Production: Guillaume de Machaut's 'Livre ou je met toutes mes choses' " *Romania* 90 (1969): 433-54.

14. Caroline Spurgeon, *Five Hundred Years of Chaucer Criticism and Allusion* 1:16 ff.; Fisher, *John Gower* 3ff.

15. The references to reading are taken at face value and expanded upon by Brusendorff, *Chaucer Tradition* 19-25; George P. Wilson, "Chaucer and Oral Reading" *South Atlantic Quarterly* 25 (1926): 283-99; Ruth Crosby, "Chaucer and the Custom of Oral Delivery" *Speculum* 13 (1938): 413-32; Bertrand Bronson, "Chaucer's Art in Relation to His Audience" in *Five Studies in Literature* 1-53; Mary Giffin, *Studies on Chaucer and His Audience*; and, more recently, Bruce Rosenberg, "The Oral Performance of Chaucer's Poetry" *Forum* 13 (1980): 224-37. But more recent critics see the allusions to reading as a literary device; see George Kane, *The Autobiographical Fallacy in Chaucer and Langland Studies*; and especially Dieter Mehl, "Chaucer's Audience" *Leeds Studies in English* 10 (1978): 58-74.

16. See Pearsall, "The Troilus Frontispiece" *Yearbooks of English Studies* 7 (1977): 68-74; Laura Kendrick, "The *Troilus* Frontispiece and the Dramatization of Chaucer's *Troilus*" *Chaucer Review* 22 (1987): 81-93, makes the interesting suggestion that the picture shows the author reciting his poem while the action is mimed by actors and brings forward evidence for such performances.

17. John H. Fisher, "Chaucer and Written Language" in T.J. Heffernan, *The Popular Literature of Medieval England* 237-51.

18. Barry Windeatt, ed., *Troylus and Criseyde* 51.

19. Williams, "An Author's Role" *Romania* 90 (1969): 97. Brusendorff, *Chaucer Tradition* 57ff., speculates about the relations between Chaucer and Adam.

20. Robert K. Root, in describing the evolution of *Troylus*, detailed the process by which the foul papers could have been created, *The Textual Tradition of Chaucer's Troilus* 256ff., expanded in *The Book of Troilus and Criseyde* lxxvii. Germaine Dempster accepted this hypothesis (see "Manly's Conception of the Early History of *The Canterbury Tales*" 380, and "On the Significance of Hengwrt's Changes of Ink in the Merchant's Tale" 328) as do Norman Blake, *The Textual Tradition of the Canterbury Tales*, esp. ch. 9; Barry Windeatt, *Troilus and Criseyde* 51; and Charles Owen, "The Alterative Reading of *The Canterbury Tales*: Chaucer's Text and the Early Manuscripts" 237-43. Eleanor Hammond, *Chaucer: A Bibliographical Manual* 262, and Robert Pratt, "The Order of *The Canterbury Tales*," *PMLA* 66 (1951): 1141-67, envisaged a neat pile of loose fascicles which were disarranged by accident or by "piracy." J.S.P. Tatlock, in "*The Canterbury Tales* in 1400" *PMLA* 50

(1935): 105n, accepts the notion of piracy, and M.L.S. Lossing, in "The Order of *The Canterbury Tales*" *JEPG* 37 (1938): 160, develops it at length, but Manly and Rickert seem to argue that the copies of *The Canterbury Tales* were usually made from bound compilations; see John M. Manly and Edith Rickert, *The Text of the Canterbury Tales* 1:316-17 and 383; 2:69.

21. Root, "Publication before Printing."

22. Windeatt, *Troilus and Criseyde* 51.

23. Windeatt, *Troilus and Criseyde* 38-42. Donald Cook, "The Revisions of Chaucer's *Troilus*: The *Beta* Text" 51-62, is the last defense I have found of the McCormick and Root hypothesis.

24. Manly and Rickert, *Text of the Canterbury Tales* 2:12-41.

25. Germaine Dempster, "Manly's Conception" *PMLA* 61 (1946): 379-96; "A Chapter in the History of *The Canterbury Tales*: The Ancestor of Group D, the Origin of Its Texts, Tale Order, and Spurious Links" *PMLA* 63 (1948): 456-84; "On the Significance of Hengwrt's Changes of Ink" *MLN* 63 (1948): 325-30; "The Fifteenth Century Editors of *The Canterbury Tales* and the Problem of Tale Order" *PMLA* 64 (1949): 23-42.

26. See N.F. Blake, "Editorial Assumptions of the Manly-Rickert Edition of *The Canterbury Tales*" 385-400. These assumptions have been recently accepted by Charles Owen, "The Alternative Reading" *PMLA* 97 (1982): 244-46. However, it should be noted that Germaine Dempster specifically dissociated herself from this hypothesis in "Manly's Conception" 385n, and in "Changes of Ink" 328, as did J. Burke Severs, "Authorial Revisions in Block C of *The Canterbury Tales*" *Speculum* 29 (1954): 512-30.

27. Sir William McCormick, *The Manuscripts of Chaucer's Canterbury Tales* xiii-xiv. These manuscripts are interlarded with the others in vol. I of Manly and Rickert.

28. Using Manly and Rickert's sigils and dates, the fragments line up as follows: *Fragments*: Ds^2 1430, two leaves; Do 1450, one leaf; Ha^1 1450, five tales copied after *TC*; Hl^4 1430, one leaf; Ox 1440, two leaves; Me 1400, three leaves; Ph^1 1450, twenty-four leaves, probably from a complete text; Pl 1430, two leaves. *Tales in miscellanies*: Ar 1450, Mel; Ct 1490, 2ndN; Ee 1470, MLT; Hl^1 1460, PioressT; Hl^2 1464, PioressT; Hl^3 1470, 2ndN; Hn 1480, Mel, MkT; Ll^1 1450, KT, ClT; Ll^2 1420, ParsT; Np 1475, ClT; Ph^4 1450, ClT; Sl^3 1477, Mel; St 1440, Mel; Tc^3 1478, Mel. *Separate fascicles*: Ra^4 1483, ClT, PioressP; Si ca. 1460, ClT and fragment D. *Written from memory*: Ad^4 1400, from GP description of Parson, written at end of *Boece*.

29. The history of the editions is summarized by Blake, *Textual Tradition* ch. 1, and in the essays on the important editions in Ruggiers, *Editing Chaucer*.

30. Charles Rosen, "Romantic Originals," *New York Review of Books* 17 December 1987: 31. This review of recent editions of Balzac, Byron, and Wordsworth cites many examples of how authors weakened their own works

in revision. Ralph Hanna III, "Problems of 'Best-Text' Editing and the Hengwrt Manuscript of *The Canterbury Tales*" 87-94, raises questions about the supposed authenticity of Hengwrt, particularly about its metrical practice.

31. Blake, *The Textual Tradition* 159. Dempster, "The Fifteenth-Century Editors" 1139-41, is, like Manly and Rickert, wedded to the idea that the early manuscripts were produced in a "shop" that preserved and worked over the original exemplars. But the idea of a shop has been pretty well discounted by A.I. Doyle and M.B. Parkes, "The Production of Copies of *The Canterbury Tales* and *Confessio Amantis* in the Early Fifteenth Century" 163-210, which presents instead the view that literary manuscripts were produced on commission by independent scribes for patrons. See note 36 following.

32. Larry Benson, "The Order of *The Canterbury Tales*" 77-120, is the most recent argument that the Ellesmere order is authorial. His detailed rejection of Blake's hypothesis is of central importance to the controversy.

33. Blake, *The Textual Tradition* ch. 4-7. Both Dempster, "Changes of Ink" 478, and Severs, "Authorial Revisions" 513, see the early manuscripts as successively derived one from the other, not as derived from different copy texts.

34. Vance Ramsey, "The Hengwrt and Ellesmere Manuscripts of *The Canterbury Tales*: Different Scribes" 135-54, and "Paleography and Scribes of Shared Training" 107-44. The latter is in response to M.L. Samuels, "The Scribe of the Hengwrt and Ellesmere Manuscripts of *The Canterbury Tales*" 49-65, and to Doyle and Parkes "The Production of Copies."

35. Martin S. Ruud, *Thomas Chaucer*,

36. Charles Owen, "The Alternative Reading" 244, sees the multiple copy texts dating from before Chaucer's death as surviving "right up to the time when the first printed editions of *The Canterbury Tales* appeared." Larry Benson, "The Order of *The Canterbury Tales*" 100 et passim, hypothesizes that two authorial versions of the compilation survived, one earlier and one later.

37. See especially George Kane, *Piers Plowman: The A Version* ch. 4. Norman Blake in *The Textual Tradition* 2-3 et passim, "The Textual Tradition of *The Book of the Duchess*" 237-48, and Barry Windeatt in "The Scribes as Chaucer's Early Critics" 119-42, argue that scribes were capable of making salutary changes in Chaucer's text.

38. In his essay "J.M. Manly and Edith Rickert," P. Ruggiers, ed., *Editing Chaucer* 207-30, George Kane has suggested how editorial decisions about the text of *The Canterbury Tales* might be made on the basis of *usus scribendi*.

39. These quotations are taken from Lawrence Lipking's contribution, "Literary Criticism" 79-97, in *Introduction to Scholarship in Modern Languages and Literatures*. Derek Pearsall, in "Editing Medieval Texts" 100, finds the editor's assumptions of unity and completeness in a medieval text "not merely difficult to apply but irrelevant."

40. Ralph Hanna, in "Problems of 'Best-Text Editing,' " raises questions about the authority of the Hengwrt text.

41. W.W. Lawrence, *Chaucer and The Canterbury Tales* ch. 4, gives a good summary of the development of the Chaucer Society order. A.C. Baugh, *Chaucer's Major Poetry*, still adheres to this order. George Keiser defends it in "In Defense of the Bradshaw Shift" *Chaucer Review* 12 (1978): 191-210. Manly was convinced that the Chaucer Society order was Chaucerian and the Ellesmere order editorial; see Dempster, "Manly's Conception" 395-99.

42. Derek Pearsall, in *The Canterbury Tales*, discounts Chaucerian order and treats the tales by genre. Paul Olson, *The Canterbury Tales and the Good Society*, and Judson Allen and Theresa Moritz, *A Distinction of Stories*, rearrange them by topic. John Gardner, "The Case against the Bradshaw Shift" *Papers on English Language and Literature* 3 (1967): 80-106, and Donald Howard, *The Idea of the Canterbury Tales*, find topical patterns within the Ellesmere order. Morton Bloomfield, in *"The Canterbury Tales* as Framed Narratives" *Leeds Studies in English* 14 (1983): 44-56, nicely summarizes the causative and authenticating aspects of the pilgrimage frame. C. David Benson, *Chaucer's Drama of Styles*, argues that the dramatic structure is editorial and the compilation should be viewed as a collection of contrasting styles. N.F. Blake, "Critics, Criticism, and the Order of *The Canterbury Tales*" *Archiv* 218 (1981): 47-58, calls critical attempts to prove the unity of *The Canterbury Tales* inappropriate in view of its fragmentary state.

VII *Piers Plowman* and Chancery Tradition

1. Chancery hand and language are treated in the third essay in this collection and in the introduction to *An Anthology of Chancery English*.

2. Kane and Donaldson, 132ff. All citations to the B version are from this edition.

3. The discussion of the chronology of *The Canterbury Tales* manuscripts in J.M. Manly and Edith Rickert, *The Text of the Canterbury Tales* 1.248 et passim, has now been superseded by N.F. Blake's treatment, *The Textual Tradition of the Canterbury Tales*, and the treatment of the chronology of the *Troylus* manuscripts by R.K. Root, ed., *The Book of Troilus*, and B.A. Windeatt, ed., *Geoffrey Chaucer, Troilus & Criseyde*. That of the chronology of the Gower manuscripts in G.C. Macauley, ed., *The Works of John Gower* 2:cxxxviiiff., and in John Fisher, *John Gower: Moral Philosopher and Friend of Chaucer* 99ff., will no doubt soon be superseded by the catalogue of the manuscripts of John Gower's works promised by Jeremy Griffiths, Kate Harris, and Derek Pearsall.

4. For manuscript identifications, see Table A.

5. M.B. Parkes, *English Cursive Book Hands 1250-1500*.

6. See the plates and discussion in Fisher, *An Anthology of Chancery*

English 1-5, but see also the strictures in the review article by Lister Matheson in *Speculum* 61 (1986): 646-50.

7. The traditional discussions of court hand are Hilary Jenkinson, *English Court Hand AD 1066-1500* and L.C. Hector, *The Handwriting of English Documents*.

8. The fourteenth-century developments are discussed by Parkes, *English Cursive* xix-xxi; Hector, *The Handwriting* 52-54; and Pierre Chaplais, *English Royal Documents 1199-1461* 52.

9. Chaplais, *English Royal Documents* 52.

10. Parkes, *English Cursive* xx.

11. On the movement outward from Chancery, Hilary Jenkinson writes in "Elizabethan Handwriting" 3-4: "Fashions in these hands were largely set by the Royal Courts and other departments of public administration, and in developments which occurred in public administration from the thirteenth century downwards we find a very close connection with those of writing, methods of authentication of executive documents, the conventional forms of these documents, the departments or functionaries which controlled and issued them, and even the language in which they were written—all these went through a series of changes closely parallel to each other and to those of handwriting." M.T. Clanchey, *From Memory to Written Record* 50-57, discusses the way in which the practice of producing authenticated documents spread from the royal Chancery and Exchequer to episcopal sees and civic guilds and corporations. The earliest bishops to inaugurate registers had both been Chancery officials.

12. The plates in Anthony G. Petti's *English Literary Hands from Chaucer to Dryden* nicely illustrate the movement of hands from public to personal (and see my review in *Speculum*).

13. That this script was recognized is evidenced when John Clopton ends a 1454 letter to John Paston, "wretyn with my chauncery hand, in ryth gret haste": *The Paston Letters*, ed. James Gairdner, 2:315.

14. Laura Hibbard Loomis, "The Auchinleck Manuscript and a Possible London Bookshop of 1330-40" 595-627.

15. A.I. Doyle and M.B. Parkes, "The production of copies of *The Canterbury Tales* and the *Confessio Amantis*" 163-210. The preceding article in the same volume (Graham Pollard, "The *pecia* system in the medieval universities" 143-61) discusses the production of texts in the universities by simultaneous copying, which might have paved the way for the commercial production of texts as described by Doyle and Parkes. Pollard describes the "bespoke" nature of book production in "The Company of Stationers before 1557."

16. Timothy Shonk, "A Study of the Auchinleck Manuscript: Bookmen and Bookmaking in the Early Fourteenth Century."

17. See Essay III.

18. E. Talbot Donaldson, *Piers Plowman: The C-Text and Its Poet* 208-19.

19. M.L. Samuels, in "Some Applications of Middle English Dialectology," introduced the term Chancery Standard to designate fifteenth-century government English. On the influence of Henry V, see Malcolm Richardson, "Henry V, the English Chancery, and Chancery English," and the introduction to Fisher, *An Anthology of Chancery English.*

20. Fisher, *An Anthology of Chancery English* 5ff.

21. See the lists in Fisher, *An Anthology of Chancery English* 31-33.

22. Samuels, "Some Applications of Middle English Dialectology" 411.

23. Samuels, "Chaucer's Spelling" 17-37.

VIII Caxton and Chancery English

1. M.L. Samuels, "Some Applications of Middle English Dialectology."

2. R.W. Chambers and Marjorie Daunt, eds., *A Book of London English.*

3. Malcolm Richardson, "Henry V, the English Chancery, and Chancery English."

4. Quoted in Essay II from Chambers and Daunt, *Book of London English* 139.

5. Susan E. Hughes, "Guildhall and Chancery English, 1377-1422."

6. Mary Patricia Relihan, "The Language of the English Stonor Letters, 1420-1483" 279, 284ff.

7. Norman Davis, "The Language of the Pastons" 130-31.

8. Henry Cecil Wyld, *A History of Modern Colloquial English* 70-98.

9. A.I. Doyle and M.B. Parkes, "The Production of Copies of *The Canterbury Tales* and *Confessio Amantis* in the Early Fifteenth Century" 163-212.

10. For Wyld and Davis, see notes 8 and 9. Albert C. Baugh and Thomas Cable, eds., *A History of the English Language* 194, 250; E.J. Dobson, "Early Modern Standard English" 25-54.

11. The ideographic nature of Standard Written English is discussed by Henry Bradley, *On the Relation of Spoken and Written English.*

12. Marshall McLuhan, *The Guttenberg Galaxy.*

13. Margaret Shaklee, "The Rise of the Standard English" 48.

14. N.F. Blake, *Caxton and His World* 173ff. See also his "Caxton's Language."

15. N.F. Blake, "English Versions of *Reynard the Fox*" 63-77.

16. Helmut Wiencke, *Die Sprache Caxtons.*

17. W.J.B. Crotch, ed., *The Prologues and Epilogues of William Caxton*; Oliver H. Prior, ed., *Caxton's "Mirrour of the World"*; W.T. Culley and F.J. Furnivall, eds., *Caxton's "Eneydos."*

18. Blake, "Caxton's Language," *Caxton and His World* 177. The four

passages are quoted from Crotch, *Prologues and Epilogues of Caxton* 2; Prior, *Caxton's "Mirrour"* 21; Crotch, *Prologues and Epilogues of Caxton* 110; and Culley and Furnivall, *Caxton's "Eneydos"* 123.

19. Margaret Bryant, in *English and the Law Courts*, illustrates the importance of precedent, uniformity, and form words in modern legal proceedings.

20. N.F. Blake, "Caxton's Language," *Caxton and His World* 128.

21. Wiencke, *Die Sprache Caxtons* 315.

22. Arthur O. Sandved, *Studies in the Language of Caxton's Malory and That of the Winchester Manuscript.*

IX The History of Received Pronunciation

1. Martyn F. Wakelin, *English Dialects* 5.

2. Robert W. Burchfield, *The English Language* 41-42.

3. Gunnar Landtman, *The Origin of the Inequality of the Social Classes*, esp. 303-4. The oldest linguistic marker is "Shibboleth" (Judges 12).

4. See Essay II.

5. See the quotation at the beginning of Essay II.

6. In Chaucer's *Reeve's Tale* (ca. 1390), the northern accent of the two clerks is provincial (Fisher, *The Complete Poetry and Prose of Geoffrey Chaucer* 72). In the Wakefield *Second Shepherds' Play* (ca. 1400), Mak adopts an aristocratic southern accent as part of his disguise: "What, ich be a yoman, I tell you, of the king," Bevington, *Medieval Drama* 391.

7. John Hart, *A Methode . . . to Read English* (1570) 234. William Matthews, *Cockney Past and Present* 201-2, gives this quotation with different wording.

8. George Puttenham, *The Arte of English Poesie* (1589) 144-45.

9. John Aubrey, *Brief Lives* 1:354, quoted from A.C. Baugh and Thomas Cable, *A History of the English Language* 250.

10. James Boswell, *The Heart of Boswell: Six Journals in One Volume* 322.

11. David Simpson, *The Politics of American English* 147.

12. Harold Perkin, *The Origins of Modern English Society*, treats the transformation of "a classless hierarchy" into a "viable class society." It discusses the rise of education (120-21, 291-302, etc.) but says nothing about language as a social marker. See also Penelope J. Corfield, *Language, History, and Class* 101-30, and Gillian Sutherland, "Education" 3:119-69, esp. 132-39, which likewise have nothing to say about language in this context. Other social historians who purport to be interested in language (such as Gareth S. Jones, *Languages of Class*; Ross McKibben, *The Ideologies of Class*) are not concerned with linguistic class markers but with the language that historians, philosophers, and the people themselves (especially the "proletariate") have used to talk about class,

which amounts essentially to deconstructive lexical and semantic concerns.

13. Nancy Mitford, "The English Aristocracy," is a classic essay on language as a class marker. This and other essays dealing with linguistic class distinctions in England are collected in *Noblesse Oblige*, ed. Nancy Mitford. Anthony Burgess, *A Mouthful of Air*, supports RP as the most attractive pronunciation but wishes that it could be relieved of its class association.

14. Hugh Blair, *Lectures on Rhetoric and Belles Letters* 1:14.

15. As S.A. Leonard put it: "the language described by the grammarians and rhetoricians of the eighteenth century was of course that of gentlemen. Writers felt that they were working to warn against the inadvertent contamination with language of the vulgar," *The Doctrine of Correctness in English Usage* 169-70.

16. James Boswell, *The Heart of Boswell* 323 (also see note 10).

17. Thomas Sheridan, *A Course of Lectures on Elocution* (1762) 30.

18. Thomas Sheridan, *A Complete Dictionary of the English Language* Introduction 6-8.

19. Johnson (see note 16) was responding to Boswell's criticism that he had not included pronunciations in his *Dictionary*. It is evident that he was referring specifically to the claims to authority in Sheridan's Introduction.

20. George Philip Krapp, *The English Language in America* 1:356.

21. Frances Austin in *The Language of Wordsworth and Coleridge*, has nothing to say about language as a class marker. *The Language of Jane Austen* by Norman Page has a detailed discussion of social dialects that turns largely on the propriety of grammar and lexicon, but it does refer to the "authoritative tone of voice" in which Lady Catherine de Bourgh questions Elizabeth (147-67, esp. 167). In *The Language of Dickens*, G.L. Brook observes that "Dickens's references to upper-class speech are generally uncomplimentary" and follows this observation with a detailed analysis of pronunciation, grammar, and lexicon (54-65). K.C. Phillipps in *The Language of Thackeray* confines discussion of dialect and register largely to grammar and lexicon (98-114) but does comment on the "languid drawl" of the upper class (96-97) and the social placement of characters by their pronunciation (106-9). In *The Language of Thomas Hardy*, Raymond Chapman observes that Hardy was interested mostly in rustic dialects but states that "Mrs. Durbeyfield habitually spoke the dialect; her daughter, who had passed the Sixth Standard in the National School under a London-trained mistress, spoke two languages: the dialect at home, more or less; ordinary English abroad and to persons of quality" (112-24, esp. 121). *The Language of D.H. Lawrence* by Allan Ingram speaks of Lawrence's mother "who spoke the King's English" in contrast to the pit language of his father, and to the way that Mellors drops "normal" English for dialect as the love relationship with Connie progresses (22-23).

22. Thomas Sheridan, *A Discourse Delivered in the Theatre at Oxford, in*

the Senate House at Cambridge, and at Spring-Garden in London. On Sheridan's life, see *DNB*.

    23. On Walker's life, see *DNB*.

    24. Noah Webster, *Dissertations on the English Language* (1789) 24.

    25. Webster, *Dissertations* 106-7.

    26. Matthew Arnold, *Matthew Arnold and the Education of the New Order* 65.

    27. James Fenimore Cooper, *Notions of the Americans* (1828) Letter V, 62-63; Letter XXIV, 360.

    28. Timothy Dwight, *Travels in New England and New York* 1:367-68.

    29. Henry Van Schaack, *The Life of Peter Van Schaack* 162-63.

    30. James Russell Lowell, *The Biglow Papers*, Introduction 234.

    31. D.J. Palmer, *The Rise of English Studies* ch. 1.

    32. Thomas Arnold said in one of his sermons to the students at Rugby:

> "But our congregation will of necessity within a few years be all scattered to the four winds of heaven; we should look for its several members anywhere rather than here. . . . [O]ur country spreads forth her arms so widely that the scattering of the members of an English school, by the various circumstances of life, is literally a scattering over the whole habitable world; there is no distance so great to which it is not within probability that some of our congregation may betake themselves. And yet once again; those very distant countries, those ends of the earth to which some of us may in the course of things be led, are new settlements, with a small population, with institutions, habits and national character unformed as yet, and to be formed; unformed, and capable therefore in their unsettled state of being influenced greatly by the conduct and character of even a single individual, so that, putting all things together, a stranger does well to feel something more than a common interest in the sight of the congregation assembled within this chapel, as it is this day." (*Thomas Arnold on Education* 146)

    33. Sutherland, *Cambridge Social History*, ed. Thompson, 135.

    34. Palmer, *Rise of English Studies* 2-6.

    35. Sutherland, *Cambridge Social History*, ed. Thompson, 138.

    36. John Wakeford, *The Cloistered Elite* 12. Wakeford gives a good description of the clientele of the public schools and the careers of their graduates.

    37. Ada V. Hyatt, *The Place of Oral Reading in the School Program* 12ff.

    38. Christopher Hollis, *The Oxford Union*, gives the history of the founding of the Union and its nineteenth-century rise to prominence. David Walter, *The Oxford Union: Playground of Power*, describes its luminous constituency from 1910 onwards.

    39. Robert Graves quoted from Randolph Quirk, *The Use of English* 88.

    40. Quirk, *The Use of English* 281.

41. Barbara Strang, *A History of English* 76. W.R. O'Donnell and Loreto Todd, *Variety in Contemporary English* 90-94, describe the deliberate program by which BBC settled on RP as its standard.

42. O'Donnell and Todd, *Variety* 27. J.D. O'Conner, *Better English Pronunciation* 5-6, begins his discussion: "The sensible thing to do is to take as your model the sort or English you hear most often. If you have gramophone records based on, let us say, American pronunciation, make American your model; if you can listen regularly to BBC, use that kind of English. . . . In this book I cannot describe all the possible pronunciations of English that might be useful to you so I shall concentrate on one, the sort of English used by educated natives in South-east England, often referred to as Received Pronunciation (R.P. for short), that is 'accepted' pronunciation" (5). The most lively discussion of the difference between RP and American pronunciation is in chapter 7 of H.L. Mencken's *The American Language* esp. 322-29. Chapter 1, "The Two Streams of English," and chapter 6, "American and English," deal largely with grammar and lexicon. Mencken summarizes and quotes objections to RP from both England and America, but his own prejudice cannot offset the statements on the continuing prestige of RP by more objective authorities like Barbara Strang, Randolph Quirk, and Robert Burchfield.

BIBLIOGRAPHY

Abularia, David. *The Two Italies: Economic Relations between the Norman Kingdom of Sicily and the Northern Communes.* Cambridge, Eng.: Cambridge UP, 1977.

Allen, Judson, and Theresa Moritz. *A Distinction of Stories: The Medieval Unity of Chaucer's Fair Chain of Narratives for Canterbury.* Columbus: Ohio State UP, 1981.

Armitage-Smith, Sidney. *John of Gaunt.* 1904. New York: Barnes and Noble, 1964.

Arnold, Matthew. *Matthew Arnold and the Education of the New Order: A Selection of Arnold's Writings on Education.* Ed. Peter Smith and Geoffrey Summerfield. Cambridge, Eng.: Cambridge UP, 1969.

Arnold, Thomas. *Thomas Arnold on Education.* Ed. T. W. Bamford. Cambridge, Eng.: Cambridge UP, 1970.

Aubrey, John. *Brief Lives.* Ed. Andrew Clark. 2 vols. Oxford: Clarendon-Oxford UP, 1898.

Auerbach, Erich. *Literary Language and Its Public in Latin Antiquity and in the Middle Ages.* 1958. Trans. R. Manheim. New York: Pantheon, 1965.

Austin, Frances. *The Language of Wordsworth and Coleridge.* The Language of Literature Series. London: Macmillan, 1989.

Bach, Adolf. *Geschichte der deutschen Sprache.* 8th ed. Heidelberg: Quelle and Meyer, 1965.

Baildon, W. *Select Cases in Chancery, 1364-1471.* Selden Society 10, 1896.

Baldwin, J. F. *The King's Council During the Middle Ages.* Oxford: Clarendon-Oxford UP, 1913.

Baugh, A.C. "Kirk's Life Records of Chaucer." *PMLA* 47 (1932): 461-515.

———. *Chaucer's Major Poetry.* New York: Appleton, 1963.

———. *A History of the English Language.* 2d ed. Englewood Cliffs, N.J.: Prentice-Hall, 1957.

————, and Thomas Cable. *A History of the English Language.* 3d ed. Englewood Cliffs, N.J.: Prentice-Hall. 1978; 4th ed. 1993.

Bec, Christian. *Les marchands écrivains: affaires et humanisme à Florence,
1375-1434.* Paris: Mouton, 1967.

Bennett, H.S. *Chaucer and the Fifteenth Century.* Oxford: Clarendon-Oxford
UP, 1947.

Benson, C. David. *Chaucer's Drama of Styles.* Chapel Hill: U of North Carolina
P, 1986.

Benson, Larry. "The Order of *The Canterbury Tales.*" *SAC* 3 (1981): 77-120.

Berry, J. "The Making of Alphabets." *Readings in the Sociology of Language.*
Ed. Fishman. 737-83.

Bevington, David, ed. *Medieval Drama.* Boston: Houghton, 1975.

Blair, Hugh. *Lectures on Rhetoric and Belles Lettres.* 3 vols. n.p. 1806.

Blake, N.F., ed. *The Cambridge History of the English Language.* Vol. 2. Cambridge, Eng.: Cambridge UP, 1992.

————. *Caxton and His World.* London: Deutsch, 1969.

————. "Caxton's Language," *Neuphilologische Mitteilungen* 67 (1966): 122-
32.

————. "Critics, Criticism, and the Order of *The Canterbury Tales.*" *Archiv*
218 (1981): 47-58.

————. "Editorial Assumptions of the Manly-Rickert Edition of *The Canterbury Tales.*" *English Studies* 64 (1983): 385-400.

————. "English Versions of *Reynard the Fox* in the Fifteenth and Sixteenth
Centuries." *Studies in Philology* 62 (1965): 63-71.

————. "The Textual Tradition of *The Book of the Duchess.*" *English Studies*
62 (1981): 237-48.

————. *The Textual Tradition of The Canterbury Tales.* London: Arnold, 1985.

Bloomfield, Morton. "*The Canterbury Tales* as Framed Narratives." *Leeds
Studies in English* 14 (1983): 44-56.

Bolland, W.C. *A Manual of Year Book Studies.* Cambridge, Eng.: Cambridge
UP, 1925.

Boswell, James. *The Heart of Boswell: Six Journals in One Volume.* Ed. Mark
Harris. New York: McGraw, 1981.

Bowers, John M. "The House of Chaucer & Son: The Business of Lancastrian Canon Formation." *Medieval Perspectives* 6 (1991): 135-43.

Bradley, Henry. *On The Relation of Spoken and Written English.* Oxford: Oxford
UP, 1919.

Bronson, Bertrand. "Chaucer's Art in Relation to His Audience." *Five Studies
in Literature.* Ed. Bertrand Bronson et al. U of California Studies in
English 8,1. Berkeley: U of California P, 1940. 1-53.

Brook, G.L. *The Language of Dickens.* London: Deutsch, 1970.

Brunot, Ferdinand. *Histoire de la Langue Française.* 12 vols. Paris: Colin, 1966.

Brusendorff, Aage. *The Chaucer Tradition.* Oxford: Oxford UP, 1925.

Bryant, Margaret. *English and the Law Courts: The Part that Articles, Preposi-*

tions, and Conjunctions Play in Legal Decisions. New York: Columbia UP, 1930.

Burchfield, Robert W. *The English Language*. Oxford: Oxford UP, 1985.

Burgess, Anthony. *A Mouthful of Air*. London: Hutchinson, 1992.

Burnley, J.D. "Curial Prose in England." *Speculum* 61 (1986): 593-612.

Cable, Thomas. "The Rise of Standard English." *The Emergence of National Languages*. Ed. Aldo Scaglione. Ravenna, Italy: Longo, 1984. 74-94.

Chambers, R.W., and Marjorie Daunt, eds. *A Book of London English*. Oxford: Clarendon-Oxford UP, 1931.

Chaplais, Pierre, ed. *English Royal Documents 1199-1461*. Oxford: Clarendon-Oxford UP, 1972.

Chapman, Raymond. *The Language of Thomas Hardy*. The Language of Literature Series. London: Macmillan, 1990.

Chaucer, Geoffrey. *The Complete Poetry and Prose of Geoffrey Chaucer*. Ed. John H. Fisher. 2d ed. New York: Holt, 1988.

Christianson, C. Paul. "Evidence for the Study of London's Late Medieval Manuscript Book Trade." *Book Production and Publishing in Britain*. Ed. Griffiths and Pearsall. 87-108.

———. "Chancery Standard and the Records of Old London Bridge." *Standardizing English*. Ed. Trahern. 82-112.

Citrin, Jack, Beth Reingold, Evelyn Walters, and Donald Green. "The 'Official English' Movement and the Symbolic Politics of Language in the United States." *Western Political Quarterly* 43 (1990): 535-59.

Clanchey, M.T. *From Memory to Written Record, 1066-1307*. London: Arnold, 1978.

A Collection of Ordinances and Regulations for the Government of the Royal Household. London: Society of Antiquaries, 1790.

Cook, Donald. "The Revisions of Chaucer's *Troilus*: The *Beta* Text." *Chaucer Review* 9 (1974-75): 51-62.

Cooper, James Fenimore. *Notions of the Americans: Picked up by a Travelling Bachelor*. 1828. Ed. Gary Williams. Albany: SUNY Press, 1991.

Cooper, Robert. *Language Spread: Studies in Diffusion and Social Change*. Bloomington: Indiana UP, 1982.

Corfield, Penelope J. *Language, History, and Class*. Oxford: Blackwell, 1991.

Crane, Susan. *Insular Romance*. Berkeley: U of California P, 1986.

Crosby, Ruth. "Chaucer and the Custom of Oral Delivery." *Speculum* 13 (1938): 413-32.

Crotch, W.J.B., ed. *The Prologues and Epilogues of William Caxton*. EETS, OS 176. Oxford: Oxford UP, 1928.

Crow, M.M., and Clair Olson, eds. *Chaucer Life Records*. Oxford: Clarendon-Oxford UP, 1966.

Culley, W.T., and F.J. Furnivall, eds. *Caxton's "Eneydos."* EETS, ES 57. Oxford: Oxford UP, 1890.

Davies, R. *Extracts from the Municipal Records of the City of York.* London: Nichols, 1843.

Davis, Norman. "The Language of the Pastons." *Proceedings of the British Academy* 40 (1955 for 1954): 119-44.

——. "Styles in English Prose of the Middle and Early Modern Period." *Actes du VIII Congres du FILLM.* Paris: Societé d'Edition "Les Belles Lettres," 1961. 165-81.

Deansley, Margaret. "Vernacular Books in England in the Fourteenth and Fifteenth Centuries." *MLR* 15 (1920): 349-58.

Dempster, Germaine. "Manly's Conception of the Early History of *The Canterbury Tales.*" *PMLA* 61 (1946): 379-96.

——. "On the Significance of Hengwrt's Changes of Ink in the Merchant's Tale." *MLN* 63 (1948): 325-30.

——. "A Chapter in the History of *The Canterbury Tales*: The Ancestor of Group D, the Origin of Its Texts, Tale Order, and Spurious Links." *PMLA* 63 (1948): 456-84.

——. "The Fifteenth Century Editors of *The Canterbury Tales* and the Problem of Tale Order." *PMLA* 64 (1949): 23-42.

Denholm-Young, N. *Handwriting In England and Wales.* Cardiff: U of Wales P, 1954.

Deutsch, Karl W. "The Trend of European Nationalism—The Language Aspect." *Readings in the Sociology of Language.* Ed. Fishman. 598-606.

Devoto, Giacomo. *The Languages of Italy.* Trans. V. Louise Katainen. Chicago: U of Chicago P, 1978.

Dictionary of National Biography (DNB).

Dobson, E.J. "Early Modern Standard English." *Transactions of the Philological Society.* Oxford: Blackwell, 1955. 25-54.

Donaldson, E. Talbot. *Piers Plowman: The C-Text and Its Poet.* New Haven: Yale UP, 1949.

Doyle, A.I. "English Books In and Out of Court from Edward III to Henry VII." *English Court Culture in the Later Middle Ages.* Ed. V.J. Scattergood and J.W. Sherborne. New York: St. Martin's, 1983. 163-82.

——, and M.B. Parkes, "The Production of Copies of *The Canterbury Tales* and *Confessio Amantis* in the Early Fifteenth Century." *Essays Presented to N.R. Ker.* Ed. Parkes. 163-212.

Drogereit, Richard. "Gab es eine angelsachsische Konigskanzlei?" *Archiv fur Urkundenforschung* 13 (1935): 543-67.

Duggan, Charles. *Twelfth Century Decretal Collections and Their Importance in English History.* London: Athlone, 1963.

Dunham, W.H. *The Fane Fragment of the 1461 Lords' Journal.* New Haven: Yale UP, 1935.

Dwight, Timothy. *Travels in New England and New York.* Ed. Barbara M. Solomon. 3 vols. Cambridge, Mass.: Harvard-Belknap, 1969.

Ebin, Lois. *John Lydgate.* New York: Twayne, 1985.

Edwards, A.S.G. "Walter W. Skeat." *Editing Chaucer*. Ed. Ruggiers. 191-206.

————, and Derek Pearsall. "The Manuscripts of the Major English Poetic Texts." *Book Production and Publishing*. Ed. Griffiths. 257-78.

Ekwall, Eilert. *Studies in the Population of Medieval London*. Stockholm: Almqvist, 1956.

Englefield, F.R.H. *Language: Its Origins and Its Relation To Thought*. London: Elek, 1977.

Entwistle, William J. *The Spanish Language*. 2d ed. London: Dickens and Conner, 1962.

Ewert, Alfred. *The French Language*. London: Faber, 1943.

Ferris, Sumner. "The Date of Chaucer's Final Annuity and of 'The Complaint to His Empty Purse.' " *Modern Philology* 65 (1967): 45-52.

Fisher, John H. "The Ancestry of the English Alphabet." *Archaeology* 4 (1951): 232-42.

————. "Chancery Standard and Modern Written English." *Journal of the Society of Archivists* 6 (1979): 136-44.

————. "Chaucer and Written Language." *The Popular Literature of Medieval England*. Ed. T.J. Heffernan. Knoxville: U of Tennessee P, 1985. 237-51.

————. *The Complete Poetry and Prose of Geoffrey Chaucer*. 2d ed. New York: Holt, 1988.

————. *The Importance of Chaucer*. Carbondale: Southern Illinois UP, 1992.

————. *John Gower: Moral Philosopher and Friend of Chaucer*. New York: New York UP, 1964.

————. Rev. of *English Literary Hands from Chaucer to Dryden*, by Anthony G. Petti. *Speculum* 54 (1979): 183-84.

————, Malcolm Richardson, and Jane Law Fisher, eds. *An Anthology of Chancery English*. Knoxville: U of Tennessee P, 1984.

Fishman, Joshua A., ed. *Readings in the Sociology of Language*. The Hague: Mounton, 1972,

Fisiak, Jacek. *An Outline History of English I: External History*. Poznan, Poland: Kantor Wydawniczy, 1993.

Fortescue, John. *De Laudibus Legum Anglie*. Ed. and trans. S.B. Chrimes. Cambridge, Eng.: Cambridge UP, 1947.

Furnivall, F.J. "The Chaucer Holographs." *The Athenaeum* 29 November 1873: 698.

Gairdner, James, ed. *The Paston Letters*. 6 vols. 1904. London: Chatto and Windus, 1934.

Galbraith, V.H. *An Introduction to the Use of the Public Records*. Oxford: Oxford UP, 1934.

————. "The Literacy of Medieval English Kings." *Proceedings of the British Academy* 21 (1935): 201-388.

Gardner, John. "The Case against the Bradshaw Shift." *Papers on English Language and Literature* 3 (1967): 80-106.

Gibson, S. *Statuta Antiqua Universitatis Oxoniensis*. Oxford: Clarendon-Oxford UP, 1931.

Giffin, Mary. *Studies on Chaucer and His Audience*. Quebec: Leclerc, 1956.

Gneuss, Helmut. "The Origin of Standard Old English and Aethelwold's School at Winchester." *Anglo-Saxon England* 1 (1972): 63-83.

Goodman, Elliot R. "World State and World Language." *Readings*. Ed. Fishman. 717-36.

Gower, John. *The Complete Works of John Gower*. Ed. G.C. Macaulay. 4 vols. Oxford: Clarendon-Oxford UP, 1899-1901.

Gray, D., and E.G. Stanley, eds. *Middle English Studies Presented to Norman Davis*. London: Nelson, 1983.

Green, Richard Firth. *Poets and Princepleasers*. Toronto: U of Toronto P, 1980.

Griffiths, Jeremy. "*Confessio Amantis*: The Poem and Its Pictures." *Gower's Confessio*. Ed. McInnis. 163-78.

————, and Derek Pearsall, eds. *Book Production and Publishing in Britain, 1375-1475*. Cambridge, Eng.: Cambridge UP, 1989.

Grillo, R.D. *Dominant Languages: Language and Hierarchy in Britain and France*. Cambridge, Eng.: Cambridge UP, 1989.

Gumperz, John J. *Language and Social Identity*. Cambridge, Eng.: Cambridge UP, 1982.

Hall, Hubert. *The Red Book of the Exchequer*. Rolls Series 99, 1896.

————. *Studies in English Official Documents*. Cambridge, Eng.: Cambridge UP, 1908.

Hammond, Eleanor P. *Chaucer: A Bibliographical Manual*. New York: Macmillan, 1908.

Hanna, Ralph III. "Problems of 'Best-Text' Editing and the Hengwrt Manuscript of *The Canterbury Tales*." *Manuscripts and Texts*. Ed. Derek Pearsall. Cambridge, Eng.: Brewer, 1987. 87-94.

Hargrave, F., ed. "A Treatise of the Maistres of Chauncerie." ca. 1596. In Hargrave, *A Collection of Tracts Relative to the Law of England*. Vol. I. London: 1787. 300-309.

Hargreaves, A.D. "Equity and the Latin Side of Chancery." *Law Quarterly Review* 68 (1952): 481-99.

Harriss, G.L. *Cardinal Beaufort*. Oxford: Clarendon-Oxford UP, 1988.

————. *Henry V: The Practice of Kingship*. Oxford: Oxford UP, 1985.

Hart, John. *A Methode . . . to Read English*. 1570. In *John Hart's Works on English Orthography and Pronunciation*. Ed. Bror Danielsson. Stockholm: Almqvist, 1955. 229-250.

Haugen, Einar. *The Ecology of Language: Essays by Einar Haugen*. Ed. Anwar S. Dil. Stanford: Stanford UP, 1972.

Hector, L.C. *The Handwriting of English Documents*. London: Arnold, 1958.

Heller, Monica S. "Negotiations of Language Choice in Montreal." *Language and Social Identity*. 108-18.

Herlihy, David. *Pisa in the Early Renaissance*. New Haven: Yale UP, 1958.

————, R.S. Lopez, and V. Slessarev, eds. *Economy, Society and Government in Medieval Italy: Studies in Honor of Robert L. Reynold.* Kent, Oh.: Kent State UP, 1969.

Hingham, Florence M.G. "A Note on the Pre-Tudor Secretary." *Essays in Medieval History Presented to T.F. Tout.* Ed. Little and Powicke 361-66.

Hoccleve, Thomas. *The Regement of Princes.* Vol. 3 of *Hoccleve's Works.* Ed. F.J. Furnivall. EETS, ES 72. Oxford: Oxford UP, 1897.

Holdsworth, W. *A History of English Law.* 17 vols. London: Methuen, 1903-12.

Hollis, Christopher. *The Oxford Union.* London: Evans, 1965.

Holzknecht, Karl J. *Literary Patronage in the Middle Ages.* 1923. New York: Octagon, 1966.

Howard, Donald. *The Idea of the Canterbury Tales.* Berkeley: U of California P, 1976.

Hughes, Susan E. "English in the Letter-Books and Plea and Memoranda Rolls of the Corporation of London, 1377-1422, in Comparison with Contemporaneous Chancery English: Their Possible Roles in the Evolution of Chancery Standard." Diss. U of Tennessee, 1978.

————. "Guildhall and Chancery English, 1377-1422." *Guildhall Studies in London History* 4 (1980): 137-45.

Hutchinson, Harold F. *King Henry V: A Biography.* New York: Day, 1967.

Hyatt, Ada V. *The Place of Oral Reading in the School Program: Its History and Development from 1880-1941.* Contributions to Education. New York: Teachers' College, Columbia U, 1943.

Ingram, Allan. *The Language of D.H. Lawrence.* The Language of Literature Series. London: Macmillan, 1990.

Jenkinson, H.F. "Elizabethan Handwritings." *Library* 3 (1922-23): 1-34.

————. *Paleography and the Practical Study of Court Hand.* 2 vols. Cambridge, Eng.: Cambridge UP, 1915.

————. "The Teaching and Practice of Handwriting in England." *History* NS 11 (1926): 130-38, 211-18.

Jespersen, Otto. *Growth and Structure of the English Language.* Leipzig: Teubner, 1905.

Johnson, Charles. *English Court Hand A.D. 1066-1500.* 2 vols. Oxford: Clarendon-Oxford UP, 1915.

Johnson, Paul. *The Life and Times of Edward III.* London: Wiedenfeld, 1973.

Jones, Gareth S. *Languages and Class: Studies in English Working Class History, 1832-1982.* Cambridge, Eng.: Cambridge UP, 1983.

Jones, Richard Foster. *The Triumph of the English Language.* Stanford: Stanford UP, 1966.

Kane, George, ed. *Piers Plowman: The A Version.* London: Athlone, 1960.

————. *The Autobiographical Fallacy in Chaucer and Langland Studies.* London: Lewis, 1965.

————. "J.M. Manly and Edith Rickert." *Editing Chaucer.* Ed. Ruggiers. 207-30.

————, and E. Talbot Donaldson, eds. *Piers Plowman: The B Version.* London: Athlone, 1975.

Kedar, Benjamin Z. "The Genoese Notaries of 1382." *The Medieval City.* Ed. H.A. Miskimin, David Herlihy, and A.L. Udovitch. New Haven: Yale UP, 1977.

Keiser, George. "In Defense of the Bradshaw Shift." *Chaucer Review* 12 (1978): 191-210.

Kendrick, Laura. "The *Troilus* Frontispiece and the Dramatization of Chaucer's *Troilus.*" *Chaucer Review* 22 (1987): 81-93.

Kingsford, C.L. *Prejudice and Promise in the XV Century.* Oxford: Oxford UP, 1925.

Kirk, R.E.G., ed. *Life Records of Chaucer.* Chaucer Society Publications 32, 2d ser. London: Kegan Paul, 1900.

Klaeber, F. ed. *Beowulf.* 3d ed. Boston: Houghton, 1950.

Krapp, George Philip. *The English Language In America.* 2 vols. New York: Century, 1925.

Landtman, Gunnar. *The Origin of the Inequality of the Social Classes.* 1938. New York: AMS, 1979.

Lass, Roger, ed. *Approaches to English Historical Linguistics.* New York: Holt, 1969.

Latham, R.E. "The Banishment of Latin from the Public Records." *Archives* 4 (1959-60): 158-69.

Lawrence, W.W. *Chaucer and the Canterbury Tales.* New York: Columbia UP, 1950.

Leach, A.F. *Schools in Medieval England.* New York: Macmillan, 1915.

Legge, Mary Dominica, ed. *Anglo-Norman Letters and Petitions from All Souls MS.182.* Oxford: Oxford UP, 1941.

————. *Anglo-Norman Literature and Its Background.* Oxford: Clarendon-Oxford UP, 1963.

Lenaghan, R.T. *Caxton's Aesop: Edited with an Introduction and Notes.* Cambridge, Mass.: Harvard UP, 1967.

Leonard, S.A. *The Doctrine of Correctness in English Usage, 1700-1800.* U of Wisconsin Studies in Language and Literature 25. Madison: U of Wisconsin, 1929.

Leopold, Werner F. "The Decline of German Dialects." *Readings in the Sociology of Language.* Ed. Fishman. 340-63.

Lerer, Seth. *Chaucer and His Readers.* Princeton: Princeton UP, 1993.

Lipking, Lawrence. "Literary Criticism." *Introduction to Scholarship in Modern Languages and Literatures.* Ed. Joseph Gibaldi. New York: MLA, 1981. 79-97.

Little, A.C. and F.M. Powicke, eds. *Essays in Medieval History Presented to T.F. Tout.* Manchester: U of Manchester P, 1925.

Lockwood, W.B. *Informal History of the German Language.* Cambridge, Eng.: Heffer, 1965.

Loomis, Laura Hibbard. "The Auchinleck Manuscript and a Possible London Bookshop of 1330-40." *PMLA* 57 (1942): 595-627.

Lopez, Robert. "Stars and Spices: The Earliest Italian Manual of Commercial Practice." *Economy, Society and Government.* Ed. David Herilhy. 35-42.

Lossing, M.L.S. "The Order of *The Canterbury Tales.*" *JEGP* 37 (1938): 153-63.

Lowell, James Russell. *The Biglow Papers.* 2d ser. Boston: Houghton, 1898.

Lydgate, John. *Troy Book.* Ed. Henry Bergen. EETS, ES 97. Oxford: Oxford UP, 1906.

McCormick, William. *The Manuscripts of Chaucer's Canterbury Tales.* Oxford: Clarendon-Oxford UP, 1933.

McFarlane, K.B. *Lancastrian Kings and Lollard Knights.* Oxford: Clarendon-Oxford UP, 1972.

———. *England in the Fifteenth Century: Collected Essays.* London: Hambledon, 1981.

McIlwain, C.H. *The High Court of Parliament and Its Supremacy.* New Haven: Yale UP, 1910.

McIntosh, Angus. "A New Approach to Middle English Dialectology," *English Studies* 44 (1963): 1-11.

McKibben, Ross. *The Ideologies of Class: Social Relations in Britain, 1880-1950.* Oxford: Clarendon-Oxford UP, 1990.

McKnight, G.H., and B. Emsley. *Modern English in the Making.* New York: 1928.

McLuhan, Marshall. *The Gutenberg Galaxy.* Toronto: U of Toronto P, 1962.

Maitland, F.W. *English Law and the Renaissance.* Cambridge, Eng.: Cambridge UP, 1901.

———. *The Year Books of Edward II, 1307-09.* Selden Society 17 (1903).

Manly, J.M. "Chaucer as Controller." *Times Literary Supplement* 9 June 1927: 408.

———, and Edith Rickert. *The Text of the Canterbury Tales.* 8 vols. Chicago: U of Chicago P, 1940.

Martinez, Lauro. *Lawyers and Statecraft in Renaissance Florence.* Princeton: Princeton UP, 1968.

Matheson, Lister, rev. of *An Anthology of Chancery English,* by John H. Fisher et al. *Speculum* 61 (1986): 646-50.

Matthew, Gervase. *The Court of Richard II.* London: Murray, 1968.

Matthews, William. *Cockney Past and Present.* New York: Dutton, 1938.

Maxwell-Lyte, H.C. *Fifty-Seventh Report of the Deputy Keeper of the Public Records.* London: H.M. Stationary Office, 1896.

———. *Historical Notes on the Use of the Great Seal of England.* London: H.M. Stationary Office, 1926.

Mehl, Dieter. "Chaucer's Audience." *Leeds Studies in English* 10 (1978): 58-74.

Mencken, H.L. *The American Language*. 4th ed. New York: Knopf, 1941.

Merilees, Brian. "Anglo-Norman Literature." *Dictionary of the Middle Ages*. Ed. Joseph Strayer et al. Vol. I. New York: Scribner's, 1982.

Mersand, Jospeh. *Chaucer's Romance Vocabulary*. New York: Comet, 1939.

Migliorini, Bruno. *The Italian Language*. Abridged and recast by T.G. Griffith. London: Faber, 1966.

Middle English Dictionary (MED). Ann Arbor: U of Michigan P, 1954-.

Minnis, A.J. *Gower's Confessio Amantis: Responses and Reassessment*. Cambridge, Eng.: Brewer, 1983.

Misra, Bal Govind. "Language Spread in a Multilingual Setting: the Spread of Hindi as a Case Study." *Language Spread Studies*. Ed. Cooper. 148-57.

Mitchell, Jerome. *Thomas Hoccleve*. Urbana: U of Illinois P, 1968.

Mitford, Nancy, ed. *Noblesse Oblige*. New York: Harpers, 1956.

Morris, Colin. *The Discovery of the Individual: 1050-1200*. 1972. Toronto: U of Toronto P, 1987.

Morsbach, Lorenze. *Uber den Ursprung der neuenglischen Schriftsprache*. Heilbronn: Henninger, 1888.

Mossé, F. *A Handbook of Middle English*. Trans. J.A. Walker. Baltimore: Johns Hopkins UP, 1952.

Myers, A.R. "Parliamentary Petitions in the Fifteenth Century." *EHR* 52 (1937): 385-404, 590-613.

Nalimo, V.V. *In the Labyrinths of Language: A Mathematician's Journey*. Philadelphia: ISI, 1981.

Nicholas, Harris, ed. *Proceedings and Ordinances of the Privy Council of England*. 7 vols. London: Public Records Commission, 1834-37.

Nicholls, Jonathan. *The Matter of Courtesy*. Cambridge, Eng.: Brewer, 1985.

Norton-Smith, John. *John Lydgate: Poems*. Oxford: Clarendon-Oxford UP, 1960.

O'Donnell, W.R., and Loreto Todd. *Variety in Contemporary English*. London: Unwin, 1980.

Ogilvie, C. *The King's Government and the Common Law, 1471-1641*. Oxford: Blackwell, 1959.

Olson, Paul. *The Canterbury Tales and the Good Society*. Princeton: Princeton UP, 1986.

Otway-Ruthven, A.J. *The King's Secretary and the Signet Office in the Fifteenth Century*. Cambridge, Eng.: Cambridge UP, 1939.

Owen, Charles. "The Alternative Reading of *The Canterbury Tales*: Chaucer's Text and the Early Manuscripts." *PMLA* 97 (1982): 237-43.

Oxford English Dictionary (OED). 1st and 2d eds.

Page, Norman. *The Language of Jane Austen*. New York: Barnes and Noble, 1972.

Palgrave, F. *An Essay Upon the Original Authority of the King's Council*. London: Commission on Public Records, 1834.

Palmer, D.J. *The Rise of English Studies*. Oxford: Oxford UP, 1965.

Parkes, M.B. *English Cursive Book Hands 1250-1500*. 1969. London: Scolar, 1979.

———. *Pause and Effect: An Introduction to the History of Punctuation in the West*. Berkeley: U of California P, 1993.

———, and A.G. Watson, eds. *Medieval Scribes, Manuscripts, and Libraries: Essays Presented to N.R. Ker*. London: Scolar, 1978.

Pearsall, Derek. *The Canterbury Tales*. Oxford: Blackwell, 1985.

———. "Editing Medieval Texts." *Textual Criticism and Literary Interpretation*. Ed. J.J. McGann. Chicago: U of Chicago P, 1985. 23-40.

———. "Hoccleve's *Regement of Princes*: The Poetics of Royal Self- Representation." *Speculum* 69 (1994): 386-410.

———. *John Lydgate*. Charlottesville: U of Virginia P, 1970.

———. "The Troilus Frontispiece," *Yearbook of English Studies* 7 (1977): 68-74.

Perkin, Harold. *The Origins of Modern English Society, 1780-1880*. London: Routledge, 1969.

Petti, Anthony G. *English Literary Hands from Chaucer to Dryden*. Cambridge, Mass.: Harvard UP, 1977.

Phillipps, K.C. *The Language of Thackeray*. London: Deutsch, 1978.

Pike, L.O. "Common Law and Conscience in the Ancient Court of Chancery." *The Law Quarterly Review* 1 (1885): 443-65.

Pollard, A.F. *The Evolution of Parliament*. 2d ed. London: Longman, 1925.

Pollard, Graham. "The Company of Stationers before 1557." *Library* 4th Ser. 18 (1937): 1-37.

———. "The *pecia* System in the Medieval Universities." *Medieval Scribes*. Ed. Parkes and Watson. 143-61.

Pollock, F., and F.W. Maitland. *The History of English Law Before the Time of Edward I*. 2 vols. Cambridge, Eng.: Cambridge UP, 1898.

Pratt, Robert. "The Order of *The Canterbury Tales*." *PMLA* 66 (1951): 1141-67.

Price, Derek J., ed. *The Equatorie of the Planetis*. Cambridge, Eng.: Cambridge UP, 1955.

Prins, A.A. *French Influence on English Phrasing*. Leiden: Universitaire, 1952.

Prior, Oliver H., ed. *Caxton's "Mirrour of the World."* EETS, ES 110. Oxford: Oxford UP, 1913.

Pugh, T.B. "The Magnates, Knights, and Gentry." *Fifteenth Century England*. Ed. Chrimes, Ross, and Griffiths. Manchester, Eng.: Manchester UP, 1972. 86-128.

Puttenham, George. *The Arte of English Poesie*. 1589. Ed. G.D. Willcock and Alice Walker. Cambridge, Eng.: Cambridge UP, 1936.

Quirk, Randolph, A.C. Gimson, and Jeremy Warburg. *The Use of English*. New York: St. Martin's, 1962.

Ramsey, Vance. "The Hengwrt and Ellesmere Manuscripts of *The Canterbury Tales*: Different Scribes." *Studies in Bibliography* 35 (1982): 135-54.

―――――. "Paleography and Scribes of Shared Training." *SAC* 8 (1986): 107-44.

Rashdall, H. *The Universities of Europe in the Middle Ages.* Ed. F.M. Powike and A.B. Emden. 3 vols. Oxford: Clarendon-Oxford UP, 1936.

Relihan, Mary Patricia. "The Language of the English Stonor Letters, 1420-1483." Diss. U of Tennessee, 1977.

Richards, Mary P. "Elements of Written Standard in the Old English Laws." *Standardizing English.* Ed. Trahern. 1-22.

Richardson, H.G. "Letters of the Oxford Dictatores." *Formularies which bear on the history of Oxford.* Ed. H.E. Salter and W.A. Pantin. Oxford: Oxford Historical Society, N.S. 4-5, 1942. 329-449.

Richardson, Malcolm. "Henry V, the English Chancery, and Chancery English." *Speculum* 55 (1980): 726-50.

―――――. "The Influence of Henry V on the Development of Chancery English." Diss. U of Tennessee, 1978.

Riley, H.T., ed. *Memorials of London and London Life.* London: Longman, 1868.

Rolls Series. *Calendar of the Rolls Proceedings of the King's Council in Ireland, 1392-93.* Rolls Series 69, 1877.

Roman de la Rose. Ed. Félix Lecoy. 3 vols. Paris: Compion, 1965-70.

Root, R.K., ed. *Book of Troilus and Criseyde.* Princeton: Princeton UP, 1926.

―――――. "Publication Before Printing." *PMLA* 28 (1913): 417-31.

―――――. *The Textual Tradition of Chaucer's Troilus.* Chaucer Society Publications 99, 1st ser. London: 1916.

Rosen, Charles. "Romantic Originals." *New York Review of Books* 17 December 1987: 22-31.

Rosenberg, Bruce. "The Oral Performance of Chaucer's Poetry." *Forum* 13 (1980): 45-57.

Roskell, J.S. "Thomas Chaucer of Ewelme." *Parliaments and Politics in Late Medieval England.* London: Hambledon, 1983: 151-92.

Rotuli Paliamentorum. Ed. J. Strachey et al. 6 vols. London: 1767-77.

Ruggiers, Paul G., ed. *Editing Chaucer: The Great Tradition.* Norman: Oklahoma UP, 1984.

Ruud, Martin B. *Thomas Chaucer.* U of Minnesota Studies in Language and Literature 9. Minneapolis: U of Minnesota, 1926.

Rymer, Thomas. *Foedera.* 20 vols. London, 1700-17.

Salter, Elizabeth. "Chaucer's Internationalism." *SAC* 2 (1980): 71-79.

Samuels, M.L. "Chaucer's Spelling." *Middle English Studies.* Ed. Gray and Stanley. 17-37.

―――――. "The Scribe of the Hengwrt and Ellesmere Manuscripts of *The Canterbury Tales.*" *SAC* 5 (1983): 49-65.

―――――. "Some Applications of Middle English Dialectology." *English Studies* 44 (1960): 81-94.

Sanders, George W. ed., *Orders of the High Court of Chancery.* 2 vols. London: Maxwell, 1845.

Sandved, Arthur O. *Studies in the Language of Caxton's Malory and That of the Winchester Manuscript.* Oslo: Norwegian UP, 1968.

Scanlon, Larry. "The King's Two Voices: Narrative and Power in Hoccleve's *Regement of Princes.*" *Literary Practice and Social Change in Britain, 1380-1530.* Ed. Lee Patterson. Berkeley: U of California P, 1990. 216-47.

Schirmer, Walter. *John Lydgate.* Trans. Ann E. Keep. Berkeley: U of California P, 1961.

Sciaffini, A. *Testi Fiorentini del Dugento e dei premi del Trecento.* Florence: Sansoni, 1926.

Scogan, Henry. *Moral Balade. The Complete Works of Geoffrey Chaucer.* Ed. Skeat. VII:xli.

Severs, J. Burke. "Authorial Revisions in Block C of *The Canterbury Tales.*" *Speculum* 29 (1954): 512-30.

Seward, Desmond. *Henry V Warlord.* London: Sidgwick, 1987.

Shakespeare, William. *The Riverside Shakespeare.* Ed. G. Blakemore Evans et al. Boston: Houghton, 1974.

Shaklee, Margaret. "The Rise of the Standard English." *Standards and Dialects in English.* Ed. Timothy Shopen and Joseph M. Williams. Cambridge, Mass.: Winthrop, 1980.

Sharp, Margaret. "The Administrative Chancery of the Black Prince Before 1362." *Essays Presented to T.F. Tout.* Ed. Little and Powicke. 320-29.

Sheridan, Thomas. *A Complete Dictionary of the English Language.* 3d ed. London, 1790.

———. *A Course of Lectures on Elocution.* 1762. Facsimile ed. New York: Blom, 1968.

———. *A Discourse Delivered in the Theatre at Oxford, in the Senate House at Cambridge, and at Spring-Garden in London.* n.d. Augustan Reprint Society, 136. Los Angeles: UCLA, 1969.

Shonk, Timothy. "A Study of the Auchinleck Manuscript: Bookmen and Bookmaking in the Early Fourteenth Century." *Speculum* 60 (1985): 71-91.

Siebs, Theodor. *Deutsche Buhenanssprache.* Bonn: Ahn, 1922.

Simpson, David. *The Politics of American English, 1776-1820.* Oxford: Oxford UP, 1986.

Sisam, Kenneth. "Aelfric's Catholic Homilies." *RES* 7 (1931): 6-22.

Skeat, W.W. *The Complete Works of Geoffrey Chaucer.* 2d ed. 7 vols. Oxford: Clarendon-Oxford UP, 1899-1900.

Spaulding, Robert K. *How Spanish Grew.* Berkeley: U of California P, 1948.

Spurgeon, Caroline F. *Five Hundred Years of Chaucer Criticism and Allusion.* 1908-17. 3 vols. New York: Russell, 1960.

Staley, Edgcumbe. *The Guilds of Florence.* London: Methuen, 1906.

Stevenson, W.H. "The Introduction of English as a Vehicle of Instruction in English Schools." *Furnivall Miscellany.* Oxford: Clarendon-Oxford UP, 1901.

————. "An Old English Charter of William the Conqueror." *EHR* 11 (1896): 731-44.

Straithwaite, T.W. *The "Six Clerks of Chancery," Their Successors in Office, and the Houses They Lived In—A Reminiscence.* London, 1879.

Strang, Barbara. *A History of English.* London: Methuen, 1970.

Stubbs, W.W. *The Constitutional History of England,* 3 vols. Rev. ed. Oxford: Clarendon-Oxford UP, 1887-91.

————. "Modus tenendi Parliamentum." *Select Charters.* Ed. W. Stubbs. 9th ed. London, 1913. 600-06.

"Students' Right to Their Own Language." *College Composition and Communications* 25 (1974).

Sullivan, Mark. *Our Times: The United States 1900-1925.* 3 vols. New York: Scribner's, 1930.

Sutherland, Gillian. "Education." *Cambridge Social History.* Ed. Thompson. 3.119-69.

Tatlock, J.S.P. *"The Canterbury Tales* in 1400." *PMLA* 50 (1935): 100-39.

Thompson, F.M.L., ed. *The Cambridge Social History of Britain, 1750-1950.* 3 vols. Cambridge, Eng.: Cambridge UP, 1990.

Toller, T.N. *Outlines of the History of the English Language.* Cambridge, Eng.: Cambridge UP, 1927.

Tout, T.F. *Chapters in Mediaeval Administrative History.* 6 vols. Manchester: U of Manchester P, 1920-33.

————. "The English Civil Service in the Fourteenth Century." *Bulletin of the John Rylands Library* 3 (1916-17): 185-214.

————. "The Household of Chancery and Its Disintegration." *Essays in History Presented to R.L. Poole.* Ed. H.W.C. Davis. Oxford: Oxford UP, 1927. 46-83.

————. "Literature and Learning in the English Civil Service in the Fourteenth Century." *Speculum* 4 (1929): 365-89.

Towle, George M. *The History of Henry V.* New York: Appleton, 1866.

Trahern, Joseph B., Jr., ed. *Standardizing English: Essays in the History of Language Change in Honor of John Hurt Fisher.* Knoxville: U of Tennessee P, 1989.

U.S. Government Printing Office. *A Manual of Style Prepared by the U.S. Government Printing Office.* New York: Gramercy Park, 1986.

Vale, Juliet. *Edward III and Chivalry.* Cambridge, Eng.: Brewer, 1982.

Van Schaack, Henry. *The Life of Peter Van Schaack.* New York: Appleton, 1842.

Voge, Wilfred M. *The Pronunciation of German in the Eighteenth Century.* Hamburg: Buske, 1978.

Wakeford, John. *The Cloistered Elite: A Sociological Analysis of the English Public Boarding School.* New York: Praeger, 1969.

Wakelin, Martyn F. *English Dialects: An Introduction.* London: Athlone, 1972.

Walter, David. *The Oxford Union: Playground of Power.* London: Macdonald, 1984.

Wardhaugh, Ronald. *Languages in Competition: Dominance, Diversity, and Decline.* Oxford: Blackwell, 1987.

Waterman, John T. *A History of the German Language.* Seattle: U of Washington P, 1976.

Webster, Noah. *Dissertations on the English Language.* 1789. Gainesville, Fla.: Scholars' Facsimiles, 1951.

Wells, Stanley. "The Publication of Shakespeare's Works." *Shakespeare: The Writer and His Works.* Ed. Stanley Wells. New York: Scribner's, 1978.

Whorf, B.L. "An American Indian Model of the Universe." *International Journal of Linguistics* 16 (1950): 61-72.

Wiencke, Helmut. *Die Sprache Caxtons.* Kolner Anglistische Arbeiten, no. 11. Leipzig: Tauchnitz, 1930.

Wilkinson B. *The Chancery Under Edward III.* Manchester: U of Manchester P, 1929.

———. *Constitutional History of the Fifteenth Century.* London: Longman, 1964.

Williams, Sara Jane. "An Author's Role in Fourteenth-Century Book Production: Guillaume de Machaut's 'Livre ou je met toutes mes choses.' " *Romania* 90 (1969): 433-54.

Wilson, George P. "Chaucer and Oral Reading." *South Atlantic Quarterly* 25 (1926): 283-99.

Windeatt, Barry. "The Scribes as Chaucer's Early Critics." *SAC* 1 (1979): 119-42.

———, ed. *Troylus and Criseyde.* London: Longman, 1984.

Wolff, Philippe. *Western Languages, A.D. 100-1500.* Trans. F. Partridge. London: Weidenfeld, 1971.

Woodbine, G.E. "The Language of English Law." *Speculum* 18 (1943): 395-463.

Workman, S.K. *Translation as an Influence on English Prose.* Princeton Studies in English 18. Princeton: Princeton UP, 1940.

Wrenn, C.L. *A Study of Old English Literature.* New York: Norton, 1967.

Wright, Sylvia. "Author Portraits in the Bedford Psalter-Hours: Gower, Chaucer, and Hoccleve." *British Library Journal* 18 (1992): 190-201.

Wyld, H.C. *A History of Modern Colloquial English.* London: Unwin, 1920.

———. *A Short History of English.* 3d ed. New York: Dutton, 1927.

Wylie, James Hamilton. *History of England Under Henry the Fourth.* 2 vols. 1884. New York: AMS, 1969.

———, and W.T. Waugh. *The Reign of Henry V.* 3 vols. 1914-29. New York: Greenwood, 1968.

INDEX